RISK – TRUST – LOVE

Learning in a Humane Environment

STUDIES OF THE PERSON

edited by

Carl R. Rogers
William R. Coulson

RISK – TRUST – LOVE

Learning in a Humane Environment

William D. Romey

St. Lawrence University

CHARLES E. MERRILL PUBLISHING COMPANY
A Bell & Howell Company   Columbus, Ohio

To Lucretia,
who has lived with the changes going on within me
and accepted them

International Standard Book Number: 0-675-09119-5

Library of Congress Catalog Card Number: 74-186448

1 2 3 4 5 6 7 8 9 10/ 76 75 74 73 72

PRINTED IN THE UNITED STATES OF AMERICA

8ה77

PREFACE

This began as a book for science teachers. I started to work for the Earth Science Curriculum Project in the fall of 1969 with the intention of helping to prepare better earth science teachers. This goal quickly seemed too narrow as I found myself more and more interested in teachers in general. As the book grew, it became apparent to me that to isolate science from other subjects is to take away its real-life qualities. It is to forget people and the way that learning occurs. The mind—whatever it consists of—does not operate in narrow boxes called "science," "literature," "math," "industrial arts," or "social studies." The mind wanders—it integrates, it tears apart, and its most significant creative acts usually occur outside of conventional boxes.

Thus it has become important to me to direct this book to learners and to any people who help other people learn. This book can be used to good advantage as either a primary or, more likely, a supplementary text in general education methods courses, in various foundations of education courses, in educational psychology courses, and in science methods courses.

The ideas to be found in the pages that follow are based on several assumptions that should be stated here in order that the reader knows in advance what is in store for him. During several years of experience in the areas of curriculum development and preparation of science teachers, I have become convinced that teachers can be divided into two main categories: those who mainly trust students and, on the other hand, those who mainly do not trust students. This book offers suggestions that will be useful to teachers who either already trust their students or feel that they would like to trust students but don't know how to go about developing the environment for trust. There are few empirical, numerical data available to prove that students really learn better in an environment characterized by trust and non-coercion. On the other hand, neither is there any proof that students in highly directive, relatively low-trust environments learn well or efficiently. What is clear is that modern-day education in all fields is characterized by extreme inefficiency, great boredom on the part of the overwhelming majority of students, and highly directive, overly managed instructional situations in which students have little or no opportunity to make meaningful decisions about what they are to learn, when they are to learn it, where they are to learn it, whom they can associate with during the learning experience, and how they are to learn it. I shall use an anecdotal approach for the most part in illustrating numerous learning situations. I shall not consciously try to "sell" the reader on developing greater freedom for his students within the learning environment, for I shall almost certainly fail in this attempt or, for that matter, in any attempt to be objective. Objectivity can only be achieved, as one aphorism puts it, "when nobody is talking to no one about nothing." Any human interaction must, of necessity, involve subjective judgments, and I shall be unabashedly subjective in the ideas I present. I urge the reader to attempt to use some of the ideas suggested in the following pages before he rejects the notion of freedom in the classroom, but, in keeping with my own philosophy of personal freedom, I recognize that how a teacher perceives his role in the classroom is a matter of personal choice. I only hope that any teacher reading this book will be led to reexamine his own posture as a teacher.

Among the assumptions that are implicit in the approaches to be described, several have been challengingly stated by Robert E. Samples* as follows: (1) "The student (at any level) is a reservoir of relevant information." As a consequence of this assumption, teachers need to reward a student for using his own experience and being recognized as an authority on what he already knows. (2) "The student is capable of making decisions about what happens to him." (3) "The student knows the difference between relevant things and crap." (4) "Nothing is more important for the student than to sense and know himself." (5) "Once he trusts the environment to provide a realization of all the previous assumptions, he will learn far more capably than we could possibly predict."

Other assumptions (previously stated in an article of mine entitled "Beyond ESCP: Emergence of a New Identity") relate more to the learning environment. These are the following: (1) A learning environment is rich in proportion to the number of alternatives for learning that it allows the students at any given time. (2) A learning environment is rich in proportion to the number of significant decisions it allows the stu-

---

*Robert E. Samples. "Toward the Intrinsic, A Plea for the Next Step in Curriculum." *The American Biology Teacher,* 32, no. 3, pp. 143-148.

dents to make. (3) The environment is rich in proportion to the freedom of individual students to be doing different things at any given time. (4) The accessibility of potential richness in the learning environment is dependent on the degree of trust between teachers and students. (5) Teachers should learn in the same kind of environment they are expected to create.

I have divided the book into five major sections. Chapter I, "Some Recollections and Reflections," is largely an autobiographical account of the influences that I consider to have been important in my own learning. In it, and especially in the section entitled "Breaking Out of the Guided Inquiry Mold," I have included many reflections on the development of my present ideas about the need for open learning environments. The sections entitled "From the Dim Past" and "Learning Experiences in the University" use examples from the area of modern languages, literature, and political science. "Preparing to be a Teacher" and "Becoming a Facilitator of Learning" describe the evolution of my ideas about teaching and learning in science and spell these ideas out in some detail.

Chapter II, "Looking at Some Elementary and Secondary Schools," gives my impressions of a number of recent visits to elementary and secondary schools and identifies what I consider to be some of the positive and negative factors in the existing educational system. My children, Cricket, Gretchen, and William, their friends, and their school situations in several different locations over the past few years have provided me with a wealth of information and ideas. Numerous visitations to schools in my role as science education teacher, student teacher supervisor, and curriculum developer have contributed to the impressions and ideas recorded. The last section in Chapter II, "Visiting Some Schools That Make Me Feel Better," describes some more ideal school situations that give me hope for the future of the educational system within the United States and its capacity for providing more and better alternatives in the future.

Chapter III is a series of essays examining various aspects of the teacher's role as a facilitator of learning. It contains many practical suggestions about how a teacher can change his perception of his role and move toward accepting and working to create a student-centered learning environment.

Chapter IV, "Some Problems of Schools," is a series of essays concerning the problem of creating open, student-centered schools in a society that is used to a highly regimented school system in which all schools are alike. Oddly, the introduction of democracy into the schools of a democratic society poses threats to the existing system, and I analyze some of these threats.

Chapter V, "Fantasy," comprises a collection of my present ideas for ideal school situations. These ideas change day by day as I learn more about the things that can happen in learning environments. The models proposed are not utopian and impossible to attain. Sections on high school teaching and administration draw together a number of things that I have actually seen working in high schools. The sections on college teaching describe models that I am presently involved in beginning to implement. The results of these implementation efforts will probably form the material for a sequel to this book.

A number of books written in recent years have been addressed to the approaches I shall discuss in this book. John Holt, in his books, has used many examples from the area of mathematics. Richard M. Jones writes from experiences in the social sciences. Neil Postman and Charles Weingartner, Ken Macrorie, Jerry Farber, and others are English teachers concerned with a new kind of education. Carl R. Rogers is a psychologist and uses many examples in this area.* No such books using extensive examples from science have yet been published to my knowledge. I am a geologist and science educator, with roots in modern language and drama, and thus some of the flavor of what I write will be recognized as having special relevance to teachers and learners of science. All of the above authors and I share the same deep confidence in our students. What we write may be found useful—or at least provocative—to anyone interested in helping other people learn, develop high self-esteem, and live together in mutual respect.

---

*John Holt. *Why Children Fail,* New York: Dell Publishing Company, 1964.

Richard M. Jones. *Fantasy and Feeling in Education,* New York: Harper & Row, 1968.

Neil Postman and Charles Weingartner. *Teaching as a Subversive Activity,* New York: Delacorte Press, 1969.

Ken Macrorie. *Uptaught,* New York: Hayden, 1970.

Jerry Farber. *The Student as Nigger,* New York: Pocket Books, 1970.

Carl R. Rogers. *Freedom to Learn,* Columbus, Ohio: Charles Merrill, 1969.

ACKNOWLEDGMENTS

It is impossible for me to identify all of the people who have influenced my thinking and being and have thus had a role in the making of this book. The least I can do is to identify some of the people who have had a more or less direct influence on me during actual planning and writing. To the many whom I inadvertently omit, I apologize.

Bob Samples first urged me to put this down on paper.

John Thompson, Jonathon Swinchatt, and Bob Lepper, you know how important you were in helping me get in touch with myself and thus getting this started. Bud Holland and Bud Stone added encouragement and loving care at important times.

Cricket, Gretchen, and William are beautiful children to live with, love, and learn with. You talked to me, took me to your classes, and shared with me your feelings about schools, learning, and grownups. You and your friends, Nancy, another Nancy, Ann, and many others, helped me relive my own early school life and showed me new dimensions from your own.

Other people I work with regularly tolerated my moods and reinforced me time and again. I especially thank Maggie Wheeler, Pat Brown, Carol Saathoff, Larry Irwin, Bob Wohlford, Gail Griffith, and Dot Curtis. Verna Todd and Phyllis Drake helped me to look at another side of the coin and thus helped me clarify my own thoughts.

Many people were with me during workshops and conferences during the writing of this book. Many of their thoughts and feelings have influenced me in various ways. I especially remember Jim McLelland, John Shelton, Ed Stoever, Léo Laporte, John Cooper, Neil Maloney, Barry Doolan, Lee Shropshire, Bill Page, Walt Dean, Yngvar Isachsen, Stan Harris, Jim McClurg, John Carpenter, Roger Bybee, Dave Newton,

George Hein, Jack Carter, Dale Hesser, O. J. Harvey, Jim Lakis, Lou Pakiser, Gene Hall, Bill Elberty, and Hugh Gunnison. Ideas and feelings from many others among several hundred have undoubtedly found their way into my mind.

I have enjoyed meeting with and growing with lots of people in Earth Science Teacher Preparation Project workshops. These have included people in the Education 401 group from 1969–70, members of the ESTPP-University of Colorado In-service Institute, 1970–71, participants in our teaching assistant conference, 1970–71, fellow learners in the University of Colorado UPSTEP program, and participants in ESTPP faculty workshops held over the past two years. I am especially indebted to the undergraduates at St. Lawrence for helping sustain my beliefs in open learning environments and also to undergraduates and graduate students at Minot State College (North Dakota), the California State College at Fullerton, the University of South Carolina, and numerous other places.

I want to thank a number of teachers and administrators who have shown me that *it can be done:* Roger Hudiburg, Larry Crowley, Jim Gladson, Pat Kelly, Don Glines, and others.

Thanks to Donna, Meg, Harriet, Ski, Joyce, several Garies, Lucie, Bonnie, Roy, and a whole bunch of beautiful people in about twenty different colleges I've visited in the last couple of years. I don't remember many of your names, but you helped me feel that I am real and that status barriers need not exist between me and people who come to learn with me.

The inputs I received many years ago from a number of friends are still apparent in several sections of this book. Among these special people are Dick Stillinger, Dick Miller, George Bard, Ed Shay, John Merrill, Bob Kilburn, Jack Lewis, and many more that will come to mind just as this book comes off the press.

The time of writing this book was also a time of reading and reflecting. I have not met all of these authors personally, but I feel that I know them well enough from their writings that I want to thank them for their influence: Carl Rogers, A. S. Neill, Paul Goodman, Dick Jones, Neil Postman, Charles Weingartner, Ken Macrorie, Jerry Farber, Herb Kohl, George Leonard, Charles Reich, and many others.

William D. Romey

CONTENTS

A Fool Loves To Teach
A Wise Man Loves To Learn

Russian Proverb—
quoted in *Cancer Ward,*
Aleksandr Solzhenitsyn

RISK – TRUST – LOVE

Learning in a Humane Environment

1

Some Personal Recollections and Reflections on Constraints and Freedom in Education

INTRODUCTION

My feelings about education are colored heavily by my own experiences. During the past few years, my philosophy of education has undergone drastic changes. The best way to understand the evolution of this philosophy is to describe some of the influences that have led me to favor free learning environments. It is easy to decide from a logical point of view what an education should consist of and then to choose the most "efficient" ways to produce an "educated person." Educational philosophers construct theories about what education is or should be; educational developers and technicians construct widely different kinds of curricula around these theories; experts in educational measurement then reduce the learner and the learning situation into integers in order to measure educational achievement. But educators rarely look back deeply into their own experiences to see what their education was about, how they felt about their formal educational experiences, and what effect these experiences have had upon them as people. Carl Rogers and others complain that education too frequently proceeds from the neck up. The kind of education I have become convinced is necessary for children and young people must involve the whole person and his deepest feelings and perceptions. Thus I feel that it may be useful to the reader if I first use my own experience to show why I believe that freedom and openness must be achieved in the educational establishment if truly meaningful learning is to occur.

As I describe my experiences, I shall try to convey my feelings about them and will often judge these experiences in terms of my present feelings about the need for teachers to operate as facilitators of learning rather than as presenters of information, imparters of skills, organizers of activities, people who make decisions for students, or classroom managers. My own experiences as a student and then as a teacher have convinced me that I learn better and that I can help other people learn better when there are no barriers between me as a person and someone who comes as a person to help me learn or to be helped by me. I want to be a facilitator of learning, a whole person who, by his way of being, helps others to realize their full potential as self-actualizing human beings.

FROM THE DIM PAST

Character and personality are said to be formed largely during the first few years of a human being's lifetime. If so, the forces that shaped me must remain hidden in obscurity, for I remember little from early childhood. There is a vague recollection of having been locked in the bathroom of a nursery school as punishment for some long-forgotten antisocial act. My response, tearing the plumbing from the walls, was rewarded by instant expulsion. Vague memories of grade school bring back visions of sitting in rows, reciting, reading aloud, trying to do story problems in arithmetic which held no interest for me, and learning to conform to the strict disciplinary patterns imposed by teachers whose main reason for being seemed to be to control us. Report cards provided no particular obstacle. The word "satisfactory" appeared for most of the work performed. Notes from the teacher occasionally made vague mention of rebellious behavior, but aside from this the child mainly conformed. Rewards for good grades were made at home in the form of a graded scale of cash payments for quality indicated by report cards. The notion of competing against other children began to come into focus.

Junior high school continued in the same humdrum manner. I remember pleasant daydreams, passing notes, and watching the pretty girl who sat beside me. In the middle junior high school years, the Second World War made it necessary for us to move, and I changed school systems.

Life at Edison Junior High School in Harrisburg, Pennsylvania, was somehow less sheltered than in Richmond, Indiana. The combination of influences and effects of the wartime years combined with a move and the onset of adolescence caused deep personal effects. Having decided in advance that I would not like Pennsylvania, I did not. My way of coping was to retreat from other people and to take refuge in the safe world of developing strategies to beat the system in school. I have few recollections of learning much in school, but I did learn to beat the system. I found out that by quickly memorizing my notes taken in classes I could get high grades on tests and be identified as a "good" student. Once labeled in this way I was given privileges of various kinds that enabled me to be excused from classes for extracurricular activities that were much more worthwhile than the classes themselves. What I learned by heart as a ticket to get out of at least some of the conventional schoolwork was then quickly forgotten.

My most significant learning during this period came from outside activities—Boy Scout meetings, becoming a patrol leader and roaming about in the Appalachians near Harrisburg, exploratory trips on Saturdays to dime stores rich in paraphernalia, frequent visits to the state library and state museum (which were never once used by any of our teachers for class visits), concerts, plays, travels with the family, the world of clarinet lessons (which replaced the cherished piano lessons previously enjoyed in Indiana), and marching in the junior high school band.

In the summer after the end of junior high school, I went to a boys' camp in Maine. Boys' camps had been a way of life for me since the age of nine. Many of my skills, much of the information I had learned, and many of my likes and dislikes were related to several years in YMCA and Boy Scout camps. This experience was to be different, however. At the age of fourteen I was trusted by my parents to travel alone on a crowded wartime train to New York City, to change stations, and to find my way to my group. I think the trust lavished upon me by my parents during these adolescent years probably had as much effect on me as any other single factor that influenced me then.

At Camp Kewanhee the environment for learning was superb. The natural setting included mountains to be climbed, lakes to be swum in, rocks and plants to awe me. Canoes, rowboats, and sailboats were there to be paddled or sailed, and instructors in handicraft, woodcraft, and nature study were available at all times. There were no grades to be competed for, no normal curves to fit onto, no system to beat. However, there were provisions for competitiveness. In each activity area there were levels to be passed with specified competencies established to mark the ar-

A Heterochotymus eats behavioral objectives. But it doesn't gain any weight because they don't have anything in them that is digestible. It consumes behavioral objectives in copious quantities and passes them completely unchanged. Its only viable offspring are known as curriculum projects. Under stress it backs into every situation. This would be a field recognition clue.—The Heterochotymus is a creation of James Gladson and friends and appears by the courtesy of the Environmental Studies project. Photo by Robert Samples.

rival at any given level. Perhaps this caused my later and temporary infatuation with behavioral objectives.[1] Each of us was in effect asked to compete with himself and to pass as many levels as he could. Elaborate reward systems were established in which level winners were announced at every campfire. The element of interpersonal competition was introduced in the organization of the camp into teams. Each member of the camp was assigned to one of two teams, the maroons and the greys. Everything we did was measured in terms of the number of points it contributed to the team. For every achievement level passed one's team received a fixed number of points. For every athletic event in which we won or placed, points were awarded to the team total. Thus there were two kinds of heroes—the first were the athletic heroes who won large numbers of points for their teams in athletic events such as the weekly swimming meets. But the *real* heroes were the level-getters, who got points for their teams by completing large

---

[1]See William D. Romey, *Inquiry Techniques for Teaching Science* (Englewood-Cliffs, N.J.: Prentice-Hall, Inc., 1968).

numbers of achievement levels. I was one of those, a beaver who worked at level-getting perhaps more for the glory of the greys than for my own pleasure. It is difficult to separate personal pleasure from team spirit, however, for the areas in which achievement levels could be obtained were many. Most of the activities were things that boys liked to do anyway, and the leaders of many activities were junior counselors and counselors not much older than we were. A sense of camaraderie developed, and much was learned by many of us in spite of the competitive atmosphere we lived in. Cooperative elements were not excluded by the competitive aspects of the environment. We did not hesitate to help each other in preparing for achievement levels—especially if we were both members of the same team. I trace my early interest in geology to the years spent at Camp Kewanhee. Collecting trips to old mines in Maine, panning for gold, wondering about the origin of the lake and the mountains, using the lapidary facilities, classifying our materials, studying the stars—we studied them all to the extent that we pleased in a completely noncoercive atmosphere. Mr. Kieffer, the nature counselor, was a gentle giant perhaps six feet six inches tall. He was a natural facilitator of learning who enthusiastically responded to our own enthusiasm and did not make an oppressive game out of the achievement level system. In general, the senior campers lived in a trust environment where we could find facilities to do pretty much what we pleased when we pleased. More effective learning, in both quantity and quality, occurred during an eight-week summer period here than in nine months at Edison Junior High School.

Upon returning to Pennsylvania and entering high school, I found that the camp experience had helped me resolve many of my adolescent problems, and I had more interest in social aspects of the school situation. Grades tumbled, at least at first, and social involvement increased. Extracurricular activities became more important than the curricular ones. I discovered an interest in drama and had my first big role in *Junior Miss,* the school play for the fall term. This activity consumed most of my energy, with other activities, even Latin, which I had especially enjoyed in junior high school, falling by the wayside.

Shortly after the critical triumph of our class play, the war having ended, my family moved back to Indiana, where I stepped into a quite different set of high school circumstances. Here it was possible to both beat the academic game and be involved heavily in extracurricular activities at the same time. Class time was mainly boring. Latin, in the hands of a tyrant, lost all appeal for me. Taking a required biology course, I found the work and assignments insipid but easy enough to get through. On one occasion I inserted the poem "Mary Had a Little Lamb" in a special block directly in the middle of an important term paper. My instructor failed to notice it and gave me the usual A on the report. Geometry and algebra were nearly unbearable. History and civics were replays of the same thing gone through for the I-don't-know-how-manyth time. I found that I had a taste for English literature and especially for poetry where much emphasis was placed on oral expression.

In the eleventh grade Mrs. Charles appeared on the scene. I was met at the door to her classroom by a teacher who greeted me entirely in French. Emphasis was on oral aspects of the language, and, although Mrs. Charles was a stern disciplinarian, I buried myself deeply in my studies in this area. Her acceptance and encouragement of my interest had a strong reinforcing effect. Outside of this one area of study my life revolved around extracurricular activities. Real appreciation and feeling for literature came primarily from participation in civic theatre and high school drama productions. Interest in music was mainly satisfied through private lessons taken outside of school hours, although one composition class had an important effect. Oddly, in cooking class there was opportunity for creative activity as opposed to the recitation and trivial projects required in most classes.

Having learned to beat the system with minimum effort, I was able to operate with a large degree of freedom during my senior year. A history and civics teacher who was a particularly warm human being although a somewhat dry teacher was responsible for my being made editor of the high school annual. Although his classes had been rigidly structured, he became a real facilitator of significant learning by providing maximum opportunity for my yearbook efforts. With support from our advisor and from the other staff members, our group managed to secure private production quarters for our efforts—the anteroom adjoining the men teachers' lavatory! The men teachers in general were none too happy about this turn of events. Frequently they would enter the lavatory area to find one or more nubile high school girls lounging about. Nonetheless they tolerated us. This room became a haven of freedom away from the normal confines of the classrooms. Several of us on the yearbook staff managed to obtain permanent passes which allowed us to leave our classes at virtually any time in connection with our yearbook activities.

During that final high school year a new French teacher arrived in the school, and she made the study of that subject ridiculous. My great interest, developed during the preceding year, carried me through, however, and I continued to work on my own, rarely doing the assigned work but rather concentrating on aspects I was personally interested in. In a speech class I became interested in an American Legion oratory contest in which I enjoyed considerable success through several rounds of competition. I thus developed a personal relationship with the speech teacher which enabled us to work together as human beings with mutual interests rather than as teacher and student. Drama and athletics provided other escapes from the dull and trivial aspects of the high school day. Life during these days consisted of five or six hours of generally dull lessons and eight or ten hours of activities related to genuine interest. We thus enjoyed a considerable degree of freedom, at least some of us did, and were able to turn our minds off during much of the trivial instruction. I distinctly recall using certain classes as places to catch up on my sleep. Frequently the sleep was not hidden, and I suppose I should be glad that some of the instructors were facilitative enough not to complain to me when they saw my head down on my arms in the very front row of their classes! On other occasions I remember taking advantage of my walletful of passes, leaving classes and going to our yearbook office to lie on the couch and read Macbeth or perform some other activity more interesting than those offered in the classes.

Yearbook activities provided opportunity for confrontations with the school administration. Our creative impulses led us to try to sneak in a photograph of an amorous couple in the midst of a chaste embrace in the school corridor, a common scene in many high schools. The principal got wind of our scheme, and, after we were threatened with dismissal and other penalties, the yearbook staff finally agreed to remove the picture. Of course, we got back at the administration in various ways, but we always had the feeling of having sold out. I recently learned of a high school annual in Denver in which the students, with the approval of their advisor, turned their yearbook into a vehicle for serious political commentary and satire on some of the sham things that occur in high schools, on their feelings about the war in Viet Nam and other important issues of the day. That particular staff exercised its freedom to the utmost and has since heroically defended itself against scores of outraged parents and townspeople. Incidentally, the teacher who had allowed this freedom to the yearbook staff later resigned in protest against the school's attempt to prevent future similarly honest expressions of student feelings and concerns.

LEARNING EXPERIENCES IN THE UNIVERSITY

King: Our court shall be a little academe
Still and contemplative in living art. . . .

Longaville: The mind shall banquet, though the body pine:
Fat paunches have lean pates, and dainty bits
Make rich the ribs, but bankrupt quite the wits.

Berowne: What is the end of study? Let me know.

King: Why, that to know which else we should not know.

Berowne: Things hid and barr'd, you mean, from common sense?

King: Ay, that is study's god-like recompense.

Berowne: Come on then; I will swear to study so,
To know the thing I am forbid to know;
As thus: to study where I well may dine,
When I to feast expressly am forbid;
Or study where to meet some mistress fine,
When mistresses from common sense are hid;
Or, having sworn too hard-a-keeping oath,
Study to break it, and not break my troth.
If study's gain be thus, and this be so,
Study knows that which it doth not know.
Swear me to this, and I will ne'er say no.

King: These be the stops that hinder study quite,
And train our intellects to vain delight.

Berowne: Why, all delights are vain; but that most vain
Which, with pain purchas'd doth inherit pain:
As, painfully to pore upon a book,
To seek the light of truth; while truth the while
Doth falsely blind the eyesight of his look: . . .
Study is like the heaven's glorious sun,
That will not be deep-search'd with saucy looks;
Small have continual plodders ever won,

Save base authority from others' books.
These earthly godfathers of heaven's lights
That give a name to every fixed star,
Have no more profit of their shining nights
Than those that walk and wot not what they are.
Too much to know is to know nought but fame;
And every godfather can give a name.

Love's Labour's Lost, Act I, William Shakespeare

Entrance into Indiana University introduced a new kind of game. I was pledged to a fraternity while still a high school senior. The attempts to make us conform and to destroy creative outbursts which might have made us appear eccentric or different were alarming. These rigid societies were coupled with dry and sterile classes in which we sat in rows in front of professors and listened. Three fortunate things happened to me during this period, however, which allowed me to establish a position of relative freedom within the constraints surrounding me. In the first place I broke my leg on the first day of registration. This got me out of most of the onerous freshman duties connected with the fraternity for much of the first semester and allowed me to operate outside of the normal situations requiring conformity in our living situation. In the second place I had a genuine interest in taking many different kinds of courses and never had the feeling of being forced to take requirements. In the third place I had a facilitative advisor who, when I came to him with a prepared list of the things I wanted to do, was pleased to let me follow my own paths. I signed up for a heavy load of courses in the humanities and included several upper level courses in French, my one true love from high school. Both French instructors were relatively structured in their approaches to lower level students, but in my eyes this was relatively unimportant, for both were Frenchmen. In that respect they became ideal resource people for me. Perhaps my negative feelings about the rigid social constraints imposed by the fraternity led to my taking refuge in my studies, much as I had done as a junior high school student in Pennsylvania. I sought every opportunity to escape the fraternity group and spent much of my time deeply engrossed in studies—especially in language. I soon discovered that high grades won me freedom from many of the fraternity constraints. One does not tamper with the few students who bring in high grades in a fraternity, for they are needed to offset the effects of the students so involved in fraternity that they fail courses and lower the fraternity's overall academic standing. High grades became a license for relative eccentricity and freedom. Although the course programs were relatively rigid, I basked in the freedom provided by having only eighteen or twenty hours of formal classwork a week. Another factor which won me additional freedom in the fraternity was my participation in athletics, which enabled me to return to the fraternity late in the evening, have supper saved for me, and escape much of the nonsense associated with the organization. Athletes and scholars were privileged, even as freshmen.

As I think back to this first year in the university, I recognize that I had a considerable feeling of personal freedom within the restrictions that surrounded me, and various subterfuges were available to minimize their effects. The absurdity of the system is shown by the fact that I was elected "Pledge of the Year" by the fraternity, a feat which I can explain only as a result of my having kept away from the confines of the fraternity as much as possible and having had reasonable success as a scholar and athlete.

I signed up for geology in the second half of my freshman year largely because of pleasurable experiences in this subject during my days at Camp Kewanhee. After the excitement of the facilitative environment provided by Mr. Kieffer in the Maine woods, classroom experiences seemed dull indeed. Occasional slides and films livened up the course to some extent, and I dutifully took extensive notes which I memorized, thereby earning A grades on all examinations. Certain subjects in the textbook, however, highly fascinated me. I became very much concerned about the problem of isostasy—the mobility of the earth's crust—and I could not come to understand why it was that the earth's crust wasn't completely leveled off. Yet this was one topic that was avoided entirely in the course. I allowed myself to digress from the topics that were assigned to me for a considerable length of time in pursuing this subject but received no help in the form of a facilitative relationship with any of the course instructors. Our laboratory assistant was a knowledgeable fellow who did his best to make fill-in-the-blank kinds of laboratory activities seem interesting. I put in my time and did satisfactory work, but found no real interest in the work there.

Several field trip experiences had a profound effect upon me. I remember the first bus trip on which someone was lecturing about the geologic features surrounding Bloomington. This provoked a mild "um-hum" reaction from a few of us and no reaction at all from the others. However, when we arrived at certain limestone caves near Bloomington and proceeded to enter and explore them the excitement mounted. Although we were lined up rather rigidly in long lines that led to the caves, and the talk of the instructor meant little to us, the physical experience of the exploration meant a great deal. Had we been turned loose and not subjected to the lengthy descriptions of what the instructor thought we should know about the various things we saw, I think a great deal more would have been learned. All that remains now is the memory of the excitement of the experience and a vivid mental picture of the configuration of the cave. Other things that remain in my mind are visits to limestone quarries near Bloomington. Here again, none of the information communicated remains—only a good feeling about the togetherness of the group and the excitement of the experience. Another visit to some of the coal mines of southern Indiana is vivid twenty-two years after the experience. The enormity of the mining apparatus and the view of the coal pit have survived.

I remember a course in federal government which I took in my freshman year. This was a large lecture group with some hundreds of students in it. Examinations were particularly onerous in that they involved an unlimited multiple-choice format in which none, one, two, three, or all of the choices relating to each question could be correct. The course was taught by a friend of my family whom I thought highly of. I was particularly distressed by the final examination in which in addition to the multiple-choice examination there was an optional essay question. The rules of the game were that we could answer the essay question if we wished to do so and we would receive extra credit. On the other hand, if we did badly on this question in the opinion of the instructor, we would lose credit. Being a gambler and thinking that I was well prepared for the examination, I wrote the essay. But I did badly on the question and my A grade slid out from under me and became an A–, perhaps a small penalty, but nonetheless the kind of penalty that discourages risk-taking. Education without risk-taking is sterile. Penalties imposed for trying things did not facilitate learning for me.

During the summer after this first university year, I returned to Camp Kewanhee as a senior counselor. In the years after my first two-month stay there in 1945 I had returned every summer, as a master camper in the second year, and then for two years as a junior counselor. In my second year as a junior counselor, I had been made the captain of one of the competing all-camp teams. My fellow senior campers and junior counselors and I had begun to find the achievement level system an artificial and unnecessary kind of inducement for activity which, we felt, put too much emphasis on extrinsic awards. The captain of the other team, Dick Stillinger, and I used to get together prior to the major athletic events of the summer and deplore the highly competitive nature of much of the camp life. Nonetheless, we were grateful for the relative freedom enjoyed by the campers and ourselves. Although there was a system of extrinsic rewards around us everywhere and a strong feeling of competitiveness between the two major teams, regular camp life held many cooperative attempts at learning. A great personal closeness grew between campers and because of the small age difference between campers and counselors, the lines between the leaders and the led were often only dimly perceived. Those of us in leadership positions did enjoy a great amount of freedom with respect to the camp administration and were able to guide the course of our lives and the nature of our experiences much as we wished to. Resources were available to us everywhere, and leadership in group situations often migrated among the members of the group so that each was recognized as leader in his own area of specialization. Throughout high school and the early college years, these camp experiences provided much of the real education my co-campers and I obtained. All of us were highly successful in our academic pursuits, and yet most of us felt a substantial sense of personal freedom.

Academic success and a sense of freedom unfortunately do not always go together. Many people I knew who carried high grades home from high school and college denied themselves many real-life experiences in order to devote themselves to their studies. Even though I look on those days as happy ones, I can think of many times when I failed to allow myself the freedom to devote myself to experiences in which I desperately wanted to participate, all because of a test scheduled for the next day. I am just now in my life beginning to realize the matchless importance of experiences that involve my whole person.

By the onset of the sophomore year at Indiana University I had set some definite goals for myself. I had decided to study in France during my junior year and was soon granted admission to a junior year group run by Sweetbriar College. Finishing off the general requirements for the bachelor's degree and working extensively on my competence in French thus became my goals for this year.

Because of my being voted "Pledge of the Year" in the fraternity, I was also made a member of the governing board of this organization, the only sophomore member. By the end of the first semester I had convinced my fellow governing board members by my actions of my unwillingness to coerce the next group of freshmen into patterns of conformity. I also moved out of the fraternity complex at midyear and participated little in their activities except for meals and occasional meetings.

The French department admitted me to advanced courses in literature and conversational French. In these courses we had a great deal of liberty. All of us were stimulated by the work because of our inherent interest in the materials, and the classes were small, permitting us to become well acquainted with our instructors and with each other. None of us worried much about grades, and for much of the time we worked in a setting where coercive elements were not an important factor—at least not so in my mind.

In one set of French grammar courses there was a particularly inept instructor whose approach to the teaching of grammar consisted of assigning us a number of sentences to translate from English into French for each class period. Our activities in class consisted of writing our solutions on the board and then having the instructor criticize our efforts. The tests embodied the same trivial approach to language learning. At the beginning of the second semester when it was clear that I would indeed be in France the following year, I decided that I really had to write in French and that my course in grammar was providing me with no opportunity to learn these skills. I therefore approached this dull-witted instructor and asked him for permission to submit to him each week an essay of my own composition in which I would try to learn to express myself in French. All I asked was that he go over my work and give me his evaluation. I made it clear to him that I wished no grade on these materials and that I did not intend for this work to get me out of any normal classroom activities. I wished to do this on the side in order to prepare myself for the forthcoming year abroad. At first he refused to do this on the ground that he was much too busy. Finally, after much urging, he accepted the task. Immediately afterwards I submitted to him an essay several pages long. When I received the essay back it was literally covered with red marks, crossouts and various criticisms which I was glad to get. But accompanying his criticisms was a long note to the following effect: "Dear Mr. Romey: You have fallen into the trap that all Americans fall into when they think they know how to write French. You have made every possible grammatical error. If you had learned your grammar first and learned it well, then you would not have these difficulties. . . ." Thus the note continued for nearly a full page, a calculated attempt to destroy my feeling that this might be the best way for me to learn to write French—namely by writing it. Fortunately I had a reasonably hard shell and took up his comment as a challenge. The second essay I wrote and submitted on schedule, as I had told him I would, dealt with a fictitious planet, an oppressive professor, and one of his students who proceeded to cause him considerable trouble. The point of the essay must have been obvious to him as I think about it now. He must have perceived that this was a very clumsy and direct attack upon him. Either he was too dull to notice it (which I suspected at that time), or else he was a good enough teacher to chuckle at my clumsiness and to accept the fact that I really meant to learn how to write French (which from a more charitable point of view twenty years after the fact I now suspect). His red marks became fewer as the term continued, and my written French improved considerably. As I look back on that experience now, I am certain my own decision about how I could best learn French was a far better one than his. I became reasonably competent, and the particular directions set for myself prepared me well for the following year.

My advanced conversation classes were a delight. We set up situations and improvised plays and enjoyed to the fullest our contact with the delightfully personable French woman who was our leader. She had assigned us a conversation book to use, and she required us to memorize certain sections each day which formed the basis for our later improvisation. The particular book she had chosen dealt with everyday scenes in the drugstore buying toothpaste, getting a hotel room, and the kinds of things which I was going to need in the following year in any case. The warm personal relationship that developed between Mademoiselle Billant and the rest of us and among her students led to an environment in which the facilitation of developing conversational skills was paramount.

My second encounter with science was quite different from the first. This was a lecture-laboratory course in psychology. The lecture sections contained several hundred students, and absolutely no clear memory of anything presented in these lectures remains behind. It is possible that some of my current interest in psychological factors of education dates from these experiences. Memories of the laboratory exercises are, however, still clear. We worked with rats in mazes and did many kinds of experiments. Most of us participated in psychological experimentation in which we were the subjects. One of the requirements of the course was that each of us spend a certain number of hours as subjects. For our course grades we were tested on vocabulary items in trivial multiple-choice tests. Getting As was no problem, but little was done by the course instructors to facilitate learning in psychology in any significant way. We saw our instructors only as performers up in front of a group of several hundred of us. We never came to know them as real people. My attitude toward psychology at that time was therefore one of indifference.

In order to complete my science requirements, I also enrolled in a second semester of geology. Here the class was relatively small, and we were able to get to know our lecturer to some extent, but not nearly as well as we would have liked to. He spent most of his time with us reading lecture notes. If he had spent this time in personal contacts with us, a much closer relationship could have been developed. I received perfect scores on most of his examinations because I gave him back exactly what he wrote on the board for us to copy down. This impressed him a great deal and me very little. In the laboratory sections we did a good deal of drawing of fossils, and although I enjoyed drawing the fossils, I frequently got mediocre grades back on my drawings. This made me feel that I probably wasn't very good at drawing, and I still avoid drawing today because of this and other experiences that have repressed my desire to express myself in this way. As I look back at those drawings of fossils from my vantage point as a geology professor, teaching similar kinds of courses, I now think that they weren't bad at all. I should have been encouraged or at least not graded. I am convinced that I do not do many different kinds of things that I am perfectly capable of doing well simply because someone in the schools was unresponsive or discouraging. Negative facilitation of this kind is one of the most common phenomena in traditional educational systems. I know now that there was no conscious attempt on the part of my lab instructor to discourage me by grading me down on these drawings. However, his lack of a more direct and personal communication with me produced a negative effect.

Again in this course, the field trips saved the day in terms of overall interest in a course where the lectures and laboratories were dull. The historical geology class had an annual three-day weekend spent at fossil localities in southern Indiana. We all were to go to these trips by bus and to stay overnight together at a small inn near the Ohio River. Almost the entire geology faculty and their families regularly went on this trip. We thus had a chance to rub elbows in an informal way with a number of people whom we perceived to be prominent geologists. The informality of this encounter did much to shape my view of geologists as people and ultimately probably had a good deal to do with my decision to pursue further studies in geology almost ten years later. At the time of the field trip I had to make what was for me a very difficult decision. I was a member of the university tennis team, and we had an important match scheduled for the same afternoon as the departure for the field trip. I consulted with my geology instructor and informed him of my dilemma. He agreed that I should stay behind for the tennis match. At the same time, however, I desperately wished to be a member of the field trip group. My compromise was to hitchhike from Bloomington to the area of the field trip as soon as the tennis match was over. My memory of this field trip is a highly visual one. I can close my eyes and recall numerous scenes at outcrops where we scrambled around hunting for fossils. The high degree of excitement of the professors when we showed them our finds had a highly stimulating effect on us. I remember that we were lectured to at a number of the outcrops, but I remember nothing of what was said. What I do remember is the physical makeup of the group. I see something like a black-and-white moving picture with no sound track. Some of the human things that happened stand out clearly in my mind, however, such as having a distinguished paleontologist lecture to our group on forgetfulness as he stood in front of us with his fly wide open!

Another factor about geology that affected me to some degree was the physical environment of the geology building itself. Although the lecture and laboratory rooms were drab, the displays available in the building attracted attention. The time I spent examining these displays during break time increased my interest. Departmental bulletin boards also had a facilitative effect on my interest in geology. The geology library was an attractive place with a remarkable view out on the student union. I spent many hours studying in this library, and many times it was not geology that I studied. However, my physical presence in this environment had the effect of increasing my interest in geology. As I passed by the shelf containing new periodicals and books, and as I browsed in the library after tiring of work on French or some other subject, I commonly leafed through books and journals that made me curious. Nothing in the elementary geology course work invited me to explore in the library. It was strictly by chance that I found this a physically attractive place, and I am sure that my browsing in this area had an effect on my later choice of geology as an area for further study. Had conscious efforts been made to encourage me to browse in this manner, my interest might have developed much more rapidly and in a better organized way. I remember walking around in the geology building looking in laboratories and in drafting rooms and wondering what was going on. Yet no effort was made to encourage us in the elementary class to see what the professional geologists were doing. Such an opportunity might not have been taken advantage of by large numbers of students, but for those of us who were curious such opportunities might have made more recruits to the profession or in any case better educated laymen.

After my second semester of geology, I had a strong desire to take an upper division course in field geology. However, the rigid scheduling and requirements of the university system made it necessary for me to do other things in order to fill blocks on a requirement sheet. I enjoyed filling the other blocks because I was curious about other subjects as well. However, had I been allowed wider latitude in my choices, I would have included further work in field geology, and the development of my own career might have progressed in a quite different way. Rigidity of scheduling had a strong effect on the sense of priorities I had to establish.

Other courses also had a profound effect during this sophomore year. One was a year-long course in Biblical literature taught by Professor Will Hale, a small, dynamic, bald-headed scholar. Hale had two lectures a week with somewhat more than a hundred students in each session. Although we were subjected to the usual kinds of examinations and had the normal extrinsic pressures to deal with, there was much interchange between Hale and his students in this course. Hale's challenges to students were not based upon memory of things Biblical or directed toward people who disagreed with him. He directly and vigorously challenged the personal belief system of each of us, leading us into a kind of personal introspection that caused great ferment in many of us. I had personally been deeply religious up until this time but for a variety of reasons had begun to reject church-oriented religiousness. One of the reasons for my growing suspicion of the validity of the church as a social organization had been my contact with a local Lutheran minister in my home town who was the embodiment of bigotry. After much reading and thought during high school years, and strongly influenced by the outdoor religious aspects of summer camping experiences, my views became strongly pantheistic. Professor Hale in essence gave us permission to introspect deeply in our own views of life and existence. His approach (which consisted of much external, rather sarcastic jabbing at many of us as individuals, but done in a non-threatening manner), facilitated, at least for me, a rethinking of my position. This freed me from the external control I had always felt from a God I had been threatened by through Sunday school, church, school, and other societal affiliations preceding this experience. Hale's facilitation and the introspection that followed it over a period of several years helped me to throw off many of my ideas about fate control of the type discussed by O. J. Harvey[2] and other psychologists.

The sense of freedom and the desire to explore that were developing in me as a result of various influences, coupled with the feeling that most eighteen- and nineteen-year-olds get of wanting to prove their independence and manhood, led me to leave home and the familiar protection of structured boys' camp situations during that summer. I obtained a ride to Estes Park, Colorado, and set out with only a few dollars in my pocket to see how I could survive. I found work as an unskilled laborer on a construction project—The Big Thompson Power Project—and proceeded to perform the various tasks assigned to me. After two or three days in a tourist home, I purchased a bicycle and moved into the Rocky Mountain National Park where I set up camp for the duration of my experience. Knowing as I did that my trip to France was to begin in only two months, I had brought a French conversational and writing manual along to work further on these skills which I perceived to be important for me. I arose each morning at five o'clock and spent a couple of hours repeating and repeating and reading aloud from this manual. Each evening I would spend additional time in this effort. At the end of several weeks, having further expressed my freedom by growing a beard and dressing in what my fellow workers considered to be a highly eccentric fashion, I set out by bicycle to return to Indiana. This 1,300-mile, thirteen-day odyssey provided a fascinating view of middle America and some of the people who live in it. Sleeping

---

[2]See O. J. Harvey, "System, Structure, Flexibility and Creativity," in *Experience, Structure, and Adaptability,* ed. O. J. Harvey (New York: Springer Publishing Co., 1966), pp. 39-65.

in church yards, school yards, city parks, and even a jail in one Kansas town and stopping frequently to talk with people in small towns along the road brought me in contact with migrant laborers, farmers, shopkeepers, and many kinds of people with whom I had had few dealings before.

The rest of the summer consisted of an extension of this journey in which I was provided with the loan of an automobile by my parents who were facilitating this experience by trusting me to do as I pleased and to explore not only the environment of the United States I was living in but also the environment within myself. The second part of this odyssey carried me to the East in the company of a friend and involved visits with friends, a prolonged visit to the camp we had worked in together, and ultimately an excursion into French-speaking Canada where I continued my preparations for going to France.

The journey to France was accomplished in the company of about thirty other students from various universities across the country. In general the group imposed no significant constraints on our overall freedom. It facilitated our transition to life in another country by removing worries about transportation and lodging details. Upon arrival in Paris we were placed in French homes where we were to live throughout our year. In order to aid in our transition from the American to the French university system, the group established a six-week training session in advance of the French university school year. We were assigned to small tutorial groups for intensive training in various aspects of French. Some of us were highly motivated and already had reasonably good preparation for what we had set out to do. Among those of us in the high-proficiency group were a number of students of French parentage or who had lived extensively in France before this experience. The lessons we received were highly structured, but they were conducted in small groups. Since most of us in the high-proficiency group were highly motivated, we established early the pattern of speaking only French, even among ourselves. Some of us carried this to extremes, considering it almost "sinful" to exchange even a few words of English with any of the other members of the group. This was a self-imposed constraint and made me feel good, and so I continued to operate in this manner. Although the instructors clearly occupied the role of authority in all cases, close personal relationships grew between us. We had no real feeling of competing against the other students in our groups, as grading was strictly on the basis of merit in comparison to the instructor's absolute scale, rather than relative merit within the group. Much of the work consisted of drill, and those of us who imposed the completely French-speaking, French-thinking mode of existence upon ourselves progressed rapidly in our ability to use French. No constraints were placed on the external activities of the males within the group. We established our own version of a student government, but I, as president of this group, felt no desire or power to dictate any rules to the group. Thus we operated in a very free and open manner. For the most part those of us who wished to have associations primarily with French people rather than with other members of the group rapidly drifted away from the protection of the group as a whole and formed our own associations elsewhere. Group activities in general were optional, with the exception of the classes in the intensive training session.

At the end of the intensive training session, there was a break of a few days before the beginning of formal sessions in the various branches of the University of Paris. I loaded my bicycle on a train and proceeded alone to the chateau country in the Loire Valley. I took a self-guided excursion through French history as reflected in these historic monuments. Plunging myself deeply into the local culture, I stayed primarily in small inns and spent my time trying the new experiences that presented themselves. I also met some people who developed into good friends helping my transition into a more French mode of life.

Upon returning to Paris the members of our group elected whatever studies they wished to pursue in any of the branches of the University of Paris. There were no limitations that I knew of placed upon us, and the administration of the group was charged with making possible our entry into any kind of educational experience we desired. For some of the people with less well-developed abilities in French language the group set up special courses which were run more nearly at the level of course work in an American university. In this way the group made it possible for unprepared participants to escape real confrontation with the rigorous French system of education. Some of the courses set up by the group were so attractive in design that nearly everyone signed up for at least a few of them. The group offered a course in contemporary French drama, for example, in which each of us was presented with a ticket for a play each week of the year. A seminar session was also arranged weekly, taught by a drama critic from one of the Parisian daily newspapers. Much of the time he simply talked about the plays we had either just seen or were just about to see and much of this preparation and many of the readings he assigned to us did not make any strong impression. However, on several occasions he arranged to have the leading actors from a play come to discuss with us their concepts of the production and their own roles. In addition, a course in dramatic diction was offered by one of the directors of the French National Theatre, the Comédie Française. These were heady experiences. There was little pressure put on us at any time. The dramatic diction group presented a series of readings to the whole group and their invited guests, but this took the form of a dramatic presentation rather than an examination. We were given examinations in the course on modern French theatre. There were only two of these, one at the end of each semester, and they consisted of essays. I must admit that I was offended by these examinations, feeling that they had very little to do with allowing me to show what I had actually learned and gotten from this course in terms of feelings and personal growth. There was no truly personal contact between the instructor of this particular group and the students, and the examinations left a distinctly sour taste in my mouth after the apparent free mode in which we had been operating.

Courses in the regular schools of the University of Paris were a revelation to us all. The total number of hours spent in lecture sessions was very small. In many courses professional stenographers took down the lectures verbatim for later publication and sale before the examinations. The American administration of our group, by way of facilitating learning for students having difficulty with courses, set up special recitation sections to assure the success of all students if possible. In my own case, since I attended no such special sections, I received from my professors in regular courses at the University only the broadest kinds of suggestions for study. We knew that a day of reckoning was ahead for all courses, however. At the School of Political Sciences, the accounting for each course consisted of a ten- to fifteen-minute oral examination with either the professor or some outside examiner in charge. We were given to understand that we were responsible not for the materials covered in the course lectures necessarily but rather for in-depth understanding of the subject being treated. Extensive reading lists were provided in most courses. During the lecture sessions there was little or no opportunity for any meaningful interchange either with classmates or with the professor. As examination day and the month of June neared, evidence of worry and unrest began to appear on the faces of the students. During the last desperate two months students who had done little during the first part of the year spent hours preparing for the ordeal of the oral examination. Examinations were public, and those of us who were listed near the bottom of the examination schedule had ample opportunity to go and listen to our fellow classmates being examined. In one large class of several hundred students an American friend and I were near the bottom of the list. We were able to sit in on oral examinations for this course as early as two weeks before our own turns came up. We went to these examinations and wrote down all of the questions and evaluated the answers in terms of the professor's acceptance or rejection of them. Then we made lists of the most commonly asked questions and prepared extensive summaries of our own around these particular questions. Each of us took half of the list of questions and shared his answers with the other. Then we put ourselves through a mock examination, examining each other. We had seen the professor literally demolish one student who came in unprepared for the examination, roaring out in rage, "You obviously have done nothing this year! Get out of this room!" When our turns came to be examined, we found that we had successfully beaten the game. Three quarters of the questions posed to us had been included in our advance preparation lists; thus we were regarded as great successes. In another course at this institute, we had been advised to write a paper of some kind on a topic in which we were interested and to bring this to the examination where it would be looked over by the professor and would certainly have some effect on the direction our questioning took. The course dealt with international relationships since the Second World War, and I had chosen to write an extensive paper on the organization and the development of the police in East Germany. I had gone to original sources and had become quite engrossed in this topic. The professor examined my report approvingly and asked two or three perfunctory questions about my own study. Then he proceeded to ask other more general questions for which I was less well prepared. I felt that I had done miserably and perhaps even failed when I left the room. My feeling of defeat after all I felt I had learned was almost overwhelming. However, when the marks were finally posted, I had received a high mark. Still, the pain and feeling of failure at the end of the examination itself had been a quite unnecessary thing to go through.

Courses in Russian at the School of Oriental Languages had progressed in a far different fashion. There we had standard lectures on grammar which were generally dull and which were available verbatim in the course notes in any case. Nonetheless, attendance was good. I never could quite understand why so many people actually went to the lectures merely to hear a man read what they themselves could read again shortly, sometimes even in an expanded form. In addition to the grammar lectures, there were practical sessions in the Russian courses. For these we had an authoritarian old bear of a Russian woman. She succeeded in scaring out a large number of the people by forcing us to recite long lists of verb conjugations and noun declensions before the whole class. There was no particular grade pressure on us during these early sessions except the threat that she might whisper bad things about us to the oral examiners at the end of the year. By the middle of the year a very large class had diminished considerably in size, and those of us who had been able to withstand her attacks found that there was a quite human woman below the gruff exterior and that she was vitally concerned about helping us succeed. Once we perceived this about her, we accepted her help and did our drill assignments not only with the same regularity as before but also with a much greater degree of enjoyment. In this school we came to know our instructors on a more personal level than had been possible at the School of Political Sciences. The oral examination, although rigorous, was devoted to subjects about which we had been warned in advance and which demanded that we demonstrate certain specific skills in conversation, translation, and interpretation of literature and history.

In the French university environment, for the most part we were given extensive freedom to study in certain areas, but then we were subjected to highly rigorous examinations at the end of the year. Very little attempt was made by most instructors to facilitate peer group interaction of any kind or to have the professors approach us in any kind of equalitarian fashion. Thus I could see freedom operating in an authoritarian framework concerned with the maintenance of extrinsic standards. Of course, in my own case the formal university life was a small part of my life. As I look back now, I realize that I spent far too many hours studying and far too few hours delving into the more human aspects of the French environment. Nonetheless, there were numerous social encounters, and my competence in French grew due to my self-imposed total immersion in things French. The delightful older French lady in whose home our group had arranged for us to live for the year had no control over our comings and goings and thus allowed us total freedom in this sense. However, she was a very human person and a motherly tutor to us at mealtimes. Coffee twice a day in her salon recreated for us the ambience of a nineteenth century French drawing room, and my fellow roomers and I learned far more about France and things French in her company than we did in any of our class work. A Christmas trip took one of my fellow students and me to the south of France, to Algeria, and to Spain. During part of this time I traveled alone by bus through numerous small French villages where I had many opportunities for personal, human contacts of various kinds.

At the end of the school year I was joined by a non-French-speaking American friend who was to spend the summer touring with me by bicycle. This ended a ten-month period devoted entirely to speaking French. We lined up positions counseling for part of the summer in a summer camp near the town of Annecy in Haute Savoie. The camp was a bilingual one, the odd days with English being the official language of the camp and the even days with French. The contrast between this camp and those I had attended in the United States was striking. Run by Donald

McJannet of Tufts University, the camp stressed cooperation to such an extent that no real competition was allowed in any way whatsoever. Swimming races, for example, were not allowed. Although tennis, soccer, and other such games were played, strong emphasis was laid upon "how you played the game" rather than upon winning. It was refreshing not to be concerned with winning things and to devote oneself to internal competition, but my friend and I, having been brought up to be highly competitive people, questioned this approach and thought it quite unnatural at first. Unfortunately, there were a number of rules which kept both the campers and the counselors from realizing any strong feeling of freedom. In the competitive framework of Camp Kewanhee, we had enjoyed considerable freedom, but in this cooperative environment many rules restricted our activities.

My friend and I also toured on our own, mainly by bicycle and hitchhiking. We were not tied to contracts with the camp and enjoyed a large measure of personal freedom. The amount of learning that went on strictly as a result of our being placed in new environments and having to cope with them in our own ways was phenomenal. All of this during the summer months occurred without the benefit of any external facilitation. Indeed, we learned all the more for being entirely on our own at this point in time.

Upon returning to Indiana University I found that I had virtually complete freedom. As an advanced French major who had done his tour in the mother country, I had no further requirements to fulfill other than stacking up credit hours. I signed up for advanced courses in French, Russian, and political science. All of the classes were small, and a more or less human, tutorial relationship existed between me and my instructors. I set up a special problems course in French composition and wrote a series of essays for one instructor. We got together weekly and discussed my essays. There was never pressure of any kind except my own pressure, and I found great joy in the learning experience. A special problems course consisting of readings in nineteenth century *Boulevard* drama was set up for me. During the course of the semester I read and discussed with my advisor some fifty different plays. In Russian language courses, although I had studied for only a year in France, I was advanced to graduate level courses in conversation, literature, and studies of the Soviet press. If there were examinations, I recall nothing about them. I had moved back into the fraternity and was now accepted as an eccentric intellectual and enjoyed complete freedom from the constraints that bothered me during my freshman and sophomore years.

After finishing the bachelor's degree at Indiana I returned to France as a graduate student. I wanted to extend my earlier experiences, and I was also engaged in a search for what I wanted to do with my life. France seemed an exciting place to continue this search, to try to finish up some degree work I had begun there previously, and to delay being inducted into the military service for the Korean War. Now I was free even of the very limited constraints imposed by the Sweetbriar group. However, I also had no access to the facilitative functions they had provided. I found my own places to live, learned to be lonely, and learned to fend for myself in many ways. There was no group to provide support.

I enrolled in a continuation of the Russian studies I had begun two years previously and also enrolled as a free auditor at the School of Political Sciences. I signed up for both second-year and third-year Russian courses simultaneously and immersed myself deeply in a program of reading and writing. I found lodging with an emigrant Russian family and tried my best to become a part of the Russian culture as represented in the Parisian colony. Because I was intent upon completing two years' worth of work at the School of Oriental Languages in a single year, I also arranged for weekly private tutorial sessions with the bearlike older lady who taught at the School of Oriental Languages. I later moved away from Prince Gagarin's house where I had been staying to a suburb where I found less expensive lodging with Mariya Yakovlena, who became a sort of Russian godmother to me for the rest of the year. Since she spoke no English and only broken French, there was good opportunity for my conversational skills in Russian to develop.

In addition, I decided to learn German. Various free courses were available, and I took two separate courses, one at the School of Political Sciences and another in a public evening school. At

Christmas I made arrangements with the French student services group for accommodations over the holidays with a German family in Nuremberg. It seemed to me that this baptism by fire —committing myself to two weeks' worth of residence with a non-English-speaking German family—would be one of the best access routes to conversational ability in that language. I returned again to Germany in the spring and spent two weeks cycling along the Rhine River, stopping in small villages and forcing myself to use only German. My reading, writing, and conversational skills developed at a gratifyingly rapid rate in this atmosphere free from external coercive pressures. Resources were there to be used as I wished to use them, and I was in a position to taste what I wanted to taste when I wanted to taste it. Fortunately, due to the trust of my parents backed up by their financial support—provided at a level equal to what it would have cost me to be in graduate school in the United States—I was able to seek whatever learning and experiences I wished during this year. I learned that I could learn by myself and that learning gave me pleasure.

PREPARING TO BE A TEACHER

Upon returning to the United States I began a three-and-a-half-year term of duty with the United States Navy. A full year of this time was taken up by schooling of the most rigid kind. Absolutely no freedom was provided, and the mode of instruction was almost entirely by lecture. The strictest information-learning and behavioral goals were imposed upon us. Almost no trace of the information obtained during this period of time remains with me now. During the navy years I made those important decisions about what to do with the next few years of my life. As is customary with important decisions, this one was based primarily on intuitive and emotional considerations rather than on any rational analysis. I decided I wanted to be a college teacher and that, rather than going on with modern languages, the field for which I was best suited, I wished to try science. After extensive inquiries I selected the University of California at Berkeley as the place to go.

After the relative freedom of my final years as a student of French and Russian, the transition back into a course-heavy program in geology was difficult. All of the undergraduate requirements for a geology major, plus physics, chemistry, calculus, and biology, had to be made up before a real graduate program could begin. I remember especially during this time that little effort was made by any of the geology faculty to make me feel much like a person. Their preoccupation was with content alone, and if you took it without complaining, that was fine, but if you didn't take it, then you'd better get out. Several of the geology faculty members seemed by their behavior to feel the weight of the role of "judge of high standards" which they had imposed upon themselves. They seemed to worry a great deal that we might fall below their standards, and as a result many of us felt little real support. Course materials were mainly highly structured, and few attempts were made to create an atmosphere that favored creative student activity. We were learning to answer questions asked by other people rather than to ask our own questions. For the first time in my own academic career I acquired a blind fear of bad grades and failure. The coldness of the relationships between faculty and students and the analytical way in which we were constantly judged had me ready to leave the program at least once a week. But some compulsion—habit and the submissiveness that gets bred into many of us middle-class Americans —kept me in. The oral qualifying examinations struck real terror into all of our hearts. Fortunately I took mine and passed them just before several of my classmates failed. And even in my own examination I was made to feel so low that it took months to regain a self-concept that would permit me to engage in any very productive activity. After the examinations I was called in by one faculty member who told me that just because I had passed the orals, I shouldn't get overconfident because he personally doubted that I could make it.

During work on the thesis I can remember being terrified that one of my advisors might decide that I was wrong in my interpretations and might somehow delay me. As a result I kept very much to myself and confided mainly in my fellow graduate students when I had problems. Many of my fellow students adopted these same defensive tactics. Such fears inhibited the creativity of many of my fellow graduate students, and they led me to do a much less competent job than I might have had I felt the truly supportive relationship that I am now convinced must be created between a student and his advisors.

BREAKING OUT OF THE GUIDED INQUIRY MOLD

Upon finishing my degree work at Berkeley and realizing that perhaps I had at least learned a few negative lessons about teaching, I went off to become one of the oppressors myself. My first experience at Syracuse University was to teach two summer session courses. I had never taught a full course before. As a matter of fact, two of my years at Berkeley had been supported by a Woodrow Wilson Foundation Fellowship. These fellowships are designed to help accelerate the graduate work of students especially interested in careers in college teaching. The effect of my receiving these fellowships was that I was freed from duties as a teaching assistant during these two years. The Wilson Fellowship thus deprived me of part of an internship in the very job it was supposed to free me to assume. The presumption must be that one teaches best who has least experience as a teacher!

These first two summer session courses were a miserable experience. I was teaching two courses I had never taught before. As far as I knew, courses meant lectures, and thus I proceeded to prepare the very best set of lectures I possibly could. I worked assiduously on lecture preparation from noon every day until late in the night. The next morning I would come with my carefully prepared lecture notes and use them as the basis for teaching the thirteen or fourteen students who were in one of my two classes and the six who were in the other. Ever since that time I have regretted missing the opportunity, with such small numbers of students, to engage in a truly open experience. I was totally wrapped up in the subject matter of the courses and consequently had virtually no time to devote to the students. Fortunately, because the classes were small, I was able to develop close relationships with most of the students in spite of the rigid arrangement I had imposed upon them. The students also had laboratory sessions in the afternoons, conducted by a teaching assistant. He treated the laboratories in equally rigid fashion, but the nature of the subject made it possible for us to get out for occasional field trips. This probably helped to personalize the relationships between us and the students.

—*Drawing by Lucretia Romey*

Because I had been appointed to a dual position in science education and geology, I found myself in contact with many professional educationists as well as geologists when the regular university year began. Because my dual position was somewhat unusual, I was regarded as "having permission" to experiment with teaching the course and to establish new and better patterns for the big elementary course in geology. During my first full semester I had my first contacts with high school teachers of science and people who were preparing to be high school teachers. I was assigned only one course to teach. I was asked to visit numerous secondary schools in supervising student teachers and took the opportunity to audit courses in educational psychology. Since my course in earth science for secondary school teachers was arranged in the form of a workshop, we worked out a format involving a great many field trips and workshop activities aimed primarily at creating laboratory activities suitable for secondary schools. I still felt obliged to give lectures but these occupied only a small segment of our time.

In spite of some of the bad things I described earlier about my graduate school experiences, I had been introduced by two instructors at Berkeley to a system of laboratory exercises involving guided inquiry. The pioneering work of these two instructors, C. M. Gilbert and M. N. Christensen, was among the first attempts at guided inquiry for large numbers of freshman college students. I had acted as a teaching assistant for both of these men and wanted badly to introduce their techniques. My first semester with the high school teachers provided an opportunity to do this. During the second semester I was given a small section of freshman students in the geology department and a budget with which to set up an experimental, guided inquiry program. This program stimualted a great deal of interest among the students. During this time I was still involved in workshop activities with a number of stimulating young high school teachers, among them John Merrill, Dale Hesser, and Jack Lewis. We worked together developing more and more open models for laboratory activities. Some of these teachers then tried the activities with their own students, and we had direct feedback. In these earth science methods workshops I had to be a learner along with my students for I had had no experience in secondary school education other than my own student days, and thus we operated as equals, at least in my view. We also had no examinations in these workshop courses. Somehow the idea that I could avoid examinations in my freshman classes still had not occurred. Everyone gave examinations, I thought.

During this period of time, plans were just being made for the new secondary school earth science program which later became known as the Earth Science Curriculum Project. Because the dual position in education and geology I occupied was rather unique, I was asked to participate in the early stages of development of this project. Participation in the three writing conferences held in 1964, 1965, and 1966 had a strong effect on my views about teaching. It caused me to move farther and farther in the direction of a guided form of inquiry. In this form of inquiry, the teacher identifies the basic problems to be solved, poses the main questions to be asked, and then turns the students more or less loose to apply whatever techniques they can to solving the problems. In some instances students were allowed to have a limited question-asking role also, but this was relatively minor in all of the National Science Foundation sponsored curriculum projects such as the PSSC (Physical Science Study Committee), BSCS (Biological Sciences Curriculum Study), CBA (Chemical Bond Approach), CHEM-Study (Chemical Education Materials Study), and in ESCP as well. In the early days of production of ESCP materials, several of us became interested in the concept of behavioral objectives. Behavioral objectives provided by the teacher tell the student exactly what behaviors he is expected to exhibit at the end of a lesson and also specify the conditions under which the student will be evaluated to see whether or not he has indeed acquired the necessary behaviors. The emphasis in these guided inquiry approaches based around behavioral objectives was on the process by which scientists obtain answers rather than on the answers themselves. We shortcircuited the process, however, by providing the students with the questions. Furthermore, we assumed erroneously that the student would automatically be interested in what we had proposed for him to do. The learning experiences we provided were certainly experiential in nature, but we allowed few opportunities for self-direction, independence, and major decision-making on the part of the student. The basic structure of the course was established by us as the writers, and we imposed our own committee-made logic on the student. The particular linearity we devised would, we assumed, help the student to master the body of content we considered to be so important.

Our elementary course at Syracuse developed along lines strongly parallel to those adopted by ESCP because of my infatuation at that time with behavioral objectives and with guided inquiry. And yet at the same time I observed that my students at Syracuse still regarded their learning experience to be largely irrelevant.

I came to view evaluation as a very important part of the educational system. We arranged to have weekly quizzes in laboratories to make sure that what we considered to be essential skills were being learned by our students. Our examinations were given several times during the term. In order to make sure that we emphasized critical thinking and problem-solving skills we made sure that these examinations consisted entirely of problems and essays. At no time did we use multiple-choice, fill-in, or true-false types of questions. The tests were all open-book examinations and generally involved analysis and discussion of situations. Average scores on these longer examinations were generally between fifty and sixty percent. I was benevolent in the grading system and allowed more high grades than any of my colleagues who gave easier examinations and obtained higher average scores for their students. At the end of the term I would often hurry down to see what range of scores had been obtained in my colleagues' classes, and I often wondered if I was being too easy on my students because I gave fewer Ds and Fs and more As and Bs than they. Grade-giving time used to be a time of trauma for me. For students who fell in the middle of grade ranges there was, of course, no problem, but for those who fell near my arbitrary border lines I sometimes spent two or three days worrying about which side of this line the student should be placed on. Once I had made this decision, I felt that the grades were entirely non-negotiable. Now it seems to me that grades serve no useful purpose other than intimidating students and that any evaluation that I make must be considered negotiable as I learn to know more about a student.

In carrying out the mandate to develop better and better courses for elementary students, my colleagues and I experimented in many different ways. Our first attempts at innovation consisted mainly in rearranging the order in which we considered topics. No matter what order we used we found that some students learned much and other students learned little. It quickly became clear that the particular linearity and externally imposed logic we used had little to do with learning that occurred on the other end.

Very early in our experimentation we began to question the viability of a survey treatment of many topics. We decided instead to substitute in-depth coverage of a small number of topics in place of survey treatment of a large number of topics. The question then became one of determining which topics to treat in depth. We experimented with many different combinations of topics and discovered two important things. In the first place, relatively in-depth coverage of a small number of topics did seem to lead to greater learning on the part of the students. In the second place, we discovered that no matter what topics we selected, some students were served well and others poorly. My original thought had been that I should choose the topics about which I was most enthusiastic in the hopes that my own enthusiasm could be communicated to my students. To some extent I found this to be true. These experiences made it clear, however, that some other scheme providing greater flexibility must be sought.

Some of the high school teachers with whom I had been working, especially Bob Kilburn, introduced me to the notion of a contract system of teaching.[3] In this system, as I decided to implement it, the teacher introduced a large number of alternatives from which students could choose. The students then made formal contracts to work for certain grades by submitting certain amounts and kinds of work. As I look back on that contract experience, I realize that I imposed a considerable burden on my students. I continued giving regular lectures and regular laboratory exercises and placed the contract activities as mainly outside requirements. Students were placed in a position where they were guaranteed a C grade in the course if they completed a certain minimum number of requirements on their contracts. These students were expected to take the examinations in the course, but their grades were not to be counted. Students wishing to receive

---

[3]William D. Romey, *Inquiry Techniques for Teaching Science* (Englewood Cliffs, N.J.: Prentice-Hall, Inc., 1968), pp. 77-87. Also reprinted in James Raths, John R. Pancella, and James S. Van Ness, *Studying Teaching* (Englewood Cliffs, N.J.: Prentice-Hall, Inc., 1971), pp. 163-172.

higher than a C grade were required to submit more outside work as part of their contracts, and there were also some specific requirements about levels they must attain on the examinations if they wished to receive a B or A grade. The outside activities allowed were many and varied. Students were invited to construct projects of their own for which variable credit was assigned on the basis of the extent and quality of this work. A large list of outside readings was provided, and students had a chance to receive "points" for each reading they submitted. We established a Tuesday film theatre where films on geologic subjects were shown twice every Tuesday. Students could attend these films and obtain credit by undergoing a short oral interview on each film. Credit for all of these outside activities was obtained when the student came to see me for a short oral interview. I set aside every Tuesday and Thursday for student appointments and kept a schedule outside my office so that the approximately ninety students in the class could sign up for five- to ten-minute chats. On some of these days I would see as many as forty students for short individual interviews. At the first interviews, students were terrified of the oral examination they were about to undergo in my office, on enemy territory. My tactic, however, was merely to ask them to tell me about what they had been reading, how work was progressing on their project, or to talk to me about the film they had seen. I asked no specific questions until they had begun to talk about aspects of the work that they had been struck by. Then I attempted to ask questions which I hoped would clarify their own feelings and thoughts about their work. When I felt that a student had not read an article carefully enough or had otherwise not done sufficient work to receive credit, I merely suggested that he ought to drop back later to talk over the same article or film or project, and I entered nothing on my master credit sheet. Thus there was no penalty for failure on these items other than a minor loss of time during the course of the term. I saw some of the students going for the higher grades fifteen times or more. Frequently, after the students discovered that these interviews were not difficult tests but were friendly chats around the subject matter, they began to bring more personal kinds of problems to me. I often didn't know what to do when such situations arose because my perception of my role as a teacher had not yet evolved far enough for me to be as accepting and empathic as I now feel I must be.

In addition to the outside contract activities students were also required to have minimum satisfactory performance on all of the required laboratory activities. Here again they had multiple chances to redo exercises at no penalty. On proficiency quizzes for the identification of earth materials, for example, we allowed them to retake these examinations several times if necessary. The ability of students to handle the material I presented in lectures became important only to the students who wished to receive As or Bs in the course.

My wife and I attempted to bring a more personal relationship to this course by having open houses in our home several times a semester. We invited students to drop by anytime between eight and ten p.m., whenever they took their evening break, and to have some cider, coffee, or tea with us and to chat about anything, either personal matters or things related to the course. Generally between ten and twenty students seemed to drop by. I envied the Lutheran chaplain across the street who always had thirty or forty students stopping in for his open houses. At first we wondered what kind of students we had at the university. They were always asking for more contact with the faculty, and then when we made efforts to allow such contact, they did not show up. As I look back now I realize what the difference was between the open houses held by the Lutheran chaplain and those that we held; he had no power over his students and thus could develop an open, friendly, non-threatening relationship. My students perceived me as having power over them because they were still tied to a system of grades that would be recorded upon a transcript. I was allowing flexibility on a number of outside assignments, but at the same time my major way of distinguishing between A, B, and C students was by very difficult examinations which showed the students that I really did not trust them to learn on their own.

At the end of the first semester of this contract system, having found the large number of student interviews plus preparation of full sets of lectures and laboratories to be an exhausting task, I was prepared to abandon most of the system. I put out an extensive course evaluation questionnaire asking for criticisms and suggestions. The response requesting a continuation of the contract system with modifications was overwhelming. Even though the students actually had to do more work in the long run under the contract system, apparently the relatively close personal contact had made them willing to pay the price again. Thus a modified contract scheme was drawn up for the second term.

At the end of the first semester of the contract system, I expected that all of the students who had successfully completed all of the laboratory requirements and had also completed a minimum of five outside units of work for their contract would automatically pass the final examination anyway. It was for this reason that I had told the students their C grade was guaranteed if they fulfilled these requirements regardless of what they got on the final examination. To my horror I found that three or four of the students received exceedingly low scores on the final examination, grades as low as twenty out of 100. I was so horrified by what I considered to be the dishonesty of these few students that I put an override clause into the contract system for the following semester. I told the students that if they fulfilled all of their contract requirements but did really badly on the final examination, I would reserve the right to give them less than a C grade. I was telling my students again that I did not really trust them. Lack of trust between teacher and students must be one of the major factors that impedes learning and prevents close personal relationships from developing.

Some of the students working under this contract scheme were freed to do highly creative project work. A number of students undertook self-directed field studies and performed outstanding work that was truly experimentative in nature. Some students spent up to twenty hours a week on their elementary geology course. This was pleasing to me, of course, but at the same time it was not fair to have caused them to neglect other studies to the extent that they must have. My compulsion to cover the standard fare had not yet been defeated.

During the course of these early experimentative years at Syracuse University I produced a fat elementary geology laboratory manual full of guided inquiry exercises.[4] There were many more exercises included than the students could conceivably do

---

[4]William D. Romey, James R. Kramer, Ernest H. Muller, and John R. Lewis, *Investigations in Geology* (Dubuque: William C. Brown Co., 1967).

in a full year of work, and the object of this was so that we could offer a large number of alternatives to our students. However, it was not the students to whom we were offering alternatives but rather to the various instructors who taught this course, because each instructor chose a definite group of laboratory exercises and proceeded to force his student through them in lockstep fashion. I also spent a good deal of time in 1966 and 1967 writing a book on inquiry techniques for teaching science. This book was intended to guide teachers in setting up more or less flexible guided inquiry programs.

The preparation of these two books represented the culmination of my love affair with guided inquiry. This was also the time when the Earth Science Curriculum Project completed its textbook *Investigating the Earth,* the first major guided inquiry textbook in earth science for the secondary schools. Having had several years of involvement in the development of guided inquiry programs for both secondary and college students, I had had a substantial chance to see the effects of such programs on the students. Although I felt that students were learning better and that I was helping in this learning in a somewhat more effective manner, I was still deeply concerned about large numbers of students who did not march to this new rhythm. I felt deeply that we needed still greater flexibility in both science education and other university programs which still did not seem to be meeting the needs of learners very effectively.

One young lady who was a student in one of my classes had read me this message loudly and clearly, but I had as yet been unwilling to understand it. The young lady in question had done slightly below average work throughout the course of the semester. At final examination time she had submitted her examination paper to me early and had left the room. When I read the examination, I was at first shocked, then amused, and then horrified. In answer to the questions, she had written a large number of absurd answers full of geological punnery, sexual overtones, and both implicit and explicit insults aimed at the university system as a whole, at the geology department, and at me specifically. It was a splendid piece of work, and the young lady had taken a huge risk in submitting such a paper. I showed the paper to several of my colleagues and finally sent a copy of it to the assistant dean of the College of Liberal Arts. He immediately got in touch with the young lady and forced her ultimately to come and apologize to me for her "insolence." I feel very sad now about my feeling of self-satisfaction in receiving her apology. I let her know that she would probably have passed the course had she written a normal final examination instead of the "insulting thing" she had submitted. She explained that she had always wanted to respond in this way on an examination and that this was the time that she had elected to do it. She apologized to me and left. As I look back on this particular situation, I feel that only now am I able to recognize that this girl was actually giving me a gift of real honesty, and I can regret that I did not seek more effective means of facilitating her learning experience and of rewarding her for helping to open my eyes to the irrelevance she found in my course.

Another experience that led me again further from the guided inquiry path where the teacher calls all of the shots was a graduate level seminar in geology. Several teaching assistants who had worked with me in the elementary course but with whom I had had no contact on a higher level asked if I would conduct a seminar for them on igneous rocks. I said that I would do this on the condition that they got one or two other faculty members to join us, that we meet in a very informal manner, that the seminar be completely participatory on the part of everyone concerned including the faculty members, and that we avoid grading schemes entirely. They agreed to these conditions, and we planned to meet weekly at the home of one of the seminar members, to drink beer together, and to have one of us each week lead a major seminar. The seminar leader was directed by the group to have a reading list prepared in advance so that other members of the seminar group would have a chance to do some peripheral reading to enrich the discussion. This seminar provided a rich experience for all of us concerned. Even here, though, some feelings of faculty power over students still seemed present, although these were less in evidence than in perhaps any other such experience I had been involved in earlier. Several of the teacher-training and methods courses I had been involved with as a teacher began to take a more and more open format in which the students had a progressively greater decision-making role.

Perhaps fortuitously I left Syracuse University in 1967–68 for a research leave in Norway, where I was totally preoccupied with rocks rather than with people. Some of the many stimuli that had been acting upon me during five years at Syracuse University began to settle and organize themselves in my mind. I spent a good deal of time puzzling over who I was and what my role with regard to students should be. Perhaps the clear Norwegian air helped to focus some of these ideas so that when I returned to Syracuse the following year, I was able to view things from a fresh viewpoint.

When I returned in 1968, a number of things happened which caused me to evolve further. As I matured as a scientist, I came more and more to the conclusion that no particular body of subject matter was of any real import to my students. I did jump back into the normal lecture-laboratory situation, but I was highly dissatisfied with requiring my students to learn anything in particular. I was concerned that they should be involved with something or the other, but I didn't yet know quite what. During this year we tried one major block of study in the laboratories where all of the students were allowed to set up their own laboratory activities for a period of about a month near the end of the year without even being accountable to their teaching assistants. As we observed the students, we found that they seemed to be getting a great deal out of their exploration. Perhaps, I thought, the students ought to be having a much greater role in deciding what they were going to study, especially in elementary courses.

Several other things happened that helped me to break away from my perception of the teacher's role as a director, manager, evaluator, grader, and judge. One of these things was the case of a science teacher back for a year of graduate study who took my elementary course. This student had clearly been one of the best students in the laboratory section of the course. However, he had considerable difficulties with the lecture examinations, consistently scoring in the low B range when compared with the undergraduates in the same course. As a graduate student, in order to receive graduate credit, he was expected to write a term paper. Normally when an especially good term paper came in, I would attach more weight to that than to relatively low marks on lecture examinations. At the time of the final examination for the course

—*Photo by Robert Samples. Courtesy of Environmental Studies project.*

this student came in with his usual middle range grade, and the term paper he handed to me was very mediocre. In spite of his high rating in the laboratory part of the course I assigned him a grade of B. He came in to me to talk the situation over and mentioned how much he felt he had gotten out of the course, speaking especially of his excellent performance in the laboratory and of the good reports his teaching assistant had been giving him. And yet he said the grade was leaving a very sour taste in his mouth. My normal procedure in earlier years would have been to raise the flag with "non-negotiable" written in large letters upon it. However, my feelings about the negotiability of grades had already begun to change. So I made a proposition to him. I suggested that if he would like to take the period between the two terms and take another crack at the term paper in the light of certain suggestions I would make, I would be happy to consider putting in a change of grade slip for him. I cautioned him that I might grade him no more highly on the second attempt at this term paper than I had on the first. After weighing the proposition for a day or two he decided that he would make another attempt. The paper he handed in to me was a superb one, and I thus advanced his grade to A. I think perhaps the first change of grade slip is the most difficult to send in. Once this is done, the second, third, and fourth come much more easily, and not only that but the whole concept of comparative evaluation in one's mind then begins to crumble.

I recently visited a colleague at an institution in the Middle West. As we talked together about removal of constraints and trusting students, he showed me a scheme that he had devised to allow students to count extra project work toward improving their course standing. He showed me a superb term paper that had been submitted by one of his students on the subject of environmental pollution. He described in detail to me the excellence of the piece of work. In jest, thinking back to my own earlier attitude toward grades, I said to him, "I suppose you gave her a C?" To this he answered in all sincerity, "Yes." When I asked him why, he responded, "Well, on the basis of this term paper, I certainly couldn't give her the F that she had coming." I then asked him, "If she was clearly an A student on the basis of this excellent piece of work, why didn't you give her the A?" To this, he gave the usual response about fairness to the rest of the students in the class, subjective evaluation versus objective evaluation, and so forth. I hope that perhaps our exchange will lead him to reconsider his position as I have had to examine mine.

Another instance after I returned to Syracuse from Norway further influenced my feelings in this matter. One of my students during my last semester at Syracuse University seemed a very average student, quite uninterested in the course, but easily able to get the "gentleman's C." I thought throughout the semester that this was a very mediocre student, especially as I saw the Cs rolling in on his examinations and his laboratory exercises. About three months after the end of the semester, however, I received a letter from this student talking about how he had enjoyed the geology course in spite of his apparently mediocre performance. Enclosed with the letter was a copy of an article he had written for a small newspaper in Massachusetts where he was working during the summer as a journalist, journalism being his major. His paper consisted of a very sophisticated analysis of a group of gravel deposits in the town where he lived and of the implications of some quarrying activities which were being planned by several contractors. On the basis of his work leading up to this article, it was clear that this student was worthy of "any man's A" in elementary geology. Yet, whenever anyone looks back at his record they are more likely to evaluate his knowledge of geology on the basis of my superficial evaluation. I had graded him on what I expected him to learn rather than on what he actually had learned.

Another straw that helped break this camel's back was the case of two students in this same last semester at Syracuse University. One, a girl, had been performing reasonably well in the course but missed a great many laboratories and lectures toward the end of the course and, as a matter of fact, did not even appear for the final examination. Consequently I placed an F on her grade card. The other student was a boy who had attended lectures and labs fairly assiduously and had appeared to be doing the minimum work in the laboratory. However, he had terrible fortune with the examinations, consistently coming in with extremely low scores. He, too, received a grade of F. Shortly after the end of the term I received a letter from the dean of women asking me if I would not change the girl's grade from F to Incomplete, in that she had had some personal problems (some of them health problems) and had agreed that she would retake the course during summer session. The dean asked if it would be all right for her to have her grade assigned on the basis of the summer session rather than having an F posted on her record. I quickly agreed that if the dean of women was willing to suggest such a remedy I would be all too happy to do what she asked.

Shortly after I received this request from the dean of women, the boy who had failed came in to negotiate about his grade. In this case I was adamant. Later he came in with his father, and he and his father pleaded with me to give the boy another chance. By this time I was mixed up enough so that I didn't know quite what to do. As a solution we finally decided that if he would retake the course during summer session, I would sign a petition to have the F removed from his transcript in favor of the summer grade. Both of these students subsequently completed the course satisfactorily.

These are a few of the instances that have brought me to reconsider seriously some of the basic assumptions I was operating under about the teaching-learning relationship. I had a chance during the summer of that year, 1969, to begin trying some of the assumptions I now felt I was ready to test.

DECISION TO BECOME
A FACILITATOR OF LEARNING

During the summer of 1969 I worked for six weeks with a group of sixteen so-called gifted high school students whose learning experience was supported by a grant from the National Science Foundation. Conditions for learning were optimal. I had a full-time teaching assistant to work with me with these sixteen young people, we had a good equipment budget, we had a thousand dollars to pay for field trip expenses, and all of the students were there because they had expressed a special desire to come learn about geology during their summer vacation. There was no credit assigned to the learning experience, and no grades were to be given. There was no particular body of subject matter that needed to be covered. So this was a time to test assumptions. Furthermore we had available all of the facilities of the geology department at Syracuse University. Most of the faculty and graduate students were away doing summer field work, and we had access to a very rich environment for learning about things geological.

When we got together with the students, we mentioned to them that the stimuli we would provide would mainly be in the form of field trips to various areas. At the field trip localities students would be free to investigate whatever they wished to study. When we were back in the laboratory, they could pursue studies of any kind they wished. We let it be known that we would suggest possible activities but that the students would be free to do virtually whatever they pleased within the limitations of the constraints imposed by the environment we could provide. We also agreed that each student would probably want to undertake some special study of his own—probably a library problem of some type or the other—and that each would obligate himself to present his results to the rest of the group. Both Ed Shay, my teaching assistant, and I let it be known that we would do virtually no lecturing but would be available to give short talks occasionally if such talks were requested. Among other optimal activities, we showed films at least two or three times a week in the late afternoon for any students who were interested. At these sessions about half the group were usually present, while the others continued to work on other things of interest to them or to engage in various social activities with other members of the NSF group.

On the first regular day of the six-week session we proceeded to a quarry near Syracuse where we suggested to the students that they might want to look around for whatever they found interesting. We spent several days during that first week working around the quarry. As I think back to that experience now, I recall that we more or less expected all of the students to be present on those field trips. In this sense, perhaps we were not facilitating to the best of our capabilities. For students who preferred to remain back and work in the library or laboratory, we should and could have provided this opportunity. Since there were two of us as instructors, it would have been easy for one of us to be in the field with the group and the other to be back in the laboratory. I fear that our own desire to be outside on those pleasant summer days may have gotten in the way of our better judgment.

In the early stages of discussion, some of the students expressed a strong desire to take a several-day-overnight kind of field trip. This was another experience that it might have been within our power to make possible. However, Ed and I, probably as I think about it now mainly for reasons of personal convenience, found excuses not to let this overnight experience take place.

There was never any real pressure on the students to perform any particular work in the laboratory or to look at any particular things in the field. Ed and I occasionally posed some general problems, and we were always available to share student excitement for things discovered and to become excited ourselves over things that we had not seen before. One student came up to me after we had been together for a couple of weeks and said that he wished we would take the group to a place where we had never been before in order that they could see how we might work in a new place. Fortunately, at the time he made that particular request we actually were at a field locality that I had never visited before, and so we were able to approach the problems posed at that particular field locality in an entirely fresh way.

After the first few days, which were spent mainly in the field in areas where Ed and I knew of many interesting things to be seen, the idea came up that we should somehow be making a special attempt to organize our data in some kind of order. Ed and I, still thinking in terms of economy of time, did make some fairly specific suggestions about how some of the data might be organized. We did not require compliance with our suggestions, but now, looking back, I regret that we did not leave the students to decide for themselves what they wished to do with their data and with their rock samples before we made suggestions of our own.

As the students began studying their materials they needed resources of various kinds. We provided chemicals, microscopes, thin sections of their rock materials, and many other things that both they and we, either together or separately, thought of. When we began to work with thin sections of rocks, the students wished to know how to prepare these, and we made it possible for them to learn to operate the machinery and prepare their own materials. Here again I have a regret: In Ed's and my compulsion to get the students out to new and more glorious field localities, we overlooked the wishes of several students to do more work preparing thin sections and working with these materials under the petrographic microscope and in other ways. Had we allowed the field trips to be clearly optional, more useful, in-depth follow-up activities could have been performed by students who wished to do such things. Ed and I still had some general notion of structure which we were not exactly imposing on the students but were so strongly favoring that the students mainly followed us. Further along some students began requesting permission to stay behind from some of the field activities to do other things. When such requests were made, we gave permission. However, we should have made it clearer at the very beginning that such permission was always available. We were still seeking the way toward greater freedom in the learning experience. In many instances, we simply weren't ready in our own minds to think of the many extra possibilities that existed. For the most part we tried to keep the students grouped and did not encourage individual digressions to the extent that we should have.

Toward the end of the very first part of the session, many students became discontented with merely working with the materials physically and wished to know more about what the literature and other people's studies could tell them about the things they were working on. They felt that a stronger base of background knowledge would help them learn more about the materials they were studying. Ed and I suggested that they might want to set up a study group and possibly a seminar. They decided to gather together in small groups to consider certain special kinds of rocks and to do some reading before their seminar which would be scheduled for sometime early in the second week. Ed and I provided extensive reference lists in order that they might know where to go for information. We were available to help them learn their way around in the library and to provide them with books from my own and Ed's library when this was more convenient.

At last the morning of the seminar arrived. Ed and I arranged the tables in our big laboratory room into a big square, and the students came in and sat down around this table. We sat with them also. We sat together in silence and the students first looked at me and I smiled back and looked around the room, but said nothing. And they looked at Ed and he smiled back at them and they again looked around the room in puzzlement. The period of embarrassed silence continued for perhaps five minutes. Finally one of the students got up and said, "Well, I've had enough of this waiting around. If nobody else is going to say anything, I'll start. I've been studying about shales. . . ." After this he proceeded to give a very sophisticated discussion of shales— certainly equivalent to anything I had heard from upper division students in courses specially devoted to sedimentary rocks. As he continued to speak, a number of students chimed in to contradict him on certain points indicating that they had other information from the sources that they had studied. Ed and I kept completely out of the discussion until toward the end when each of us pointed out other things that we thought were interesting also. We had expected the entire seminar covering all of the major rock types they had been working with to last only an hour and a half or so. The session actually continued, with many breaks, and another field trip as an interruption, for a total of perhaps six or eight hours. The peer group interaction was extensive, and the contributions that Ed and I made were relatively few.

For another major group of activities, the students and we together decided that it might be interesting to make some studies of a local lake in the Green Lakes State Park. We obtained the assistance of Walter Dean, also of the geology department at Syracuse, as a resource person. Neither the students nor Ed nor I knew anything about problems of studying lakes. Dean provided us with the paraphernalia of the limnologist. We arranged with the State Park Service to provide us, free of charge, several boats in which our expedition was to take place. The students grouped themselves according to the various kinds of measurements they wished to make, and we spent several hours taking core samples of bottom materials, water samples at various depths, temperature measurements, oxygen measurements and resistivity measurements and gaining other information that would be useful in interpreting the nature of this particular lake. Dean then was available to the students for an afternoon of laboratory work studying the particular data they had gathered. Here again Ed and I more or less arbitrarily cut off this activity too early. A number of the students might have gone on for days or even weeks pursuing further kinds of lake studies had we made this opportunity available. However, we kept luring the students onto other tangents. We did not demand that they go off on these tangents with us, but we cut short their natural desire for following through on activities they had already begun.

The sixteen students in our geology group made up only one section of the NSF students at Syracuse that summer. There were similar groups in chemistry, physics, and biology. Interestingly, the students in these other sections had somewhat more structured programs, and many times I had the nagging feeling that maybe we ought to have something more definite that we were covering rather than trying to follow up as we were on student activities. We did impose some special constraints through the large number of field trips in which we expected students to participate, but we had very little by way of definite studies that we expected our students to perform for us. We encouraged them to pursue their own lines of interest for most of the time. I no longer have any guilt feelings about allowing them to do many of the things they wished to do. My guilt feelings rather are for not giving them more freedom than we did.

Toward the middle of the six-week session, all of the NSF students decided to have their own group symposium on problems in science. They set up this symposium entirely on their own and made it known that the faculty members associated with the program were welcome to attend the symposium but were not invited to participate in its planning and execution. During the symposium the students became heavily involved in the interdisciplinary nature of science and in considering the responsibility of scientists to society, their own roles as future scientists or persons at least interested in science in a very important way, and environmental pollution.

For the section on water pollution, a well-known water pollution expert was called in to give a special presentation. His presentation was not very scientifically done but was instead a moralizing sermon on the evils of water pollution. The students in my group were rather incensed by the shallowness of this presentation and began to ask the speaker for more details. The speaker conducted himself in a very authoritarian manner with the group. At one time during the course of his slide presentation, which was rather dull, a few students somewhere in the middle of the room apparently began whispering to each other. We on the other side of the room were not even aware that there was any disturbance. The lecturer suddenly shouted at these students in front of the entire group and invited them to grow up and be quiet and respect him or else to get out. The students in our own particular group, who were not involved in this incident, were nonetheless highly disappointed in this authoritarianism (of which they said they had seen plenty in their own high schools and needed no more).

Before this lecture several of our own students, knowing that they were to have a presentation on water pollution, had decided that they wished to study Onondaga Lake, a highly polluted body of water just adjacent to the city of Syracuse. We got out the measuring apparatus we needed for our study and spent the better part of a day studying the water along the shoreline, the water coming into the lake from various tributary streams, the water leaving the lake, the nature of beach deposits, and the nature of material being piled up along the lake shore by the Allied Chemical Corporation. Thus our students had made a detailed study of the lake already and were eager to talk in detail about the actual nature of pollution rather than dealing with emotional and political approaches to the issue. One of the most important parts of these lake study activities we engaged in was that neither Ed nor I knew anything at all about lake study at the beginning of the exercise. We were involved as co-learners with our students, and the working relationship that developed was one of real partnership. We turned out to have as much if not more difficulty operating much of the apparatus than the students did. We were operating on an equal basis, and learning crackled in the air.

Many of the special student projects based on library studies turned out to be extremely interesting. Here again we erred in more or less requiring all students to be present at the talks given by their peers. In course critiques we received later, some of the students felt that some of these were boring or dull. Had attendance at these sessions been more optional they would perhaps have had a better feeling about them. As students worked on their library project reports, they became interested in many things that Ed and I knew little about. One girl was very much interested in the effects of geological factors on architecture. She and I spent many hours sitting on the floor together in the library pawing through books in attempts to find references that might get her started. We gradually found some access routes, but these did not seem entirely satisfactory. At a cocktail party one evening, I was talking to a friend of mine, the head of the Department of City Planning, about this young lady's interests. He said to me, "Send her over, and I'll be glad to put her onto some things I know about." He later guided her to suitable resource materials, and she produced a remarkably good study. In the meantime, she and I found on *my own bookshelf* a long memoir dealing with architecture and geology among the proceedings of a recent international geological congress. Thus Susan helped me to learn more about the resources that I actually had available on my own shelf.

We became, as it were, facilitators for each other. It seems to me that a true facilitator must be a co-learner with the people he is associated with in the learning experience.

Another student, whom we seemed unable to help very effectively, was interested in pollution of the deep ocean. With this student I spent hours, again sitting on the library floor, getting acquainted with journals such as *Ecology,* which I had never known about before. I was able to put this student in touch with a professor of civil engineering who had a great deal of experience in studying pollution of inland waters. This resource person was able to help the student to a considerable degree. A facilitator's acquaintance with large numbers of resource people becomes a critical factor in helping students pursue lines of their own inquiry. Thus a facilitator must develop a network of contacts if he wishes to provide the best possible support for his students.

*   *   *   *   *

The preceding description of some of the incidents that happened during this summer session has been intended to describe a first real attempt at conscious facilitation as opposed to teaching. It was largely during this session that I finally decided that I never wished to "teach" again. Many of the things we did during this summer session still smacked strongly of "teaching," and these were the things I have identified in the text above that I would now definitely do differently. We facilitated to the extent that we allowed the students to follow their own lines of inquiry and to the extent that we were able to provide unusual resources that we had not thought of before. Our first attempt at facilitation was clearly marked by many incidents of inflexibility. Nonetheless it pointed out to both Ed and me that students are capable of making significant decisions about what to study and that the more freedom we allowed them the more effectively they learned.

Although we became personally involved with the students, we still allowed many little things to keep us apart from them— faculty versus students. There are many ways I am now aware of in which we could have been more real as human beings confronting each other. We gave up most of our "power" over the students, and this made a close personal relationship possible, but we did not really share personal feelings and emotions to the extent that we should have. We broke off our dialogue whenever personal considerations began to become strong. This was the single thing most lacking in our first attempt at facilitation. Further attempts will certainly have to make a special place for truly human factors to come into the picture rather than be avoided. There was relatively little role-playing in our relationship but our next endeavor must go further toward removing status barriers.

2

Looking at Some Elementary and Secondary Schools

FEELINGS ON A DAY IN GRADE SCHOOL

This morning I went to school with a grade school friend of mine. The children seemed relaxed and at ease. Several of them came up to talk to me.

Mrs. B., the teacher, was bustling about helping a few of the children who had come in before the bell rang. At the bell, the children playing outside lined up and marched into their classrooms. For several minutes they roamed around the room talking to each other, getting books and other things they needed.

"Danny," said Mrs. B., "you didn't hand in your math paper. I want to see you at recess."

Then she said, "Good morning, children," to which they responded in unison, "Good morning, Mrs. B."

A science teacher aide named John was in Mrs. B.'s room today, and she had asked him to bring out a model celestial sphere and one of those little models you use to demonstrate the astronomical reasons for summer, winter, and eclipses. A group of children were playing with these seductive pieces of apparatus, and the science aide was standing there with them.

"Now don't play with those," said Mrs. B. "We'll tell you about them later."

Mrs. B. started a little question and answer game about stars, orbits, and planets. Many of the children had books on the stars, and some began to leaf through them. A few carried on with the question and answer game Mrs. B. was playing. Gradually children drifted away, although Mrs. B. was trying to be the central attraction with her questions. The activity of the students became more diversified, and many were communicating with each other or were reading, looking at the celestial sphere models, looking at plants in the corner of the room, or talking to me or John.

Having lost center stage, Mrs. B. asked the students to take their seats. She talked for several minutes, and the children gradually grew more fidgety. Then she asked John to tell the children about the models. While he talked, Mrs. B. moved around sorting through some books and writing on the board the page numbers the children could read to find out more about what John was describing. The children moved around the classroom without asking permission, and the feeling of the classroom was fairly free.

One little boy, Larry, asked for a book. Mrs. B. denied it to him with the statement, "You have things I already gave you yesterday." Then Larry came back to me to tell me about his insect collection.

Mrs. B. then gave the children an assignment to do some research on the stars. During the next thirteen minutes some children looked through their star books; others gravitated back to those exciting but untouchable models (which they touched anyway to the tune of frequent warnings from Mrs. B.). The activity of the group again became highly diversified as each child followed his own bent.

At the end of these thirteen minutes Mrs. B. got out some plants the children had been observing. One was a shamrock and, since Saint Patrick's day was near, she launched into a question game about where Ireland is. "Is it a continent? Is it an island? What oceans surround it? We should try to know these things. Look at a map. Maps are very interesting. (Crossly) No talking now because I can't cover all this if you do! Leave that book alone." Then she moved back to her lecture.

Suddenly she diverted the one-way conversation to Irish family names in the class and national origin of other family names. At this, the children all became very attentive and began to talk both to her and to each other. The Scandinavian peninsula was brought up, and she asked, "What's a peninsula?"

By this time I was beginning to feel like a ping-pong ball as she bounced from one topic to another.

Her little lecture and discussion held the class into a more or less unified group for about six minutes before the activity of the children began to diversify again, with each child aiming toward some personally chosen activity. Two minutes after the diversification process was well under way she stopped them. "Are we going to listen please?" She returned to her plants, stressing words like "rhizome." Very important to ihe children! Certain children were designated as flower pot carriers, and they carried the various plants around the room for other children to see. As the plant parade went on, the children who remained seated moved back into the books on the stars, their arithmetic lessons, talking about their insect collections, or playing with the celestial sphere model.

But seven minutes later Mrs. B. pulled them all back again to give a little lecture on the plants. She asked John to give his ideas, too. He did this for a while, but he quickly let the children diversify.

John *responds* to the children and encourages diversified activity.

Mrs. B. *manages* the children and discourages diversified activity.

The plant discussion led Mrs. B. back to Ireland again with suggestions that the children do a little research (a favorite word of hers) on Ireland and also that they start a dinner table conversation that evening at home about their own ancestors. She then asked the children to look up the word "tuber." Several children without dictionaries started over to get them, but she stopped them, reminding them that it was the "book committee's" job to distribute the books. She pointed out to the children how they were combining spelling and language with their science.

At four after ten, the librarian came into the room and half of the class disappeared with her. Those who remained engaged in diverse activities. Several worked on math and Mrs. B. went around helping individuals. The room felt warm and at ease as the children worked along on their own. In the library, they browsed, checked their own books in and out, read, and carried on casual conversations with each other. The children in the class communicated well and regularly with each other and seemed to show care and concern for each other. Each half of the class had about fifteen minutes to browse in the library.

When all had had their chance at the library and had had some individual attention from Mrs. B., it was recess time, and there were twenty minutes for roughhousing. There was nothing particularly rigid about the movement of the children from one activity to another. They were not ordered about, but they seemed to come and go more or less together without any strong or obvious managing by the teachers.

About a third of the children went off to their music class while the others were asked by Mrs. B. to work on their math.

Some children asked Mrs. B. about their grades. She said she didn't like to give grades, and it was clear that she certainly didn't like to discuss them. But the idea of grades as a game to play ("How much work do I need to do to get ... ?") was already strongly implanted in their nine-year-old minds.

A discussion broke out on how to get more people from the community to come to their classroom. An Indian lady from Bombay had visited the class earlier in the year, and the children decided they wanted her back. No one remembered her name, address, or phone number, and so they mapped out a campaign for finding her again. One of the children referred to her as an "old woman," and Mrs. B. jumped on the child, insisting that he say "elderly lady." Mrs. B. turned the discussion partially into an etiquette lesson, asking the children how they would approach the lady to invite her, how to inquire to find out where she lived, how to introduce people to each other, and how to find out someone's name discreetly.

Later, Mrs. B. required the children to write down a resume of what had been discussed during the morning. She had her own summary written on the board, and all of the children dutifully copied down what Mrs. B. had done rather than writing about what they had done, learned, or felt. One child who started to ask a question was met with Mrs. B.'s answer of, "You know, there are times when you keep your mouth quiet and then you'll learn things."

Mrs. B. moved the children on in their math. She proceeded to drill the class rapidly, leaving an occasional child behind. They were working on least common multiples, which must be very important because it's in the "new math" books. All the children had to do was learn a system by heart and then follow the memorized rules to get an answer for which they saw little use. Learning the vocabulary of the system was emphasized. Old test papers were handed back and corrected. Mrs. B. encouraged the children to work together, and some of the more successful students were specifically designated as teachers to help the less successful. But she said firmly to several children, "If you're helping each other, that's all right, but no visiting!"

Several children assembled around John and me in the back of the room. They always clustered around John whenever they could without being sent back to their seats by Mrs. B. One child had a little broken motor for a toy car. So we all figured out together how to take it apart to see if we could fix it. John cut his finger slightly, and two of the little girls solemnly led him off to bandage the tiny cut. They came back talking about cuts, bleeding, and blood clotting. We then decided that the motor was hopelessly broken because some of the magnets inside had disintegrated and kept the shaft from turning freely.

Mrs. B. hovered over the children doing their math, telling them to hurry. They appeared nervous. She told one little girl that if she was going to be a helper, she must *help.* "A teacher's job is to make sure people get it."

John talked with the children about what they wanted to talk about. He didn't have to *manage* them.

Lunch was a leisurely time. There was some standing in line that had to be done, but the children were free to chatter and had ample time to eat. A half-hour recess followed lunch. Some children played outside while others read or talked in their classrooms. On the playground I saw Mrs. B. glaring at several children and striking a little metal triangle. At the ringing of the triangle many children looked to see whom she was glaring at. Some overly rambunctious boys saw her looking at them and abruptly stopped their rough game—only to move it to another part of the schoolyard out of her sight.

The afternoon continued, with primary attention to the math. John was asked to come up and help the class with fractions. Several students, as Mrs. B. said, already knew about these and didn't need the drill, but she asked them to repeat the exercise anyway. John used a number line to talk about fractions, and even though the discussion was led as a drill by John, the class pitched in cheerfully, and the game became a pleasant one.

Mrs. B. continued in her role as the enforcer. Whenever a child let his attention wander, she was on top of him telling him to pay attention and checking to make sure he was writing things down properly in his notebook. Finally she interrupted John and moved in using another technique than the number line to illustrate the fractions. I had the feeling of being bludgeoned. John good-naturedly tolerated her interruption and seemed to be almost in cahoots with the class.

Mrs. B. asked the students to draw circles and divide them up into five equal parts. Looking at one child's circle she said in front of the whole class, "Yours is too irregular. I couldn't give you credit for that."

At this point, completely exhausted, although the children still had an hour to go, I left. I had been "managed out" for the day.

*   *   *   *   *

Mrs. B. is an experienced teacher. She cares about children. But she has a hangup about covering ground, and she thinks that children learn best when they are managed and when all are jumping from topic to topic as she has "logically" arranged things. I saw them learning best when she wasn't managing and when they weren't being treated as little beings who couldn't be trusted to learn on their own. Mrs. B. is trying. She is allowing resource people to come in. She is allowing diversified activities to break out. But before they have a chance to develop, she puts the children down. She is afraid to give them real responsibility for their learning. But she is seeking new ways. Perhaps she can become a facilitator, if she is willing to give up her power.

OPEN SPACE DOES NOT NECESSARILY MAKE A GOOD GRADE SCHOOL

Physically open environments as in the currently favored open-space schools do not guarantee that teachers will become facilitators. Some observations by Mrs. Verna Todd of the Earth Science Educational Program illustrate this. Her comments on a visitation to an open-space school are reproduced here with her permission.

First let me describe the physical surroundings. The three grades occupy one large, carpeted area that can be partitioned off with accordion-fold doors. Each teacher can almost isolate her class if she chooses. Several of the teachers have done this, so for all practical purposes these teachers have self-contained classrooms, except that they may receive several groups of students and teach the same subject to each group. It seemed that each teacher I talked with complained about the lack of equipment. The chairs hadn't come, and the cabinets were the wrong size—as were the tables. The cassette recorders didn't fit the headphone jacks, so neither were being used. Only one teacher's area (out of about twelve) had windows.

Now for what the students were doing. In almost all of the areas most of the students were doing one activity, whether it was reading, arithmetic, or art. They either had been given assignments that they were working on or they were all (supposedly) listening to the teacher or discussing with her whatever she was explaining. Clipboards seemed to be standard equipment for the students instead of notebooks. Tracking of students is used and students are grouped according to their ability, determined by test scores and classroom performance.

Perhaps a series of vignettes will tell the story better.

In one area about twenty children are lying on the floor or leaning against a wall, each reading silently from his copy of the reader. I am amazed that all actually seem to be reading, despite the fact that no teacher is in evidence.

The only male teacher has his students on the floor in front of him with their clipboards and readers. They are discussing point of view (first person, omniscient—a word he's urging the kids to use instead of "all knowing"—and historical) as used in the stories they've been reading. Several children volunteer answers to the questions the teacher is asking, and they seem to have a good grasp of the concepts.

Almost all of the children seem to have their attention focused on the discussion. I confess I find the teacher interesting, and I think I'd have learned a considerable amount if I had been in his class.

An older, plump teacher is talking about "citations" to a group of about two-thirds of her students seated in a semicircle in front of her. (I don't remember what she said about citations, but I think she was talking about the dictionary kind and not the traffic kind. I don't think her students remember what she said about them either, for it was easy to see their squirms, vacant expressions, and conversations with their neighbors.) The other third are working with dictionaries and clipboards. One girl explains to me that she is choosing from the dictionary words to write down. She can choose any word. This third of the class apparently can talk or move around as they choose.

Another plump (this time, young) teacher is talking to all her students about starving. I catch, "I don't suppose any of you have actually felt like you were starving, but many people do." I find it more interesting to watch a boy in the back pull out of his desk a folded paper missile and show it to me. His neighbor pulls one out, too, and they discreetly go through the motions of throwing them.

In the one area that has windows I find more my idea of an open environment. Three girls are at the blackboard in the back of the room working arithmetic problems and consulting a "guide" that contains the answers. Several students are working on SRA (Science Research Associates) units and others seem to have pages of dittoed problems. Some students are sitting at tables and others are lying on the floor. A small group is clustered around the teacher at the front blackboard and the few of them (teacher and students) are discussing division— the teacher talking like one of the students and not as an "explainer."

In probably the most central of all the areas is a group of students sitting at tables and answering dittoed sheets of questions by consulting their copies of *Scholastic.* The teacher is sitting on a stool at the front. As the students complete their sheets they bring them up to her. It appears that they can read library books when they have finished. Two students come up to the teacher to ask a question. Before they speak, she asks them, "Is this recess?"

"No."

"Then wait till recess and ask me then."

Another boy has stopped to talk to a friend.

"Doug, is this recess?"

"No."

"Then what are you doing there?"

"I was going to look for my pencil."

"Over there? You're kidding me!"

A boy with a long, rumpled shirttail comes to ask about a word.

"Were you here after recess?"

"Yes."

"Didn't I explain that word right after recess? Tom (getting the attention of another boy nearby and pointing to the word in question), didn't I explain that word after recess?"

"Yes."

The first boy turns and walks away.

It seems to me that most of the teachers in this school are trying to teach as if they were in self-contained classrooms. They aren't really utilizing the open space.

Wow! Does the difference between teachers show up when one sees several in succession! I wonder if a good teacher who *cares* (I hate to use the cliché) about her students isn't still the key. Changing the environment isn't going to make a bad teacher good and vice versa.

FEELINGS IN SOME
JUNIOR HIGH SCHOOL CLASSES

Well before school began, they were there. The gym was full of boys and girls rehearsing for tomorrow's gymnastics exhibition. Several teachers spoke to me as I wandered through the halls. At the office I received a pink room-to-room pass—the same kind the students get—so that I could get by the vice-principal if I were challenged. And there he was in action already. When I went back to watch the gymnastics rehearsal, I saw him stop some boys to work them over for some peccadillo unseen by me as I had watched them earlier.

At 8:20 the first bell rang, and students who had been outside came rushing into the building. Locker doors banged and the din increased.

I met some science teacher friends in the hall. They were friendly and open as usual. They were teasing each other and me about relative merits of open versus "structured" approaches to education. Suddenly a thirteen-year-old girl came dashing up to the four of us and blurted out to me, "Who are you? What are you here for?" One of the teachers, a little on the defensive about quality of teacher-student relationships said, "See, how's that for openness?" I felt good. I always do when students feel free enough to approach me, a stranger, with such open candor and friendliness.

The teachers were mainly informally dressed. Few of them wore ties, and some of them even dressed "mod." For the most part the students communicated with each other in the halls without apparent regimentation or repression. I stopped to talk to Jenny, a thirteen-year-old friend I had come to visit, who was getting books out of her locker. She mentioned that she and Barb shared their lockers—keeping both of their coats in the one near the door and all of their books and supplies in another one near the center of the building. After all, they only had four minutes between classes, and they had to change books in a hurry. They weren't allowed to share lockers, the girls said, but lots of people did anyway. When the vice-principal inspected the lockers or found them out some other way, they would change back to singles for a day or two and then double up again.

I went off to a physical science class and sat down at a lab bench with a couple of girls. The 8:30 bell rang, and all fell silent while a well-known voice presented the morning's announcements over the P.A. system—lunch menu, announcement about a convocation, no faculty meeting today. . . .

After announcements the students were told to continue work on their circuit-wiring lab activity. They split into groups of four or five, got what they needed for their work, and proceeded to experiment with batteries, bulbs, wires, ammeters and voltmeters. They communicated freely, bantered with the teacher, helped each other, and asked the teacher for help. She was readily available, moving about from one group to the other, never imposing herself, but always available. The other day when I saw Jenny, she said, "Mrs. R. isn't so bad after all when you get to know her a little bit. She really wants to help us." One of the girls in the group was busily writing a letter to President Nixon, asking him to support some conservation measures. Another girl had a green pass to get her out of school early so she could go to a wedding. The wedding was a more important topic to these fifteen-year-olds than were their circuits. Mrs. R. didn't bother them, but let the conversation continue. She recognized that the conversation was important.

The groups were following some explicit instructions about how to set up their circuits, what to measure, what to record, and what questions to answer. They worked along mechanically, paying little attention to what they were doing. Several boys who had finished the exercise asked to go out into the courtyard in the sun to do their calculations. Mrs. R. gave them permission right away.

Mrs. R. mentioned her hope that the class would finish their experimentation that day, ready for discussion the next. The girls and students at the other tables began to work more purposefully. Nancy discovered a better way to wire the meters, and the data began to come in faster. The wires to the meter kept getting crossed and causing a short. I finally reached over and separated the wires, without saying anything. The girls then started playing with the wires, crossing and uncrossing them and watching the effect on the meters.

The students were all active, and there seemed to be a warm feeling among them and between them and the teacher, but from the conversation it was pretty clear that the girls at my table didn't care a hang about circuits and were learning little. They knew the formula for passing the quizzes without understanding, but their perception of the class was that it was a painless way to pass the time—better during labs because they could talk about what interested them, dull during the lectures and "discussions" which occupied most of their hours in science.

We had a full four minutes to sprint from science to algebra class, clear at the other end of the building. No time to exchange books, so Jenny carried her books with her for the whole morning. Four minutes is a short enough time so you don't really have to worry about further regimentation. Too short a time to get into trouble!

Mr. P. came in and began taking roll. Casual conversation continued among the students, and Mr. P. seemed unconcerned. He mentioned their horrible results on the test given the day before. He said he wasn't even going to hand the papers back— at least not yet. Linda wanted hers back. Mr. P.'s response was, "Do you want it back so you can frame your first F, Linda?" Others clamored to get their papers back in order to see what they had done wrong. But Mr. P. was adamant. "Let's see first how you do these problems *right.*" He then set out to explain how to work out the story problem involving factoring of trinomials. Some students obviously followed the discussion. The confusion of others seemed to increase. Mr. P. talked over eighty percent of the time, occasionally addressing simple questions to class members to try to keep them involved. I looked at my watch. Only half of the period was over. I began to squirm. I wasn't the only one. Most of the kids looked like they were daydreaming. What in the hell do they need to know this for? What does this have to do with their lives?

Every now and then, after my mind wandered, I would look at the board and see several new steps to a problem written up

—Photo by Robert Samples. Courtesy of Environmental Studies project.

there. Frequently they didn't make sense to me until I realized that some steps had been covered orally while I daydreamed. Occasionally Mr. P. had written down something not related to the immediate problem. I could see kids writing this stuff down every now and then—going back to copy down a bunch of steps without any understanding of intermediate steps or of the problem being studied. My mind wandered back to my own tenth grade algebra class, and I saw my own boredom of twenty-five years ago reflected in Jenny's eyes.

Some of the students shook their heads in what I presume was disbelief and doubt when Mr. P. turned his back.

Mr. P. made a mistake in a problem—perhaps on purpose. A few members of the class caught him and corrected him. He admitted fault, and the mood lightened as students and teacher chuckled over the teacher's error. The heaviness and perplexity returned soon.

A bell rang and I thought, "Finally, it's over," but this was a bell for something else. We had another ten minutes to go. Several students were totally non-participating, taking no notes, looking out of the windows, and otherwise uninvolved.

After the final ten minutes, Mr. P. announced that they would try another test tomorrow. Panicky comments from the class followed.

Later, as I talked to Jenny about the class, she mentioned that several friends had come up to her to confirm her feeling that Mr. P. had yelled a lot less than usual that day. He had seemed quite calm and at ease to me, but apparently he "loses his cool" with students who can't understand his explanations—when visitors are *not* there.

A friend who knows Mr. P. mentioned to me that Mr. P. used to be quite a rebel—wanting to do away with grades. My question was, "Well, why didn't he?" Any teacher can subvert the grade system any time he wants to. Apparently he tired of fighting the system and now applied grades rigorously.

Jenny went to study hall next. She used to take art in third period, but the teacher "hassled" her so much, had such rigid ideas about how students should draw and what they should draw, and used grade threats in such an unpleasant manner that she dropped the course. It's a good thing her mother is an artist so that Jenny gets turned back on at home after such colossal turn-offs at school.

The study hall is a good hour—at least for Jenny. The school has two kinds of study halls: the old-fashioned kind I used to sit through where everyone was supposed to study but no one did and where the helpless teacher in charge had to be a bad-guy disciplinarian to keep some semblance of order; and a lounge period held in the school cafeteria where students can play cards, read, chat, study, or do pretty much what they want—even go outside (with the study hall teacher's permission). The story of how this second kind of study hall came about is an interesting one. A teacher suggested such an open study hall at a faculty meeting. The principal tried to evade the issue on the ground that there weren't enough staff members to cover it. The teacher who proposed the open period asked if it would be proper to poll the faculty to see how many teachers were willing to help in establishing such a period. The principal had no alternative but to establish the open period concept. The principal continued to try to obstruct by requiring written parental permission for students to be in the open study hall.

A similar situation occurred in another nearby school. The school was pressured into allowing students to leave the school grounds to have lunch outside—many of them in a nearby park —rather than being confined to the school cafeteria or yard as in most schools in this district. This sounded very advanced until I read the rest of the newspaper article indicating the strict rules the "free" students had to abide by and the written parental permission that was required. Trust a junior high school student?

I went to visit Maggie, an eighth grade friend from our neighborhood, in her social studies class. The students were all in rows, looking at the backs of other students' heads as usual. The teacher, Mr. M., was young, dynamic, and friendly. He talked a lot, easily eighty percent of the time, throwing out occasional questions requiring one-sentence answers from the students. He started with the Industrial Revolution, sidetracked to the Barbary Pirates, and ended with student reports on whaling and clipper ships.

Some of the class was like a quiz game. Mr. M. succeeded in getting the students to ask him questions, and when they did, he obviously enjoyed his role as a talking encyclopedia.

At times Mr. M. took up a storyteller's role. He was a good storyteller, too.

Maggie tells me that his tests mainly ask them to answer questions about subjects "covered" in class. Maggie is getting pretty good grades so she doesn't mind it. She's figured out the game.

Sometimes—about once a week on the average—Mr. M. has the students move their desks into a circle, and they all discuss current events. Maggie says they really argue sometimes and that they have fun. Mr. M. is trying very hard and doing his best within the framework of the philosophy he now accepts. But I wish he'd make every day a little more like current events day. So does Maggie.

As I look at the social studies book, talk to the students, and sit with them in class, I keep wondering: What part of the subject matter here has ever been important to me and to my life? What will be important to Maggie's life? Only she can decide that. Mr. M. cannot, and the curriculum makers cannot. I am just beginning to take pleasure in reading history and political science books now. Perhaps I would have enjoyed it more and started reading in earnest earlier if I had been able to choose what aspects of history and social studies I wished to learn about. I am very recalcitrant when people tell me what I *have* to learn. So is Maggie. Most of my students have been too, in the days when I thought of myself as a "teacher."

I went to Maggie's science class taught by Mr. H. Mr. H. got tired of "laying crap on his classes." Now they have Monday, Tuesday, and Wednesday of each week to do their own project work. Mr. H. asks them to sign a non-binding contract—more a brief statement of their goals—each week. The class votes on a "class topic" for study, but individuals need not confine their studies to it. The students grade themselves. Mr. H. talks to them about their grades but accepts their own self-evaluations. On Thursdays Mr. H. frequently has a film for the class. Friday is *teacher's* day. H. tells them about something he is interested in or asks them to perform an activity that he has set up.

Maggie is turned on to science. Last year another science teacher, Mr. C., gave her freedom and a loving environment in seventh grade science too. Why can't her other classes be like that?

I have seen some good people teaching in this junior high school. Some of them (like Mr. H. and Mr. C.) have taken the risk of allowing their students to make significant decisions, but even these fine teachers have to put up with a system that requires their students to be present in class five days a week at the same hour every day regardless of the students' interests or desires. Without significant change in the organization of the system even the best of the teachers, the Mr. H.'s and the Mr. C.'s, find their attempts at creating a humanistic learning environment thwarted. The primary villains I see within the system are the following:

1. Linear curricula. These are curricula created by people other than individual students. Any curriculum that forces students to proceed through a series of required stages with few or no deviations permitted is implicitly coercive, non-responsive, irrelevant to the needs of the student, and, to me, intolerable. It has never been and will never be possible to create a linear curriculum that can serve the needs of more than a small fraction of students in any group. Giving students the right to proceed at their own rate through a linear curriculum does not materially improve the situation. Externally imposed linearity has to disappear for a truly humanistic educational experience to be possible. Self-actualizing people cannot develop without freedom to choose goals.
2. Threats as exemplified by teacher-given grades. As long as a system requires teachers to rate students, it will be difficult or impossible for a truly humane environment to exist.

3. The classroom. As long as self-contained classrooms exist in a school and students are confined to them, humanistically oriented teachers will continue to work under an extreme handicap. Learning occurs best when students decide how long to remain in a given part of the learning environment.
4. The locus of decision-making. As long as the system requires or encourages teachers to make decisions for their students and to impose these decisions, the school will remain a basically hostile environment for learning.

WHAT TURNS WILLIAM ON

William is a turned-on nine-year-old tonight. Pat was at school today. Pat is a young physicist from the National Center for Atmospheric Research. He likes grade schoolers, so he spends two mornings a week in Mrs. W.'s class working with the kids. The kids call him Pat, too, when Mrs. W. is not within earshot.

When I walked in the door this evening, late for dinner as usual, William had a large pan full of corn starch and water. Instead of "Hello, Dad," he shouted, "Come see what Pat showed us. See what happens when I jab my finger in this stuff? It's hard! But look what happens when I put my finger in slowly. I can move it around just like in water."

Lucretia hurried us all in to dinner at that point.

After dinner, but before dessert, William was at me again. Sure enough, the mixture he had made was stiff and tacky when I tried to move a finger through it rapidly, but quite watery and liquid when I moved the finger slowly. William's pants were covered with dried cornstarch by this time as a result of his experimentation.

I had scarcely sat down to read the paper when William was after me again: "Look how I can multiply two numbers together." I groaned after my full day of committee meetings and laid the comic page aside. William then taught me how to multiply by using magic squares—something I had never done before. Then he and I tried some other more difficult problems using the magic squares, and everything seemed to check out. William finally decided really to test the system we had worked out starting from Pat's original simple problem. He multiplied 3796 times thirty-nine. It worked.

Then as I went to the bathroom, comic page still unread, William followed me. He wanted to show me the new "code" Pat had taught them. It turned out to be pig latin. So I chimed in in fluent pig latin. William then told me the rules Pat had taught them, and we argued over some of the finer points of pig latin.

Again I picked up the paper, but William was back at me to tell me that Pat had showed them another way of multiplying. The fingers were used in the fashion of a small digital computer. At first I drew a complete blank, but William persisted with his instruction, and I finally mastered the system. Cricket, Lucretia, and Gretchen, attracted by William's guffaws at my slowness, saw our finger play and were at a complete loss until William and I, together, helped them learn the system.

Back to the paper again—but, no, William still had to tell about a veteran from Viet Nam who had visited school and showed slides. It was amazing that it wasn't all one big battlefield, William said. There were pretty trees, flowers, and villages, except when people were dropping bombs.

William doesn't usually talk about school at night—only when Pat is there. William learned lots today—science, math, linguistics, social studies, and political science. School worked today. It could work that way every day if full-time teachers were like Pat, the amateur. Pat knows enough not to lay it on kids. He does exciting things but doesn't apply force or evaluation. It's less fun when Mrs. W. makes the kids take notes on Pat's demonstrations. But today she let Pat do it his way without interrupting.

And now I'm going to read the comic page.

CRICKET, DOTTY, AND GRETCHEN

Cricket, Dotty, and Gretchen are all junior high schoolers. Cricket has spent two years in science classes where she has been highly regimented under teachers who allow little freedom. Dotty had one term of a very free science class in which she was allowed to study anything in earth science she wanted to and to grade herself. During the rest of the time she has been highly regimented in conventional science courses. Gretchen has spent two years in science classes where she has a large amount of freedom. In the first part of her first year she still had assignments and grades, but her teacher then adopted a freer classroom. This is a verbatim transcript of a conversation among the three girls.

Cricket: I think I like science, but I don't like the teacher teaching it. For science to be interesting the teacher has to be enthusiastic. You need to do lots of experimenting and go out and find out things for yourself. Last year I had to worry about points for grades instead of about learning something.

Dotty: When you think of school, you think of a teacher standin' up there tellin' you what to do.

Gretchen: I like science. It depends on the teacher, whether he is exciting or the dull old routine type. My teacher lets us do what we want. I do more when I can do things I want to do. I have more freedom this year because I don't have to worry about grades at all. We grade ourselves.

Dotty: In the free class we went to last term you could do whatever you wanted. Like if you liked rocks like Cricket does, more than anything else, you could just go off and do that, and like if you wanted him to talk about it, like if you were reading in a book and you didn't understand something, he would explain it. But if you did, then you wouldn't have to just sit around and listen to what he had to say, you could just go off and do whatever you wanted. And like in my class now, all the teacher does is sit there and lecture and stuff. The other class was sorta better because if you got bored, you didn't have to listen to him. And like say you really hate rocks like I do, if you really hate 'em, you don't have to do 'em. If you like them like Cricket, you can do whatever you want.

Gretchen: In the first three quarters of the year our teacher was giving us study guides and tests. We didn't have to do this, to study the guides or the tests. He'd lecture about three-fourths of the time, and then the rest of the time we'd do research on it, and now and then we did an investigation on it and had a lab. And some of the labs I thought were really good; they showed the point. And the last quarter, well now, he's really letting us do what we want. He gives us our grades, but he doesn't stand up in front of the class any more and lecture to us or give us tests or study guides. Right now nobody's really doing very much because it's the beginning, and they don't know what to do because they usually have been told what to do, and now they have been given the privilege of doing what they want. Some of the kids are just goofing off, running around the class screaming and yelling, but others are working on articles in the school paper and really doing something and talking about things like cleaning up streams and lakes and just all over.

WDR: Which way do you think you were learning more, the first part or the last part?

Gretchen: I think the last quarter because you can sort of study what you want. And you really get more out of it if he doesn't just sit up there and lecture cause you get sort of bored, and some people go to sleep. I think it's really better when you just get to do what you want.

WDR: Which part do you think you learned most in, Dotty, the first (free class) semester or this one with the tight schedule?

Dotty: I think I learned more the first semester.

WDR: Even though you got to do what you wanted to all the time?

Dotty: Yeah, I think I learned more because you could go off on your own and do whatever you wanted. I still think I worked harder and got the best grade in the structured class.

WDR: But you learned more in the free one?

Dotty: Yeah.

WDR: What would you like your teacher to be like?

Dotty: Well, I'd like him to be really free, not like last year. I never like to hear teachers lecture because I never listen. I get bored. But I'd like him to just sort of stand around and if we wanted help to ask him. But I really get bored when I listen to a teacher talk. I don't think I understood anything he said 'cause I just don't seem to be listening.

I think a teacher should, you know, if you want to ask questions, he should let you ask questions. I don't think he should lecture much either. Sometimes he should and sometimes he shouldn't because people do go to sleep a lot in our class. Like if you feel like reading a book or something during his class, like that time that I did, he started lecturing, and then he told us we could do what we wanted, not really what you wanted but you could work on your thing, so if you got that thing done and you didn't feel like going on to other things, I think you should be able to like read your book or something for another class. He should let you. He shouldn't take your book away from you for three days. I think that's stupid.

WDR: He took it away from you? For three days?

Dotty: Yeah, he said he'd take it away 'til Friday which was three days from then. And he said he wouldn't give it back to me. And he never told me that, that he was going to take it away. But I think that's kind of dumb.

Gretchen: I think a teacher should be sort of nice to the kids instead of being grouchy if a kid drops a pencil and saying GO OUT OF THE ROOM, instead of telling them to pick up the pencil or paper or whatever they dropped.

Dotty: Like my teacher. He loathes me. Whenever you misspell a word and want to ask your friend or something like that, it makes him mad. You say one word, and he says, "Be quiet," even when you're not doing anything noisy, just whispering. He makes you stand up all the time. I think it's stupid.

Some kids, they don't say anything really. They're asking about the questions 'cause they don't understand, and he's up there saying, "I don't want to be bothered." So you ask the person next to you. You got to stand up. Even if you're just looking at the person, you got to stand up.

"Stand up—you're talking."

Like in class, he'll either make you stand up or he'll make you write a report on why you shouldn't be late.

WDR: How well do you feel you know your science teacher?

Dotty: I'd like to know my teacher better.

WDR: What would they have to be like in class for you to know them better?

Dotty: I guess they'd be just regular teachers in class, but I think they should take you as individuals and talk to you. Like at the beginning of the year they should get to know you as an individual. Just go around the room and talk to each person. That would get you started. And then you could tell them your opinions, and then like when they were discussing in class, they'd bring up somebody's opinion, and then you'd start talking and that would get other people started. Even in my free science class the teacher never really talked to me. He just asked us if we had any problems, and we would say no even if we did 'cause we didn't know what to ask him. We just didn't understand what was going on. We didn't know what to do, and we didn't understand what we were reading. Once we wanted him to tell us what to do 'cause we couldn't even get started because we didn't know what was going on.

WDR: How could the teacher have helped you get started in this free class?

Dotty: He could have helped us find a subject we were interested in. *If he knew what we were like, then he would know what we would want to study.*

WATCHING WILLIAM AND GRETCHEN LEARN

On a trip to the Grand Canyon last weekend I found myself noticing the kinds of learning activities that William (now ten) and Gretchen (now fourteen) became involved in on a completely informal basis. We had taken them out of school for a Friday and a Monday to make the trip possible, and I was curious about the kinds of obvious learning behavior they would engage in.

During the first part of the day-and-a-half trip there were general conversations about what we would see. In addition they played cards and engaged in various forms of sibling rivalry. At lunch stop in a small park in Saguache, Colorado, Gretchen became interested in some of the rye grasses there, and these led to discussion of grasses in general. The cottonwood trees, yellow in their fall attire, led to further discussion of leaf colors and of the differences between willows and cottonwoods. Then all five of us, adults and children, climbed around on a large jungle gym made of iron pipes. While in the car we also looked at and talked about some geologic road maps we had brought along. William called our attention to a huge bird perched on a phone pole. It was a golden eagle. William continued to comment on this bird for the rest of the trip. It was the first one he had ever seen in the wild.

As we approached the four-corner area at the boundaries of Colorado, Utah, New Mexico, and Arizona, the children's excitement mounted. When we stopped at Four Corners, there was a race for the monument. William was there first, and the other four of us from the car were soon with him. I joined Gretchen and William in a ceremonial "dance of the four states" as we jumped from state to state, occasionally pausing on the point where all four intersect.

After a late evening supper it was already dark, and we were incredulous at the brightness of the stars in the clear southwestern air. We looked at constellations and talked about the movement of stars. Gretchen pointed out to us that Venus had already set, and William shouted to us about a meteorite he had seen. As we looked, we saw more of them.

Although it was dark already, we drove on, hoping to find a more sheltered campsite than the windy plain of Four Corners. The wind increased until great clouds of dust and sand were pummeling the car. The car swayed from side to side, and we shared the scary feelings of a desert dust and sand storm—the first one that any of us had experienced. We found a somewhat sheltered campsite at a small rest area in Arizona called Elephant Feet, so named for a pair of huge pillars of sandstone. Our fantasy made it easy to imagine the rest of the elephant perched atop these two front legs, which were complete with what looked like elephant toes and toenails. It was still very windy, but we found some shelter. As we lay there, the sand grains made a rat-a-tat-tat on our sleeping bags.

In the morning, I woke up a little glum at having had a poor night's sleep. William, on the other hand, jumped out of his sleeping bag and went running over to a sand dune just behind us. He pranced around on it, throwing sand into the air. "Hey, look how soft the sand is." He and Gretchen played with the ripple-marked sand and then ran up a steep, rocky outcrop behind the elephant feet. The rock itself consisted of sandstones which had in them the traces of having themselves been formed in a desert climate much like that of present day Arizona. However, they came to be nearly a hundred million years ago—or at least so our geologic maps and my previous geological experiences suggested to us.

For breakfast we stopped in Tuba City, Arizona, at a restaurant operated by an Indian-American proprietor. The place was filled with Indians. Some were dressed in traditional Hopi and Navajo garb. Others were in cowboy dress, and yet others were dressed "mod." The faces were beautiful, and so were the traditional costumes worn by some. Long conversations about the Indians of the Southwest and their conditions and customs were generated by this short stop. We began to notice some of the boarding schools out in the desert as we drove by. The difficulties of getting children from remote settlements to these reservation schools made Gretchen's and William's short bike ride to school seem no inconvenience at all.

—*Drawing by Lucretia Romey.*

We stopped by a roadside marker that indicated nearby dinosaur tracks. Both children leaped into the tracks and plodded about, following the dinosaur tracks across the ground, making appropriate dinosaur noises. Gretchen said, "It must have been pretty muddy and wet around here for them to have made these deep tracks." As we looked about, we found fossil mud cracks in the same bed of sandy shale, confirming Gretchen's idea.

On the long drive in from Cameron, Arizona, to Grand Canyon Village, William and Gretchen wanted to stop immediately and photograph the canyon of the Little Colorado. When we arrived at the watchtower near the west entrance to the Grand Canyon National Park, we all ran out to get our first view of the canyon. It was to be our last for the day, for heavy clouds, rain, and then snow were soon upon us.

In the Visitor Center we bought necessary geologic and topographic maps and also some post cards for William's collection. We picked up camper tags enabling us to camp at the bottom of the canyon. The weather got progressively worse, however, and we finally decided not to risk a trip to the bottom of the canyon but rather to stay at the top in a cabin. We did walk down about two miles along the Bright Angel trail. There were no vistas to be seen, just massive rock walls looming beside us. We looked at all of the trail markers, picked up bits of rock, slid around in the mud, and noticed differences in the consistency of the mud as related to the rock type at each elevation. We lunched in a tunnel through a rock mass that extended across the trail, being careful to save all of our trash to take back up to the top. We looked at the spectacular cross-bedding in the Coconino sandstone, and when I became enthusiastic as I discovered the Bright Angel fault, Gretchen and William seemed to share my excitement. We met mules along the trail, and William learned that he had to move quickly to avoid having a sharp hoof applied to the seat of his pants. Gretchen, William, and I got into a long discussion about genetics as we talked about the mules. Hybrids and differences among species came up. They then carried the conversation to people and their inheritance of certain characteristics. This led even to discussion of the Second World War and of Hitler's plans to abolish Jews and other groups.

Back in our cabin, we faced a long evening confined together in a small space. William had nothing to do, and, after grappling with this problem for a while, he decided to draw. (He had seen Lucretia drawing sketches all day long in the car on this trip just as on all of our outings.) But what to draw in a small tourist cabin? He finally settled on lamps. Then he spent the whole evening doing drawings of every lamp in the cabin—each sketch meticulously detailed. Gretchen read a book on survival, very appropriate given the fierce storm howling around us. William also read some of A. A. Milne's poetry from *The House at Pooh Corner.*

The next morning we succeeded in catching glimpses of the inner parts of the canyon. Gretchen and William quickly shot up all of their films. William bought himself a Grand Canyon pennant only to decide later that he didn't like it. At our suggestion,

—Drawing by William Romey.

he personally took responsibility for doing something about his dislike. He returned the pennant and had to fill out several forms to get his fifty-two cents back. He then bought a copy of *Brighty of the Grand Canyon,* which he proceeded to read during free moments for the rest of the trip. Occasionally he would read long sections to us aloud, just as he had heard Lucretia reading other things aloud to us.

The trip home from the canyon was also beset by storms. We had problems of acquiring chains to get over the mountains, and William and Gretchen learned a whole set of new words from me as I had great difficulty getting the chains on. (That is not entirely true. Gretchen had attended a summer workshop with me this year. At the workshop we posted on the walls many big sheets of paper on which we could list our ideas about trust, honesty, and love in education. Gretchen had scrawled up a statement criticizing the adults in our group for modifying their language in front of the children. She wrote, "We say worse words in junior high school than some of the ones you use. You talk about treating us as people, but then you keep on not being yourselves when we're around.")

On the way home, we got into the game of figuring out how long, at a certain rate of speed, it would take us to get from one point to another. William began the game and kept it up for some time.

As she watched Lucretia and William draw, Gretchen became interested in various ways of reproducing sketches. She asked Lucretia how you make etchings. Then we had a long discussion

—*Drawing by Lucretia Romey.*

on this subject, and all of us learned something about the techniques involved in the art.

The drive home was filled with discussions of many more things than I can reconstruct in my mind. It is clear that the things which we dealt with through our experiences and through strictly informal conversation included geography, geology, astronomy, weather, wind, biology, anthropology, photography, physical education, conservation, sex, business, art, art history, history, reading, and a whole host of other things.

All in all I think it may have been worth missing two days in school.

VISITING SOME SCHOOLS
THAT MAKE ME FEEL BETTER

I will not bore you further with any extended description of the educational wasteland that exists in most American classrooms. You probably lived through between twelve and twenty years of them yourself depending on how many diplomas and degrees you put up with. All of us know about people sitting in rows listening to teachers talk and responding only when spoken to. Much of this is like being incarcerated in a prison. In what industries or jobs would free people in a "democracy" tolerate being forced to sit all day for six or more periods of forty to fifty minutes at a time without being allowed to talk, go to the bathroom, or get a drink and then being allowed only four minutes to move to the next period?

In many classes where the new curriculum materials in social studies, physics, chemistry, biology, and earth sciences are available, students are allowed to move about in the classroom and to converse about their work. But even here the students are commonly required to be in subjects they have not really chosen and where all of the goals and means of reaching them are specified from outside. *Directed inquiry,* in which the teacher and curriculum cleverly lead the learner to discover predetermined concepts and generalizations, does cause the learner to be more actively involved in classroom activity. But dependency of the student upon the teacher and the curriculum is still one of the end results except when these techniques are used by extremely sensitive and caring teachers. And extremely sensitive and caring teachers usually earn this designation by the way in which they *depart* from a standard curriculum rather than by the way they *cover* it.

But the kind of tinkering with individual courses represented by the new science, social science, math, and other curricula is unlikely to have any profound effect on the educational system. The new curricula do not provide very fertile ground on which a teacher can easily become a facilitator of learning. In this section I shall describe some bold new attempts to improve the whole school setting, and I shall describe how some facilitators work in these environments. Excellent descriptions of attempts such as the Parkway School in Philadelphia, the Murray Road Annex in Newton, Massachusetts, and the John Adams High School in Portland, Oregon, already appear in *Crisis in the Classroom,*[1] and I shall attempt to add some new examples.

THE JEFFERSON COUNTY OPEN LIVING SCHOOL

In Jefferson County, Colorado, a group of interested citizens and educators went through normal school administration–school board channels to establish a kindergarten through sixth grade open school in which about 250 children are free to study what they will. Play and work are not separated in this school because the staff have put into operation the view that play is the child's work. Staff members in the school do still make the mistake occasionally of saying, "This is worktime, not playtime," but I was impressed by the way in which work and play become one.

The school occupies three cottages formerly used as a normal elementary school. When I drove up on a chilly winter day, there were a number of children playing outside. There are always a few children outside playing, but individual children may not be outside for very long periods unless the weather is particularly fine.

On the inside the cottages are rather like well-lived-in family rooms. All sorts of paraphernalia, books, and "junk" are everywhere. Neighborhood cats and dogs join the caged mice, gerbils, chinchillas, and other animals that are present in every room. Bulletin boards are covered with things the children have made and arranged. (This calls to mind my young son's plaintive comment, "I wish our teacher would let us put up our *own* bulletin board.") Staff members have also hung up all sorts of attractive word, number, and idea posters. There is a sign-up list by the door, and children are expected to (and do) sign in and out when

---

[1] C. E. Silberman, *Crisis in the Classroom* (New York: Random House, 1970).

they are in school. The school is open from 7:30 A.M. until about 5:00 P.M. when those remaining are shooed out.

In a conventional school, I always feel somewhat embarrassed as a visitor. Visitors aren't supposed to talk to the children or interrupt the rigid classroom activities in any way. Here, the visitor passes unnoticed, unless he sits down somewhere. Then he suddenly finds a seven-year-old climbing on his lap to show him a picture or to tell him about something or to read him a story or to ask to be read to. I sat down in a corner where three little six-year-old boys were having an animated conversation. One came over to me and said, "Do you know what 'C' begins with? —Charlie!" Then one of his friends said, "And what does 'A' begin with?—Allison." They had made up a spelling game of their own and were drilling each other on names of their class-mates. I joined in the game for awhile and then moved off.

One of the directors of the school was busily engaged in a number game rather like bingo with a group of small children. In the art area several children were making signs such as, "Ask an adult before you take these," "Put your drawings here," and so forth. I made a comment to one of the staff members who said the children had insisted that these rules be made. They decided that if an adult always knew where the various supplies were

located, then the children would always be able to obtain what they needed. One little girl took me by the hand and led me over to a big "Peace Book" in which all of the children had included drawings for the holiday season.

I sat down in a big broken-down arm chair beside a mouse cage, and a little boy was up beside me in a minute to tell me about the mother and father mouse, when the babies were born, and how they lived together. He then told me about his own small rodent pets, and I exchanged information about our own family rodents.

In a corner, a staff member was reading *A Christmas Carol* aloud to several children sprawled around on chairs, on the floor, and two lying under a table. The listeners ranged in age from about six through twelve. I sprawled with the group and listened for a while. Over in the corner I noticed a boy opening his lunch box to eat. The children eat when they are hungry, and the staff members bring box lunches too. They help themselves to milk in a big old refrigerator. A couple of larger boys began a rowdy game, and the staff member and listeners all in chorus asked the boys to go outside and not disturb the reading group.

In one of the cottages, the custodian got down his guitar and some children joined him for singing. A boy in the basement of one cottage started to tootle on a saxophone.

I sat down with a little girl who was eating her lunch. She was playing with an educational game in which you looked at a picture of a flower, flag, animal, or other object and were supposed to identify it. When you turned the card in a big frame, a new picture would appear, and, in a different little box, so would the correct name for the previous picture. She identified several flowers for me, and I several for her. She confided to me that sometimes she cheated a little when she couldn't wait to find out what certain pictures were. There she sat, eating her lunch, playing, learning to identify flowers, and making a visitor feel very much at home.

All of the staff and children are on a first-name basis, giving a pleasant informality to the place.

A boy who must have been about twelve came up to ask me about some crystals he had found inside an old dry cell battery he had dissected. He had been told I was interested in mineralogy and thus wanted to tell me about the studies he had been performing on these crystals in trying to identify them. I tried a few simple tests and had to admit that I was at a loss. I told him that what I'd do would be to try to get an X-ray pattern of the crystals. We talked about how an X-ray machine would help solve the problem, and from the nature of his questions it was clear that from a conceptual point of view he understood quite clearly how the X-ray machine could help him. Later, one of the directors of the school, the boy, and I got together, and the director agreed that they should go up to the Colorado School of Mines when a friend could get them access to X-ray facilities. The boy's project and the way he wanted to solve it were not in any way abnormal for this school.

A study done on the Jefferson County School during its first year of operation showed that the school had one of the lowest absentee rates in the district and had produced strongly positive attitudes in over ninety percent of the children enrolled and in their parents as well. Furthermore, the average gain in plain old cognitive learning was equal to or greater than that in all other schools in the district. The success of the school during its first year led the school district to open up a second open school, and both branches of the open living school now include children from kindergarten through grade seven.

JAMESTOWN, COLORADO

The fourth, fifth, and sixth grade children in this small village are all in their own little one-room school situation.[2] In discussing the Bill of Rights, they decided to make up their own, reproduced with their own spellings, punctuation, and grammar.

WILSON CAMPUS SCHOOL[3]

When Donald Glines became principal of the Wilson Campus School in Mankato, Minnesota, in 1968, he did away with

---

[2]The facilitator for this group was Elvin Sayre.

[3]Donald Glines, *Creating Humane Schools* (Mankato, Minn., Box 1005: Campus Publishers, 1971).

Room Council Bill Of Rights

① The right to think and work Independently.

② The right to talk over your work.

③ The right to set and think thing's over with a friend.

④ The right to do your work and not be questioned.

⑤ The right to talk to the teacher alone.

⑥ The right to work alone.

⑦ The right to be trusted.

⑧ The right to help make out Report Cards.

courses, classes, bells, grades, and all of the normal trappings of the school. The school now operates twelve months of the year, and students and faculty come and go as they please each day and take their vacations when they wish. There are about 600 students in the school ranging from pre-schoolers through twelfth graders. A daily schedule is posted every day listing specific activities that may be going on in any given room at any given time. For much of the time rooms are simply open so that anyone wishing to use the space or resources in it may do so. Each student has a staff member as an advisor and can change advisors if he feels he cannot communicate with an advisor he first selects. The halls, schoolyard, and courtyard are all places that are constantly in use. Within the school, all sorts of alternatives are available. For the child who wants and needs a grandmotherly "teacher" to boss him gently, such teachers are available. For the mature student of any age, complete freedom is an option.

The school is arranged into centers: a communication center, a mathematics ("systems") center, a science center, an industrial arts and art center, a music center, and other centers including a "people center" where the school ombudsman has his office.

As a visitor, I was impressed by the politeness and courteousness of students to each other, to visitors, and to the staff. I was also surprised to find that many rooms appeared to be almost empty—with only a few children in them. And yet the building contained the normal number of children one would expect in a place of its size. There was no crowding observed because all of the plant was in use all of the time. Young people were in the halls, outside, in the gymnasium, in the library, in the audiovisual center, in the auditorium, in the lunchroom playing chess or cards as well as eating, in short—everywhere. A number of the high school age young people take some courses at the Mankato State College. I rarely saw more than a few young people together in any one place at any time. When someone started to play a guitar in the music room, fifteen students materialized from nowhere. Many small seminars, both formal and informal, also occur.

Here, as at the Jefferson County School, I felt very comfortable, accepted, and at home. At the end of a day in the school, I knew a number of children by name and even more by sight. I kept running into people I had seen in another area.

In many of the centers at Wilson, students may be involved in fairly rigidly structured curricular programs, but the student has a big role in selecting the program he will follow and can easily change it. In some centers (e.g., math), students keep personal portfolios in file cabinets. When they come in, if they wish to, they may take out their own files and see where they stand with respect to certain standards and can get suggestions about what to do next. When they enter the center, they are not required to do this, however. If they prefer to lounge on big pillows in a carpeted corner and play math games, monopoly, or just read or look out the window, they may do so. There is a good deal of gentle nudging by parents, advisors, and members of each center staff—perhaps too much for many students—but the staff are working hard at developing their capabilities as facilitators as opposed to the conventional teacher role that it has been impossible for them to play since Glines arrived and removed the rigid structure in which they and their students had previously been confined.

—*Photo by Robert Samples. Courtesy of Environmental Studies project.*

Some staff members have not come to trust their charges very completely, and they succumb at the slightest provocation to a more or less authoritarian interventionist position. None of the staff members I met had adopted a completely romantic laissez-faire attitude toward his students. One consequence is a still somewhat formal personal relationship between faculty and students. The fact that there are people of all ages in the school helps to reduce the formality, but few students and teachers are as yet on a first-name basis, and most teachers wear the uniform of adulthood.

In the science areas students are expected to work through the new science curricula, at their own rates, to be sure. Oddly, although in many schools science is an area where observable student activity may be greatest, at Mankato the more or less rigid new curriculum programs (PSSC physics, Intermediate Physical Science, BSCS, ESCP, etc.) seem if anything to strangle the teachers and students, preventing effective facilitation by their relative rigidity.

In the Wilson School the absurd constraints of time, space, and rigid curricula have been removed. But the human relationships between facilitators and young people remain to be improved and made stronger. Many of the staff members are becoming more comfortable in their new roles, but others have more difficulty in adjusting. Almost all agree that they could never go back to situations like the ones that existed before the open school came into being.

The Wilson School is probably the only public K-12 school in the country to date that has moved so far in the direction of responsible student freedom and involvement. Other schools allow the student forty or fifty percent of their time, or in some instances slightly more, for freely chosen activities. Wilson potentially allows every student 100 percent of his time free just as does the Jefferson County School. The constraints that now exist there are not in the system, but rather in the people who live within the system and their relationships to each other.

We need many more model schools of this type in order to train more and better facilitators of learning for the public schools.

Plans are underway in other school districts (such as the Boulder Valley, Colorado, and the Jefferson County, Colorado, districts) to create similar kinds of K-12 alternative schools. Such schools are not being created to replace conventional schools as we know them, but rather as alternative schools for young people and facilitators who wish to explore this promising model that may ultimately lead to major reform in our entire educational system.

3

Reflections on Some Aspects of the
Facilitator's Role in Creating a
Humane Learning Environment and in
Facilitating Learning

BEING REAL

Said the Skin Horse to the Velveteen Rabbit:

It doesn't happen all at once. . . . You become. It takes a long time. That's why it doesn't happen to people who break easily, or have sharp edges, or who have to be carefully kept. Generally, by the time you are Real, most of your hair has been loved off, and your eyes drop out, and you get loose in the joints and very shabby. But these things don't matter at all, because once you are Real you can't be ugly, except to people who don't understand.

From *The Velveteen Rabbit* by Margery Williams.
Published by Doubleday and Company, 1958.

Thanks to Donna Christian for introducing me to the Velveteen Rabbit.

—Photo by Robert Samples. Courtesy of Environmental Studies project.

EGO

Teaching is an ego trip. I am the most important person in the room. Everyone looks in my direction—perhaps not *at* me, but they make me think so. When I talk they write things down—perhaps they have nothing to do with me or what I say, but I think so. When I ask a question, they have to answer. If they ask questions, I can avoid answering in many ways. When I give them lab exercises to do, I am one-up. They have to answer my questions. I can make them tremble when I give them a test. I can embarrass them. I can say things that expose them to others, but they cannot expose me. When they are rude to me, I can punish. When I teach, I am powerful. When my students do well in assignments I give them, I feel good because of my success as a teacher.

I cannot be a teacher any more.

But I still want to help people learn. I still have an ego, and I still think I can help them. But I will not use power on them. When I am effectively facilitating, I will listen a lot. I still have trouble with this because I like to talk. But when I get to talking, I will be glad when the people who came to learn with me will feel free enough to walk away when they get tired of listening to me. I accept responsibility to help them feel that free.

George Brown and George Ladd started a seminar for teaching assistants this year. After a few months, their teaching assistants came up to them and said, "Don't come to our meetings any more. We don't need you. We may invite you to come sometimes. Will you come then?" It hurt, but the hurt felt *good.* George and George are becoming facilitators.

Jim McLelland went out with a field trip group. After several days he came up to his students and asked them how they were doing and what they were up to. They said, "Bug off, Jim. We don't need you now." It hurt good. Jim is used to it. He has been facilitating for quite awhile. Jim has an ego, too, but he has given up his power. And people are learning better now.

I want to be a learner. If both the people I used to call students and I are learners together, we can go on a beautiful ego trip together, the trip called learning, liking it, and feeling good about ourselves and about it.

REDUNDANCY

When I lay my thing on a group of learners, I assume they know nothing about it. The trouble is that someone in the group has probably already heard about it.

Cricket came home from ninth grade last week and told me about a science activity on static electricity. Shrugging her shoulders, she said, "We already did that in third grade."

I used to hate American history. I had the same thing every year for what seemed like a hundred years. I'm just now beginning to like history because I'm reading history I want to read instead of something someone tells me I have to read. And I don't have to read the same thing over many times unless I want to.

Some students I used to have in freshman geology told me that they had studied about rocks in grade school and junior high school and were doing it again in college so they wouldn't have to work on it. For the ones who went on into upper division courses, the faculty treated them as if they'd never had freshman geology either.

A couple of years ago I was giving a brilliant lecture on the evolution of new species. I had taken some examples from an advanced textbook and was playing a nice little questioning game with my class of about 100. I asked one student in the front row what he thought would happen in a certain set of circumstances. His answer was, "I've already read the book you got this out of, and here's what it says. . . ." Devastating! And I deserved it.

I often found that teachers who listed "prerequisite courses" treated us all as if we'd never had the prerequisites anyway.

Over and over and over and over and over again.

If learners are allowed to choose what to study, they choose new things to learn about—unless they want to pursue an old favorite in greater depth or review an area of interest like savoring a favorite old poem.

INQUIRY

Soon after my book *Inquiry Techniques for Teaching Science* was published, David Newton wrote an article entitled "The Dishonesty of Inquiry Teaching."[1] He claimed that guided inquiry is a sham in which the teacher artificially leads or greatly manages the student through processes that are unlike those used by a true inquirer. The teacher and student play a game in which the teacher always knows the answer in advance.

I now agree with Newton that inquiry teaching is manipulative. It certainly does not lead learners to learn more independently. In a free, humanistic learning environment true inquiry takes place under non-coercive conditions where the learner can explore, fail, succeed, and learn in an atmosphere of trust and caring support. There is no material to "cover." Things that are truly "fundamental" are learned without being assigned. Things that are not generally learned by learners in a free, humanistic learning environment are probably not truly "fundamental." There is no single way nor is there any set of ways to inquire. Students who find their own ways and ask their own questions are true inquirers. When the question is provided by a teacher or by the curriculum, inquiry is short-circuited. Formulation of questions is at least as important in inquiry as the seeking of their answers.

---

[1]David Newton, "The Dishonesty of Inquiry Teaching," *School Science and Mathematics* 68 (1968):807-810.

PROCESS VERSUS CONTENT

In my early curriculum project days with the Earth Science Curriculum Project (ESCP) and as a teacher at Syracuse University, I became convinced that students should learn how scientists work and that they should focus on the processes of science rather than the content. Concern with "process" approaches was the hallmark of all of the major federally supported elementary and secondary school science and social studies curriculum projects that spent tens of millions of dollars during the sixties. Several projects still continue to urge that we impose the learning of processes rather than content on students.

My view now is that imposition of process goals on students is just as detrimental to learning as imposition of content goals. Imposed goals inhibit the development of self-actualizing learners who can set their own goals.

Learners in a free learning environment will of necessity work at the process level but not in any sequence that we can necessarily predict. They will frequently devote much time to content of their own choosing. Process and content become inseparable. They will miss some content and miss learning some processes. They did that under both the imposed content and process schemes, too. But in a truly free learning environment they will learn how to learn both the processes and the content necessary to reach their own goals. They will learn to ask personally relevant questions, to evaluate their concept of relevance in the light of concepts held by others, and to evaluate and set goals rather than accepting the goals of others.

RELEVANCE

Only the learner can determine what is relevant to him. I can tell him what I think is relevant, but I decline to try to impose my value system.

As another learner and I talk about an issue and about our feelings on the issue, I am prepared to see my ideas change about what are relevant issues. His ideas of what is relevant may change just as mine do.

AMBIGUITY

Specificity is limiting. As long as I make specific suggestions to learners, they can limit themselves to doing my thing rather than taking responsibility for setting their own goals. If I make a specific suggestion, a student is likely to come to me with a product I expect. I am always more comfortable when I know what to expect.

If I make an ambiguous suggestion, students will interpret me in many different ways, and different students will come back with results of different kinds. The learning situation is rich in proportion to its diversity. Ambiguity leads to diversity.

If I am ambiguous in the suggestions I make to students, I cannot call their results wrong. I can only observe that they are different.

I am learning to feel comfortable with ambiguity because ambiguity often leads to a rich learning environment, and it places me in situations where I am more likely to react as a human and as a fellow learner rather than as an authority figure.

SELF-CONCEPT

"My parents came to this country from Greece, and I was born here.
. . . They took me back to Sparta when I was two." (Pappas returned
to the U.S. at age ten and comments further:) "I knew no English
though I was an American citizen. I was put in the first grade. I was
so big my classmates called me "dummy," but my arithmetic was as
good as the teacher's. I continued to the ninth grade. It took that long
for my English to become fluent. I can't recall one teacher who encouraged me or helped the other kids to understand me. I was disillu-
sioned when I left school, but I was determined not to let lack of
education interfere with my ambitions."

—quoted from Gus Pappas, a highly successful Greek businessman in
Washington, D.C. Printed in *Blackie's Circuit,* v. 1, no. 4, 1971.

Many schools systematically undermine the self-concept of
all but the "best" of their students. (Best means the ones who
play the game most successfully. I know; I was a good player in
the game of school.)

Displays of creative behavior are too often criticized rather
than praised. They upset the schedule. Different children in a
single classroom can't be allowed to work on different things at
the same time.

Gretchen still has some trouble reading in the eighth grade
because teachers in the early grades made her feel like a dummy.

Cricket painted a beautiful watercolor still life of a cup and
saucer. It was sensitively done and showed a good sense of color,
form, and perspective. Her art teacher failed her at mid-term
report time because he said she failed to hand in one of the tight
little drawings he forces them to do. Cricket has talent. She
dropped art and took study hall instead because her teacher made
her feel *less than.*

Gretchen and Nancy took a quiz and used crayons to write
their answers. The teacher asked Gretchen, "Do you think it's all

right for me to give you a zero since you used a crayon on this quiz?" Gretchen burst into tears. He asked Nancy if he could say something "personal" to her. Nancy is more resistant to torture than Gretchen, so she merely said no, turned on her heel, and walked away.

In a recent encounter group dealing with self-concept, several young people said they considered the grades they got to be indicative of themselves as human beings. "C grades make me a C human being." Since teachers give only a small percentage of their students As, there must be a lot of human beings going around with less than an A self-concept.

Love and personal closeness can help people develop a good self-concept. How they cope with life depends to a large extent on their self-concept. Can I afford to undermine it?

HELPING PEOPLE LEARN TO BE FREE

—You can't be free if someone else lets you be free.

—Harlem subway graffito

One of the primary tasks of a facilitator of learning is to help the people that he works with learn to cope with intellectual freedom. Many teachers who have decided to abandon their role as teachers and become facilitators of learning have been perplexed about what happens when they tell a group of learners that they are free to study what they wish for as long as they wish in the way that they wish. A common reaction on the part of the learners from junior high school through graduate school is one of disbelief. Students who are presented with this opportunity frequently cannot cope and may end up being very unhappy. The facilitator of learning may also begin to backslide into didactic teaching when he sees that students working with him are floundering and seem unable to take any positive action. In its worst form we can imagine a student's becoming like Oblomov, the Russian author Goncharov's famous character who spends his life stretched out on his couch, unable to commit himself to any action other than reflecting.

Some learners, on the other hand, seem immediately able to cope with freedom. They rapidly become engaged in intensive creative activity, pursuing subjects of interest to them to great lengths. These people who use freedom effectively have basically free personalities, whereas those who seem not to be able to cope with free learning situations at all are basically unfree people.

What are the characteristics of a free person, and how can a facilitator (or a teacher, for that matter) help unfree students become freer people? The model of the free person I shall consider as an ideal is the kind of person described by Carl Rogers[2]

---

[2]Carl R. Rogers, *On Becoming a Person* (Boston: Houghton-Mifflin, 1961); *Freedom to Learn* (Columbus, Ohio: Charles E. Merrill Publishing Co., 1969); "Learning to Be Free," in *Conflict and Creativity,* ed. Farber and Wilson (New York: McGraw-Hill Book Co., 1963).

and John Gardner.[3] Basically the free person is a self-determining person. He does not believe that there are forces beyond his control which cause him to act and feel in certain ways. The truly free person enjoys making significant decisions about his own life and how he will spend it. He is a self-renewing person who does not allow himself to be mentally trapped by the systems that surround him. He is a real human being in whom feeling and intellect are integrated to form a sensitive instrument which accepts the feelings of other human beings and is willing to let them be as free as he is. He has a profound respect for the independence of others and thrives on his own inner independence. As a self-renewing man he finds joy in continually learning new things and in expanding his own perceptions.

Many of us are prisoners in some respect or other. Almost anyone who has gone through twelve or more years of schooling in America or western Europe is to some degree a prisoner of the culture that has been imposed upon him. Some are partially imprisoned by their religion. Others are imprisoned by family. How, in the midst of all the restrictive elements in our society, can facilitators of learning help learners treasure and use freedom? It should be pointed out as a cautionary note that if we do help learners become more truly free, our society may undergo important qualitiative changes. Given some of the problems that now face our society, I personally will welcome such changes.

In general, when very young children are given freedom, they need little help in learning how to use their freedom effectively. The way babies learn to walk, manipulate things, and talk are examples of how unconditioned human beings are able to learn independently through trial and error and without elaborate reward-punishment systems. This ability to learn independently, without direction, can be seen to persist into nursery school, kindergarten, and perhaps the first grade. Children play, they make mistakes, they succeed and take pleasure in success without needing external reinforcement, and they go on to other games. Most of their learning during their early learning years occurs through play. A colleague of mine, Robert Samples, describes a situation in which a pre-schooler was being observed during a play session. It was estimated that on the basis of his movements alone, this pre-schooler made a total of eighty decisions in only

---

[3]John Gardner, *Self-Renewal* (New York: Harper and Row, 1965).

two or three minutes. A very large number of other decisions which did not involve physical movements must also have been involved during this short period of play.

And yet, rather than trying to expand the creative capacity and intellectual and emotional breadth of young children, we commonly place them in the first grade into situations where they sit in rows and perform highly directed tasks which are externally evaluated. The children are then rewarded or punished, depending on the extent to which they perform according to externally established criteria. The schools in general seem dedicated to restricting these young minds and causing the young people to conform to a meaningless set of standards. (Can you imagine a system in this decade that requires a group of highly different six-year-olds all to be able to read at a level specified by a rather meaningless test at the end of a certain period of time? Or can you imagine in this decade a system in which a young child has to ask permission to go to the bathroom? Or can you imagine a system in which a group of effervescent, energetic six-year-olds are expected to sit quietly in a classroom without talking for a period of four or more hours per day?)

I recently attended a meeting in which a group of interested citizens were pleading for the establishment of an alternative open school within a city school district. One very antagonistic woman, not even a mother, who had come to criticize rather than to explore alternatives, asked us, "How can you trust a kindergarten child to use freedom well?" My comment to her was, "If you ever really can trust a child to use freedom well, it's at that time, when he is still an unspoiled unconditioned young thing." All one needs to do is watch little children play to see how they exercise their fantasies as well as their voices and bodies.

The problem of tolerating freedom becomes a much more substantial one after young people have been in the system for a period of many years.

Many teachers say that they can't give their students freedom because the students wouldn't know what to do if given this opportunity. I suspect that these people usually really mean that they themselves are afraid to offer freedom for fear that their students *will* be able to use it well. Once these teachers discover that their students no longer need them, they feel that they have no real function.

One of the most important things necessary in helping people learn to be free is a feeling of real trust between the facilitator and the learners who are working with him. In the first place, the facilitator himself must be perceived by the learners as a fellow-learner rather than as a constant leader to be looked to for detailed directions or as an encyclopedia to be pulled down off the shelf and consulted for definitive answers. If the facilitator is perceived by the learners working with him merely as a more experienced learner also engaged in pursuing knowledge and in trying to determine his own course, the way is open to truly human encounters between the facilitator and the less experienced learners. The kind of relationship I suggest here is not an anarchical one in which the facilitator says, "Do your own thing," and then disappears from view. It is a relationship in which the facilitator is constantly available to the learners who are working with him, is vitally interested in them as people, and is constantly concerned about providing an opportunity for them to develop emotionally, physically, and intellectually.

A. S. Neill, in *Summerhill,*[4] describes a new student who, after being unable for some months to cope with the freedom offered in the school, came to him and said, "Teach me something. . . . I'm bored stiff." Neill sent the student away when she couldn't say what she wanted to learn. She returned several months later with a definite plan to pass the college entrance exams. This may seem a somewhat brutal put-down, but it did ultimately work in the case of this particular student. I personally would be inclined to help the students to a somewhat greater degree. It seems to me that there must be transitional stages by which people can be helped toward freedom.

It is clear, however, that any facilitator who wishes to move students toward greater freedom as learners must require his students to make significant decisions as soon as possible, whether these students are six or sixty. As mentioned earlier, small children are quite prepared to play and to learn from their

---

[4]A. S. Neill, *Summerhill* (New York: Hart Publishing Co., 1960), p. 31.

play. Older learners have commonly forgotten how to play and fail to realize that most significant creative intellectual activity is very much akin to play. Learning to play all over again requires one to peel off the heavy veneer of cultural values and inhibitions that may have required years to establish themselves.

One of the most significant tasks of the facilitator who wishes to help people learn to be free is to help point out alternatives. Most students brought up in the conventional education system are used to being presented with single alternative situations. They are presented with a task to accomplish in a given time. The facilitator's job when his students have been offered freedom is to help the learners to identify alternatives. Thus, for a facilitator who operates best in the area of science, it is clear that his own knowledge of science must be great enough so that he can help identify alternative directions for learning about science. The facilitator also needs to be able to organize or otherwise provide an extremely rich environment for learning that is full of seductive possibilities for activity. In a physical area arranged for the learning of mathematics, for example, the facilitator would need to provide cuisinaire rods, geometric forms, mathematical games, counting devices, calculators, and a large variety of books, workbooks, and puzzle books. In addition to this, he would need to provide access to places and people in the community who could help students pursue topics of interest in mathematics. A facilitator in the area of science would need to provide an environment full of animals (both live and preserved), chemicals, materials for conducting physical experiments, plant materials, rock and earth materials, models, and science games, plus access to an extensive collection of readings and books, to transportation for field trips, and to people in the community, who as amateur or professional scientists and naturalists, would be in a position to facilitate for children involved in individual studies of various kinds. The facilitator concerned with languages would need to provide tape recordings, music from the country concerned, extensive access to reading and pictorial materials concerning the culture and history of the country whose language is being studied, access to transportation that might allow students to travel to the country being studied, and so forth. Facilitators concerned with literature would need to provide a whole host of reading materials, access to cultural events in the community related to literature and drama, a performing arts capability so that students could be involved in readings and in production of dramas. He would need, furthermore, to be able to provide a sympathetic ear to listen to poetry and to read essays contributed to him on a voluntary basis by students wishing to learn with the help of his facilitative efforts.

One could list extensive facilities that might be necessary to help facilitate the learning and appreciation of music, studio arts, art history, industrial arts, and the social sciences. No list that I could offer could begin to show the full range of possibilities that a facilitator would need to consider in helping to form an environment chock-full of exciting educational alternatives for students to choose from. Highly important is the notion that a true facilitator will never consider the environment that he has constructed to be fully satisfactory. He should always be seeking new alternatives to offer to his students, and he should be adding to the environment new materials and alternatives suggested by the learners who are working with him.

The true facilitator will always encourage those learning with him to depart completely from the alternatives easily identifiable in the learning environment and to create alternatives of their own. The more the learners are working with him to create their own alternatives, the more successful he will have been in helping them move toward more complete freedom and independence.

Another important role of the facilitator in helping people learn to be free is in helping students to clarify situations in their minds. As a clarifier, the facilitator may use techniques somewhat like those described by Raths, Harmin, and Simon.[5] In asking clarifying questions, the facilitator may challenge the value system of the students working with him by asking very simple open questions such as, "Do you really believe that?" Raths, Harmin, and Simon suggest that after asking such a question the facilitator should simply turn away and leave the student with this query. The facilitator should not, if he is a truly free person, pass judg-

---

[5]Louis E. Raths, Merrill Harmin, and Sidney B. Simon, *Values and Teaching* (Columbus: Charles E. Merrill Publishing Co., 1966).

ment on the learner's value system. He should merely invite the learner to examine the alternatives to his belief system and the consequences of his values.

*   *   *   *   *

Some students, perhaps as many as one-third of them according to the estimates of some educators, may have been too much psychologically damaged by their early educational experiences ever to become truly free and independent learners. Yet even the student requiring the most help—the student who is the most completely dependent—can move in the direction of greater self-determination and independence. The facilitator needs to be a perceptive enough human being to recognize the acute distress of some unprepared students faced with a free environment in which they have nothing to "hang on to". The best facilitator will thus provide as much human support as he can to help sustain students with such problems. These students may at first need to have a restricted number of alternatives provided for them so that the making of choices becomes a less traumatic experience. One of the most important things for the facilitator to remember, however, is that he must never underestimate the decision-making abilities of his students—even those that he perceives to be highly dependent in their personal characteristics. All of the students, even the most conservative and dependent, are capable of far more self-direction and independent growth than we could possibly imagine.

INVOLVEMENT

What do you do when a student placed in a free learning environment does nothing? Here are excerpts from an answer I recently sent to a teaching fellow at a large western university:

In your letter you ask the question about what you should do with students who don't do anything at all. If I tell students that each may design his own experience and evaluate himself, I realize that I give good students a chance to flower, and students who don't care a chance to be totally uninvolved. What I must do then is not only to make myself available regularly as a facilitator to students who seek me, but also to actively seek out students who do not seek me. I personally will obligate myself to seek contact with every individual at least several times each term. I will make sure that I visit with each student early in the term, so that each will have a chance to take stock of himself and his own work. I will make it clear to each individual student that the one expectation I have is for each student to be honestly involved in work that to him is intellectually sound and aesthetically pleasing. The student will work out for himself the criteria for establishing such soundness and pleasingness, but I shall want to have him tell me about his criteria and to discuss his evaluation of himself in terms of his own criteria. If I feel lack of trust or anger with the student, I take responsibility for letting him know about my feelings. I also take responsibility for letting him know that if I am angered and am led to distrust him, I reserve the right to turn in a grade of incomplete. Incomplete is as far as I am ready to go at the present time. I would not give a student a failing grade under any circumstances. In seeking out the uninvolved student, I would probably recommend that he drop the course if he cannot honestly find a reason for involving himself. I feel I must let such a student know that his lack of involvement in something like geology has nothing to do with my feelings about him as a person. I want to accept each person for what he is and for what his goals are, but at the same time I wish to let him know that if he persists in being uninvolved in work he has signed up to do with me, I would prefer that he leave and come back at a later time when he has some degree of commitment, rather than causing me to devote time to him that could be spent better with students who desire to use my facilitative efforts.

In short, I will approach uninvolved students as human being to human being, and we must recognize that a problem exists: uninvolvement. Once this problem is brought out, we can deal with it without my having to assume an evaluative or power-based, professorial role.

One other thing: I am not willing to talk about "poor students" at a place like your university or for that matter at most other institutions of higher learning. I am willing to talk, however, about uninvolved students. I cannot and will not try to force involvement. What I will do is try to get together with uninvolved students and help them clarify their positions and, thus, either become involved, drop the course, or accept "incomplete" as an evaluation of their work.

QUESTIONS AND ANSWERS

I will never again ask a learner a question to which I already know the answer unless he has asked me to play an inquiry game with him.

I will never deny a learner who asks me a question an answer that I know unless he tells me that he wants me to play a guess-the-answer game with him. I reserve the right in the case of a compulsive questioner to tell him I am not an encyclopedia, however, and to ask him, before I provide an answer, if he thinks my giving an answer will help him to become a freer and better learner.

INTERROGATION VERSUS DECLARATION

Bob Lepper once suggested to me the idea of dealing with learners in a non-interrogative manner. When I greet a learner with a question such as, "What are you up to in your education methods course this week?" I put very tight limits on the learner's potential responses. If, on the other hand, I confine myself to declarative sentences such as, "It's good to see you today," or "That's some dress you have on," or almost anything else, I free the person I have engaged to talk to me about his own interests of the moment. Or I may simply talk in a declarative way about something I happen to be excited about at the moment. The conversation may die quickly if the other person doesn't wish to be engaged, but I respect his refusal to pursue a conversation, and we can part friends and try again another time.

I find it very difficult to keep from asking questions when I meet someone. After all, most of my teaching up until a couple of years ago consisted of trying to think up better, more stimulating questions to ask people. But I don't want learners to be confined by my questions any more. I want to learn what their questions and concerns are. We must trust each other not to pry with questions but to be ready to receive each other's offerings. It's hard for me to do, but it feels very good when people start to talk to me at a deeper level than ever before.

STRUCTURED VERSUS UNSTRUCTURED

In a manuscript recently returned to me for revisions, the editor of the *Journal of Geological Education,* Tom Hendrix, protested against my use of the word "structure" as a verb. He threw out "structured" and "unstructured" too.

At a recent meeting a group of conference participants who thought our conference staff was trying to use an "unstructured" approach started to examine what we were up to and came to the conclusion that we were actually "managing" (structuring) the conference to a substantial degree. They decided they had not been aware of the structure because it was a different structure from what they were used to.

At another conference the staff was accused of knowing exactly what was going to happen next through some vague omniscience.

Tom Hendrix was perhaps right in throwing out "structured" and "unstructured" on grammatical grounds, but I think they should be indicted on more serious philosophical grounds.

Freedom to learn in one's own way is as much a "structure" as the structure that a teacher sets up on a minute-by-minute basis. It is simply a different structure. The most basic difference is that in a free learning environment the learner has permission to decide what his activities will be on a minute-by-minute basis. The structure for setting goals differs, too. In a free learning environment the learner sets his own goals.

In learning to cope with a free learning situation, one of the first things a learner must accept is the responsibility to set up his own structure within whatever constraints exist around him. The facilitator's first task with a new group of learners is to help these learners recognize this responsibility to set up their own structure and to enjoy it.

Structure is in the eyes of the beholder. It is always there in some form whenever people work alone or in a group. Who establishes the structure is what is important.

INFORMALITY

When people talk about a "structured" program, they usually mean a formal one. To me, a formal situation is one that is not like real life. I think of myself as putting on a special suit of clothes for occasions that are formal. I think of operating on a superficial level of manners dictated from some outside source. A formal lecture means to me a stiff, uncomfortable one.

I do not believe that learning is facilitated under formal conditions. Therefore I seek informality when I study or work with a group of learners or when I learn by myself. I seek an informal relationship with the people around me and the physical world around me at all times and in all circumstances. Formality stifles me and hinders the development of close relationships with people around me.

RESPONDING

Helping people learn and helping them become more self-actualizing means responding to what they bring me. It also means accepting that they may not respond to what I bring them.

Responding does not mean that I have to *like* everything they bring me. But it means accepting it, looking at it, and reacting to it.

I do not have the power to reject what a learner brings to me. I can tell him I like what he is doing, or I can tell him I do not like it, and I accept responsibility for doing this even though it may hurt me to do so for fear that he may like me less. If he likes me less, that hurts my ego. He must know that he can tell me he dislikes things that I do, say, or produce, too. He can help me grow just as I can help him grow as long as we value each other enough to communicate.

EMOTION AND LEARNING

Why is emotion excluded from the learning environment we make available to students? I grew up programmed to believe that emotions were meant to be concealed in public. This attribute is rewarded by middle-class, anglo-American culture. Teachers are free to be human beings, with all of their strengths, weaknesses, and faults, when outside of the classroom and away from places where the community in which they teach might judge their behavior, value systems, and life styles. Children are free to be human beings—occasionally—in their homes and with their friends, although in a large number of homes they are expected to act out roles dictated by their parents which may have little to do with their real feelings.

Although I value and treasure my memories of affection, love, and trust in my own boyhood and adolescence, I recall, even there, elements that have made it difficult for me to feel emotion deeply and even more difficult to share my emotions with others and to receive and value the emotions of my wife and children and of the larger family of students and colleagues with whom I spend at least a third of my life. All of this is, I believe, because of the cult of self-control imposed on us first in our families, then in the schools, and finally in our work.

In returning to some of those early influences which cause us to build barriers to the forthright and honest expression and use of feelings, I return to family experiences. I cannot write from a background of studying families in any abstract or so-called objective ways. As a matter of fact, these ways probably give erroneous ideas anyway, for they attempt to attach statistics and outside observation and evaluation to things that are too personal to be seen but must, on the contrary, be felt. Thus I retreat to the one area where I can claim expertise—the growth of my own feelings and barriers. And even these cannot be fully expressed, for I have only recently begun, through a series of experiences that have involved an attempt at intimate reexamination of feelings and emotions, to perceive them in all their real complexity.

Physical expression of emotion was commonly discouraged when I was a small boy. I soon learned that "boys don't cry," and, over thirty years later, I have only begun to learn to cry openly again and to realize that the feeling of freedom to express my emotions in this way requires strength rather than weakness. When I cry openly I take a risk—the risk that others may consider me to be less manly by comparison with the American stereotype. And yet crying can provide a release for my creative impulses that allows me to accomplish things in science and in helping students learn that I could never manage before. The influences that affected me in boyhood allowed me to weep silently in the darkness of a movie theatre when I was moved with empathy and sympathy by situations portrayed on the screen. But they caused me to feel shame for my lack of self-control, even though no one else observed it, rather than the joy I now begin to feel. Another arena where I found release was in amateur dramatics where I could step into a character's shoes and let my own feelings, concealed as his, flow freely. Perhaps this was why dramatics were so important to me and perhaps even got me over some emotional rough spots in high school and college. The availability of drama as an important extracurricular activity may, for many students who participate, be one of the main things that help them to retain their humanism in the midst of the hostile, sterile, emotionally featureless environment in which they are expected to learn.

Love is another emotion that the influences of my childhood led me to conceal. I wonder if lack of expression of an emotion does not perhaps dull one's capacity for feeling the emotions? Now that I begin to feel freer to express love for other human beings I sense that I begin to feel love more deeply. When I was only eight or nine years old, I remember that my father and I had a "man-to-man" talk (perhaps another institution that leads us to repress our feelings) in which the decision was made that boys do not hug and kiss each other, and that physical contact other than a firm handshake was not what went on between real men. (Becoming aware of some of these things has, in recent weeks, led to a deepening of my own relationship with my father. It has become more a person-to-person relationship than I have ever allowed myself to accept before.) We find here the American middle-class fear of homosexuality and what influences lead to it. I suspect that the effect is an opposite one and, although I have no evidence to support the hypothesis, that homosexuality is more likely to occur in those who have repressed their emotions and love than in those who have felt free to love openly where sexual overtones have no need to develop. The American equation of love and sexuality is a distortion.

I remember acute embarrassment when my Grandfather Dowden, a fine physician and real human being, hugged me once when I was a gangling six foot three inch teenager and, sensing my feeling, said to me, "You must never feel too grown up to kiss your old grandfather."

In 1967 I had occasion to visit the Soviet Union as a representative of the National Academy of Science. While in Akademgordok, the academic city near Novosibirsk, I was entertained frequently by young geologists and their families. I had seen many Russian films and read much from Tolstoi, Lermontov, Pushkin, Chekhov, Dostoevski, and other prerevolutionary writers and knew that Russian men were often characterized as being able to express their emotions openly. Yet the reality and depth of the emotions I witnessed in these people came to me as a revelation. I was hugged and embraced on several occasions, and, carried away by this unaccustomed openness, I found myself able to express my own deep feelings back to them. It was as if they had brought me a gift, which, finally, I could accept with joy.

Thus I begin to have a good feeling when others touch me out of genuine affection, and I find it easier to touch them. Some of this feeling has been facilitated by my personal experiences with the staff of the Earth Science Educational Program, which took the form of a prolonged encounter group situation. What leads me to write this chapter at the present moment was a set of experiences in a weekend-long encounter group which focused my attention on the importance of people as whole human beings rather than as secretaries, staff associates, editors, or directors. When I perceive people for what their roles or functions are rather than as real people, I help to undermine the very environment in which we could all "feel good" together, and at the same time I erect all sorts of barriers that impede my own creative capabilities and productivity as well as the creativity and productivity of my colleagues. Our group needs to be an organism rather than an organization.

And yet the old culturally imposed taboos die hard within me. Today, Jim, one of the participants in our group process function, and I traveled together to the airport. We had felt great closeness during our encounters of the preceding days. At the airport when I extended my hand—back to the handshake between men!—Jim advanced to hug me. There was a momentary embarrassment on my part that this should happen in public ("What will people think?"). But this feeling passed quickly, and I was able to receive his gift of trust and love and to reciprocate by expressing my own feelings.

Are feelings everything? And must feelings be related to groups? Jim and I discussed this for a while. Each of us lives according to several conflicting lists of priorities. These include

—*Photo by Robert Samples. Courtesy of Environmental Studies project.*

agendas for how I feel, what I want to produce, how I relate to my co-workers and friends, and how I relate to my wife and children. At any given moment, most of these agendas are involved, and I must choose among them. If I dwell exclusively on how I feel, I will probably accomplish little and may well feel little. A part of me—the doing part—would atrophy. If I am too much preoccupied with what I produce, my feelings dry up, and what I produce becomes sterile and meaningless to me and to others. If I spend all of my time in a group situation and feel bad every time I leave the group, I lose my independence and I sacrifice completely the loneliness that is probably a pre-condition to truly creative activity. If I am not myself first and if I do not accept myself for what I basically am, I contribute little that is real to the group. If I dwell entirely on and with my wife and children, I fall into the same trap of overdependence and attendant personal sterility that I can create in my work group. Feelings are thus not everything, but it may be that they make all human creativity and growth possible.

Another experience that helped me to begin freeing my own feelings took place at the International Geological Congress in Prague during the summer of 1968. It forms an interesting counterpart for my experience in Novosibirsk, for Soviet troops invaded Czechoslovakia while we were there. My emotions—fear, hate, love—all erupted violently during three days in Prague. In addition to the empathy I felt for the Czechs, I also felt continuing affection for my Soviet friends from Novosibirsk, with whom I spent some anxious moments as tracer bullets split the night sky outside of the hotel room where my wife and I drank with them. Upon returning to the United States I made numerous talks about our experiences in Czechoslovakia, and I cannot to this day make a talk about them without a visible display of emotion. At first I tried to avoid these displays—back to the self-control syndrome —but now I realize that what I say has far more impact and that the audience and I have a far stronger feeling of communicating if I allow myself to show my "weakness." (Is it therefore strength? Expressing my emotions is a risk to me—the risk being that the people I am with may not receive my gift of openness and may consider me to be weak. But this is not so important to me now, for I want to feel free to be myself, whatever the circumstances and whatever the risks.)

As I think back over my teaching experiences of the past ten years, I realize that I have consciously avoided emotion in dealing with my students. I suspect that many teachers would find the same to be true of their own relationships with students. One student, let us call him Lee, who had been doing badly in one of my courses several years ago came to my office to express his problem. He had been told that he had a lung tumor and was very apprehensive about an operation. This was near the end of the semester, and after I reassured him, he left, perhaps feeling a little less threatened by his course work. During the final examination, two weeks later, I was notified by phone that Lee's father had died. When we communicated this information to him, he was visibly shaken, but continued with the examination. Returning the next semester, he came in to see me. As we talked he became visibly agitated, and finally, with great emotion and with tears in his eyes, he said that I reminded him a great deal of his father. I was moved, but at the same time embarrassed and kept distant from him. My impulse was to put an arm around him and to accept his emotion and trust, but I failed him because I insisted on separating my role of teacher from that of person.

I know I have caused fear in many students. Being concerned about standards, I used to write examinations that could not possibly be completed in the time allotted and on which average students received about half of the total credit. I recall the fear I saw on the faces of many students that made me recognize their nervousness and discomfort. Yet I made little effort to accept this fear, to let them know I cared about them, and to try to make them comfortable. This will not happen again, for I will never give a conventional written examination again.

But there are other, more subtle ways in which I can inspire fear. I recently learned in an encounter group that some of the people who have worked with me for months fear me and have been afraid, on occasion, to approach me to share their anxieties and problems. As I think back, I remember students who have knocked on my door and, upon finding me obviously occupied in some task, have asked, "Are you busy?" This question used to annoy me because they could see easily enough that I was. But my reaction showed a misunderstanding of their intent. The question intended was really, "Is there anyone here who cares enough about me to help me?" Staff members in my office have actually admitted in encounter sessions that this was what they meant. The compulsion I often have to get on with the job I am doing causes me to forget that if I want to facilitate learning or group productivity, I must be prepared immediately and as often as possible to shift from my production priority system to my people priority system.

True enough, I am a human being with weaknesses too, so I may not always be able to receive someone else. I want, however, to learn to be honest, and if I am too preoccupied to "receive," I want to let others know that my lack of receptiveness is my fault, not theirs. Patient listening without attendant hearing, accepting, and exchange of feeling is too often recognized as indifference to a student or co-worker as a real person and makes them hesitate to "bother" me any more.

I experienced this same feeling at the hands of many of my own teachers. One of my advisors in graduate school, a compulsively busy man, was often gruff with all of his students. It used to take me hours to screw up enough courage to knock on his door to ask for information or help. When I finally did knock, I was often received curtly and would go away wondering for days what I had done wrong and why he had been angry. His failure to receive me and to encourage free and open communication was strongly detrimental to my own productivity and commonly left me in a state of despair. I consciously avoided him for fear of being evaluated, judged, and perhaps even asked to drop my program. When problems in my work arose, I concealed them from him rather than seeking the very aid I needed. The feeling of mutual supportiveness was not present.

On certain occasions I was called upon to act as "departmental interpreter" when visiting Soviet scientists were in town. On such occasions I was genuinely "needed." I remember one chilly night on a trip with this advisor and a visitor when I had failed to bring a sweater. My advisor became concerned about me lest I take cold and insisted that I get a sweater of his own. I believe he touched me physically, too, in a warm interchange which had a "father-son" feeling to me. This and one or two similar incidents were the only real moments of warmth that I remember to temper a cold, inhibiting relationship. From this vantage point, years later, I see that I, too, was at fault. This advisor held occasional open houses to which his students were invited, but I never attended, preferring to be relatively anonymous for what I thought to be safety's sake. And yet from my present vantage point as a fellow educator I recognize that if I want to facilitate learning and productivity in my students and junior co-workers, *I* must be the one to initiate an open relationship that supports others and helps them to feel self-worth, satisfaction, joy, and comfort. They, just as I once did, commonly feel themselves in an underdog position, and the smallest kinds of neglect that I show and my own failures to let them experience me honestly as a fellow human with doubts, problems, and fears can be destructive to them. This does not mean that I need approve the quality of their work at all times, but it does mean that I will not dwell on their failures, but will, rather, help them to accept their failures as steps toward later success. An open, truly human relationship does not lead to a lowering of standards. On the contrary, it paves the way for creative behavior on the part of the learner and probably on my part also.

Some of my colleagues have complained to me about students who come to them with boy-girl problems and other personal matters. They may even feel anger, as well as impatience, when students bring in personal problems. Indeed, I can remember a few such instances myself. Their reaction is, "Why don't you stick to the point?" because they do not accept that the real point of the visit may have been to seek out some human warmth. Their response to students is akin to the military man's answer, "Take it to the chaplain." Such matters come before us more frequently than we may realize. I suspect that many students who came to see me may not really have come to ask about a point of subject matter but rather to ask for recognition of their own humanness. I want to seek out their real questions, and this requires me to move toward the level of feelings and away from rational analysis.

There must be ways in which we can encourage expression of feelings in large-group learning situations also. I recently visited a small college in which I sat in on a conventional laboratory exercise on rocks and minerals. The superficial level at which students were engaged reminded me too much of what I had seen in dozens of similar laboratories, so I asked the instructor in

charge if I could take over the next lab group. When they entered
I used the following "lesson plan":

1. Go anywhere you want in the lab, stock room, or outside and
   bring back three rocks or minerals that you love and three that
   you hate (forty-five minutes).
2. Place the samples you have brought in two separate piles at the
   front of the room.
3. Now, working in two groups, agree on an order in which you
   should love the samples in the "love" pile and the order in
   which you *should* hate the samples in the "hate" pile.
4. Open discussion
5. How did you *feel* about the exercise you have been involved
   in?

Many students became engaged with the problem with little
hesitation. There was great diversity of student behavior. Some
left the lab, returning later with some samples. Some may have
gone to the student union to drink coffee, but they must be
trusted if they are to learn how to deal effectively with freedom.
After all, why should I necessarily insist that they play my stupid
game from ten to twelve o'clock every Wednesday? They don't
insist that I play theirs. I am learning to accept apathy in students
as well as enthusiasm. The acceptance of apathy may pave the
way for future enthusiasm. Some students snooped in the stock
room, something not normally permitted to freshman students.
A few had "permission," because of the relatively ambiguous
assignment, just to look at samples in the display cases around the
room, something they never have really been able to do as part
of an "assignment." Many simply studied minerals from the
standard trays normally used for this laboratory. The students
had many alternatives.

When they had made their value judgments as to which they
should hate and love the most, they hated slag, dusty red hema-
tite (iron ore), soft coal, tar, and other things interpreted as pol-
luting agents. One student, having decided in advance what he
hated, actually spent much of the time hunting for a piece of coal.
Another student hated a specimen because he couldn't figure out
what it was. This is a feeling I have shared many times in the field
and laboratory when I have had difficulty adequately describing

or interpreting a sample or an outcrop. The specimens they loved most included gold, enshrined in a special little plastic display box and surrounded by colorful ores of copper, lead, and other economically valuable minerals. Paradoxically, the minerals they loved most were closely related to those they hated most so that the closeness of the materials seemed to reinforce the affinity of strong emotions such as love and hate.

We had a relatively open, friendly discussion on minerals during this time. Some students thought it stupid even to try to approach minerals from an emotional viewpoint; others enjoyed the experience. All of their feelings, fears, likes, and dislikes were accepted. All were engaged in a real way with the topic. Great good humor was apparent in the classroom.

If science is to be recognized as a human enterprise including many esthetic values and institutions as well as reason, and if students are to develop the capacity to use and express their emotions and thus to be whole human beings rather than intellectual cripples, we must, as facilitators, find ways of engaging and accepting emotions in all contexts, from the large or small group situation of the classroom to the individual contacts of facilitators with learners. Until we, as facilitators, learn to encourage the honest expression of emotions in learning situations and to accept and value these expressions, there will be no real revolution in education.

ALONENESS

I have to be alone and even lonely sometimes in order to function creatively or to form feelings about other people. I come to know myself better and to be able to look inward when I am alone. Groupness sometimes stifles me. Only I can know when I need to be alone. It is important for me to feel free to go and be alone at the appropriate times.

I find that ideas often come to me when I am riding my bike to work in the morning, when I walk the dog at night, or when I am flying to a meeting somewhere. In the latter situation I am alone in the middle of a group of people with whom I am not engaged. The best moments of creative functioning often come just after a conference or meeting where I have been interacting intensely with many people. I often leave such meetings high as a kite, but then I must be alone for things to fall into place. Sometimes, when I feel lonely and low as well as alone, my thoughts combine and recombine to produce new mental images and ideas. I have come to value moments of aloneness and loneliness because of what often comes out of them.

I accept that others have these feelings too, and I want them to feel free to go off by themselves without feeling that they must even excuse themselves. I want to create and be in an environment where each of us in it experiences this kind of comfort.

TRANSIENCE

A hundred people to deal with in a term. Fifty people to get to know in a weekend workshop. It frightens me. I have a compulsion to want to know everyone's name and to know something about what each one is like and to share his uniqueness in some way.

I'm frustrated when I can't do this.

But suddenly I've discovered that I can share a moment of being together and feel good about a relationship without needing to make it a continuing thing.

I'm finding that transient relationships can be beautiful and full moments that have a completeness of their own. I'd like to have a "together" feeling with more people that I meet casually. Sometimes just an exchange of smiles is enough.

At St. Lawrence University I participated in a small encounter with three other faculty men. We were surrounded by fifty educational psychology students. An empty chair was in our circle, and as we explored our own feelings and apprehensions in front of the group, individuals from the group occasionally came up to join our circle and make statements or ask questions about our interaction. We in the circle had no chance to form relationships with the people around us, and yet we were exposing deep feelings before them. That afternoon as I was walking across the campus I heard the clatter of wooden, Scandinavian-style clogs behind me. The clatter quickened as their wearer ran up toward me. I had a first feeling that the person was running up to me, but I resisted the temptation to turn. A pleasant female voice called out, "Bill!" I stopped. A pretty girl of twenty said, "I'm Jane. I was with you this morning in the group." We exchanged a few sentences—not casual, cocktail-party, see-you-around-the-campus talk, but feelings that were deep and meaningful to me. And from her animation and glow I knew that our meeting and talking was important to her. We parted after a few minutes. I saw Jane later in the week several times, and all that we needed was to smile at each other and say a word to recall a beautiful transient moment. We may never come in contact again, but I feel richer for having experienced that moment. We may meet again, and the transient encounter may deepen into a longer friendship.

A few weeks ago as I sat in the St. Louis airport waiting to catch a connecting flight, I was struck by my isolation in the center of a huge air terminal full of milling people. Yet I felt no desire to engage anyone, to share any of me, or to take anything from them. I feel a paradox. In many circumstances I don't feel that the environment invites me to engage people or to be engaged by them.

Sometimes I initiate a transient relationship. Sometimes someone else does, and I accept it.

For me, the basis of a satisfying transient relationship is a sharing of deeper level feelings. I've always disliked cocktail-party transience—because I encounter only the surfaces of people. As I am willing to share more of my own deep feelings, I find that other people reciprocate more readily.

I want to share more of me with the people around me and to be ready to receive more from them.

Transient relationships can provide me with beautiful moments. In the transient relationships I once had with students I used to accept a controlling, managing role. The relationship was rarely a satisfying one. When I enter a relationship now as one unique person entering an encounter with another unique person, the way is cleared for a moment of sharing.

TOUCHING

Physical contact between teacher and students seems taboo in many schools. Harry Wong, a well known science teacher and curriculum innovator, mentions how loath Americans are to touch each other and contrasts with them the Chinese who are "always touching, touching, touching." So do the Italians, Greeks, and people from many other countries. Wong points out that about the only people who hug and demonstrate emotion physically in the U.S. are athletes!

I recently was drinking beer with some friends in a small upstate New York village when an Italian friend of theirs joined us. As we conversed he put his hand on my arm and remained in physical contact with me through much of our conversation.

Touching can facilitate communication. Good facilitators I know feel comfortable touching people who are learning with them. I feel comfortable when such people touch me. I am beginning to feel more comfortable touching other people too. An arm around the shoulder, a hug, or a pat at the right time may be an important part of facilitation. But such contact must result from an honestly felt desire for physical contact. And the touch may be rejected. I am prepared to risk such rejection.

INTERVENTION

Teachers are interventionists. They have power to interrupt a learner whenever they want, whether the learner wants to be interrupted or not. Students generally do not have the right to interrupt. Neither do children in their homes. Most parents have been through the "Don't interrupt, Johnny," routine at some time or another, but few parents ever think twice about interrupting their children. Administrators and employers frequently don't hesitate to interrupt people who are "below" them in a hierarchy. Some principals don't think twice about using a loudspeaker system to interrupt a whole school with trivial announcements. I have certainly exercised this double standard as a parent, as a teacher, and as an administrator, and the double standard has been exercised on me. What gives me this right to interrupt other human beings and yet prohibit them from interrupting me?

In education, intervention is widely accepted as a part of the teacher's role even though it establishes a relationship in which one person may be looked at as having lower status than the other and thus be less important. For a long time some educators have been worried about intervening. Neill, in his book *Summerhill*,[6] describes a highly non-interventionist model of child-rearing and of education. His non-intervention goes to the point where children in his boarding school are never required to engage in any activity they have not chosen. In Neill's opinion children (and adults, for that matter) will learn little that they have been forced to study and are likely to form poor attitudes towards required subjects and skills. Neill cites a number of instances in which children spent months or even years "playing" before becoming involved in any more school-like activities. Silberman[7] repeats a description given by Agnes de Lima of a school teacher in the

---

[6]Neill, *Summerhill.*
[7]C. E. Silberman, *Crisis in the Classroom* (New York: Random House, 1970), p. 210.

progressive Walden School who spent most of his time with his back to a class of children, waiting for the children to ask him something.

Some "open" schools such as The Wilson Campus School in Mankato, Minnesota, discussed in some detail on p. 94, have attempted to compromise by allowing their students wide latitude to choose among various activities, including activities completely designed by themselves. However, each student has one teacher, generally selected by the student, identified as his advisor. Each teacher becomes a "guidance counselor" as well as an instructor. The relationship established depends on the student, his parents, and the teacher-advisor. Some students are expected to see their advisor each day and to make up, together with him, a schedule of their plans for the day. Very small children of grade school age may have more "outside structuring" of their time than some of the older students. Other students may be free to wander, study, and relax as they please. I observed one teacher in the Wilson School who actually followed certain of her charges around, checking to make sure that they performed on schedule. I saw her jerk one nine-year-old boy with little interest or aptitude in reading or arithmetic out of an industrial arts area where he was busily engaged in productive activity. She had scheduled him for arithmetic at that particular hour. When I asked her why she had done this in an "open" school, she said she felt it was her responsibility to make sure that he got to certain levels in the 3Rs at certain times. Other teachers in the school intervened in a less vigorous manner. In most of the conventional subject matter areas at the Wilson School, a number (but not all) of the teachers had standard achievement levels that they expected students to satisfy but not necessarily in any particular order and certainly not at any particular rate. I doubt if any student would be allowed merely to wander aimlessly for very long, however, before a staff member would intervene.

The idea of "structured time" versus "unstructured time" has come up in a number of schools, among them the former middle school at Kansas State Teachers College in Emporia, Kansas. Many students had up to half of their time free to study or work in any area of interest. They were required to keep a schedule of the rest of their time and even to study in some areas. They were allowed to change their schedules easily, and their rate of progress in any area was largely up to them, but teachers intervened regularly with most children.

A far more romantic, Summerhillian type of school, The Jefferson County, Colorado, Open Living School (a public school with kindergarten through sixth grade age levels) started out in Fall, 1970, to be as completely non-interventionist as possible. (See p. 91.) Within four months after the school opened with over 200 students, the staff decided to establish a system under which each adult would assume primary responsibility for about twenty children of various ages. One of the directors of the school, Christine Samples, mentioned to me that she felt most of her twenty could be allowed virtually complete freedom. She would have to keep track of four or five, however, until they showed evidence of being more responsible. Thus she had them either follow a loose schedule or come and inform her when they decided to go outside to play or to migrate from one area to another. One of the big goals of the "primary responsibility" scheme will be to make it possible for the advisor to know at least where to find his or her charges at any given time. Thus a "romantic-type" open school has moved toward at least some conscious intervention.

At Summerhill, there has always been a town-meeting kind of democracy, according to Neill. Here, the group as a whole has the right to intervene whenever the behavior of any individual student causes difficulty, danger, or unpleasantness to other members of the community. Neill himself, as a psychologist and psychotherapist, scheduled "P.L." (private lessons) for many Summerhill students whom he diagnosed to need psychological help.

As I aim myself in the direction of being a facilitator rather than a teacher, I ask myself: What do I do on the sixteenth day if I have seen two boys playing chess for fifteen days? If I am a real facilitator, I don't think I will intervene as long as the boys are not interfering with or interrupting the activities of any other students. I can schedule activities that I think may be interesting to some of the young people I work with, but I will no longer force any of them to lay aside other activities to come with me, to watch me, or to listen to me. I *will* intervene when I sense danger or when I find any person disturbing another or denying another's rights. I *will* intervene whether this happens to be another staff member or visitor as well as when it is a young person whom I perceive to be a violator of another's rights. I am also prepared to have a student or a staff member intervene when *I* do something that is perceived to violate another's rights. No facilitator should have any illusions about his own perfection or infallibility.

Silberman, in discussing the English infant and junior schools, quotes Nora Goddard, chief inspector of infant schools in London, as saying that teachers must know when and how to intervene in order to help ". . . children learn how to think, to form judgments, to discriminate."[8] Silberman keeps emphasizing the role of the teacher's discretion and the teacher's "central role." There is great danger in putting stress on the teacher as the one who makes the rules, for this orientation can be used as an excuse for adults to establish or reestablish a defensive, arbitrary, non-facilitative power relationship over young people. Neill's concept at Summerhill of a participatory democracy in which his own vote counts only as heavily as that of any five-year-old or fifteen-year-old can prevent the formation of the often abusive power relationship that many adults assume with respect to young learners.

I am likely to intervene or interrupt when I deal with other people simply because I am a human being. The Plowden Report on the British infant schools is quoted by Silberman[9] as stating, "Children like to know where they stand and what to expect. . . . They must depend upon adults for their moral standards and for guidance on what behavior is tolerable in society; an adult who withholds such guidance is in fact making a decision which involves as heavy a claim for his own judgment as is made by the martinet." Although I do not agree that a facilitator at any level should have power to dictate standards on morality and behavior, I agree that I should not "withhold" my ideas. *Withholding* my own views is in a way as dishonest as imposing them. If I am to be a facilitator, I must be a real human being who expresses his views in an honest way without attempting to impose them. How

---

[8] *Ibid.*
[9] *Ibid.*, p. 226.

much I intervene depends on who I am and where I am as a human being. My intervention, if I am a real facilitator, will be peaceful rather than forceful, with the possible exception of forceful intervention required to protect myself or any people I am working with from bodily harm or what I perceive to be real psychological harm at the hands of another person. Non-intervention is equated by some opponents of open learning situations with permissiveness. I cannot accept this equation. Permissiveness usually implies that the teacher or facilitator cares so little about the people he is working with that he refuses to intervene in any situation. Facilitators who really care about the young people they are working with establish an environment of mutual trust in which the discipline problems usually associated with permissiveness will simply not exist. I have never seen more purposeful, considerate young people than those who attend open schools such as the Wilson Campus School and the Jefferson County Open Living School. Young people who are charged with governing themselves and who care *can* be trusted to live in harmony and to learn efficiently.

DOOMED TO SUCCESS: NO PLACE FOR FAILURE?

You'll never get anywhere without it.

Nothing helps a young engineer's career like being given a challenge. Which is another way of saying a *chance to fail* now and then. To make his own mistakes.

At Western Electric we give our newly recruited engineers responsibility almost immediately. They make their own decisions. Learn from their own errors. Don't get us wrong. We keep our demands reasonable enough so that our recruits can make their decisions at their own pace. But our thinking is, a man feels awfully good about even a small decision when it's his.

If you're the type who'd like the chance to make your own moves, see our recruiter or write College Relations, 222 Broadway, New York, N. Y. 10038.

A lot of hard work never hurt anyone.

 Western Electric

—Courtesy of Western Electric

In his recent book, *Schools without Failure*,[10] Glasser proposes that everything possible should be done to help children succeed in school. Macrorie[11] suggests for college level composition courses what he calls a "third way" of teaching. The third way consists of letting students operate with freedom and discipline. As an example of third way teaching Macrorie points out the importance in the early stages of identifying good points in student writing, emphasizing the positive, and only much later dealing with the correction of deficiencies.

---

[10]W. Glasser, *Schools without Failure*, (New York: Harper & Row, 1969).
[11]K. Macrorie, *Uptaught*, (New York: Hayden Book Co., 1970). The "first way" he describes considers teaching to be the handing out of information. The "second way" has the teacher providing complete freedom but no direction.

I am entirely in accord with many of Glasser's suggestions and wish that I could have begun writing under the tutelage of someone with Macrorie's ideas. But the idea of eliminating failure is not entirely satisfactory to me. I think it is more important to accept the idea of failure but to change our attitude toward it. In a humanistic learning environment no negative connotation is attached to failure. Lord Rutherford and Albert Einstein are two of the many scientists who have emphasized the important role that failure played in their careers. These men and many like them in the sciences, arts, and humanities have regarded failure as positive feedback rather than as a basis for long-lasting negative value judgments. Failure defines a limit or in some cases a dead end and thus allows us to reject one path, approach, or configuration and to move along another path or to try something else. If failure results from a limitation in our skills, we have a basis for considering whether or not we wish to do what we set out to do enough to work toward acquisition of the skill or whether we wish to abandon an original goal for another we might reach more easily as a result of greater aptitude in another skill area.

Failure needs to be recognized as positive feedback in learning situations. It needs to be identified as an integral part of the trial and error process that learning is. Students need to be helped to recognize failure and mistakes, but a facilitator of learning does not penalize learners for failure and does not treat failure as "bad." In all areas of learning, students should be encouraged to form their own standards of "success" and "failure." Success becomes the achieving of a result that I am personally satisfied with—be it a drawing, a sum, a piece of writing, or some data obtained from an experiment. Failure is creating something I am not satisfied with. Failure is usually at least partially identified as a result of external standards. A teacher should help to make these standards available for students but should not, in my opinion, try to force them onto a student. In the case of a solution to an equation there may be a "right" answer, and I may need help in recognizing my failure to achieve it. In the case of an essay, opinion becomes important in judging success (and the degree of success) or failure (and the degree of failure). Honest exchange of opinions about each other's work becomes an essential part of the human interaction between "teacher" and "student."

Learning to value failure as a step toward success is part of the behavior of many creative people. A "creation" normally comes about only after a period of intense involvement with a problem. Many creative people I know not only learned to live with the uncomfortable period of searching that precedes "success," but they actually value its onset, for they know that their deep involvement *may* be followed by a result that pleases them.

Learners at all levels need to recognize and value failure as an essential forerunner of success. Teachers need to recognize this too, and, having recognized it, they must remove from their students the idea of extrinsically identified failure which can damage or even destroy self-confidence, enthusiasm, and the learner's concept of self-worth.

EVALUATION IS A THREAT

The significance of this "free" course hit me as I was coming out of a sociology prelim on the family. I felt the test had not adequately tested what I had learned. Perhaps I will get a C or a B, but in any case, by that mark and others I will have typed myself as to intelligence and how good I feel about myself and only because it is a comparison with others. This is why geology is so significant for me. It breaks down at least some, not all, of the competitive motivation involved in learning. It makes the learner view himself from his own viewpoint, his own excellence, and not from another's.

—Dana Oviatt, a learner in an open geology course at St. Lawrence University in which students evaluate and grade themselves.

On Grading

. . . a grade (is) . . . an inadequate report of an inaccurate judgment by a biased and variable judge of the extent to which a student has attained an undefined level of mastery of an unknown proportion of an indefinite amount of material.

—Paul Dressel, *Basic College Quarterly,* Michigan State University, Winter, 1957, p. 6.

Evaluation is a threat to learners, especially evaluation that takes the form of *relative rating.* Many schools are attempting to reduce the threat by changing the evaluation system, but most of these schools still retain a system that is extrinsic to the student. That is, a teacher assigns the evaluation that ultimately becomes a part of the student's permanent record. I think that as long as extrinsic rating techniques are used, changes will do little to improve the existing situation.

Many grade schools have done away with A,B,C,D,F ratings and have substituted notes from the teacher or parent-teacher conferences. Even in many of these schools, however, papers are still corrected by teachers, and extrinsic records and punishments in the form of numerical scores and gold stars prevail.

A few junior high schools, high schools, and many colleges now allow students to take at least some of their courses on a pass-fail basis, but the teacher commonly keeps a hidden grade list anyway. Interestingly, in many colleges the instructor does not even know which of his students are taking his course on a pass-fail basis. Many college students enrolled in pass-fail courses have said to me, "Gee, I should have taken that one for a grade—I was getting an A in it!" The implication is that you should only take a course on a pass-fail basis when you are really afraid that your grade point average will suffer if you take it for a grade! Another interesting and unusual situation is that students are rarely allowed to elect pass-fail grading in courses that are part of their major. In some colleges only upper division students may elect pass-fail grading, the implication here being that freshmen and sophomores need to have *more* pressure on them than do juniors and seniors. What an odd approach! It seems to me that freshmen and sophomores, who are faced with tremendous personal readjustments as they make transitions away from home into a relatively free world, are denied the right to a relaxed world of learning. I have seen too many transcripts showing that students had very low grades during their first two years of college and then blossomed out as upper division students. The tragedy is that those poor grades from the first years remain on a student's transcript and are calculated into his grade point average. Graduate fellowships have been lost and jobs have been denied to many students who made a bad beginning. Students are evaluated on the basis of a long-term average rather than on the basis of what they are at the moment they finish their academic work.

Some colleges, which I shall not name here, have a *real* hidden evaluation system. These institutions provide their students with no numerical or letter grades in any of their work, and yet when a student applies to transfer to another college or to enter graduate school, a transcript *with grades on it* suddenly materializes!

There is a story of one girls' college in which professors write short comments on each student's performance and submit these to the registrar. A legendary little old lady receives these written comments and translates them into letter grades: "Let's see, Professor X writes that Linda did her lessons, went on the field trip, and wrote a pretty good term paper. We'll make that a C+."

Colleges such as Brown, Earlham, Colorado College, the University of South Carolina, Stanford, and a host of others have changed their rating system from A-B-C-D-F to A-B-C and no-credit. In these colleges, students cannot "fail" a course. If they do not receive passing credit, no one ever knows they were enrolled in the course. This system invites students to try courses without risk of failure becoming part of their permanent records. Students are thus invited to experiment and to try new subjects rather than confining themselves to things they already know they can do successfully anyway. The relative ranking of the A-B-C's is still a major threat to many students, however.

A few brave instructors in both secondary school and college who disagree with the system have simply told their students, "Grade yourselves." Self-evaluation poses a real threat to many instructors. Some of them fear the loss of power over their students that is involved. Others, including some very thoughtful educators, believe that the lack of ability to conduct self-evaluation may be a characteristic of the human organism. In order to allow self-evaluation schemes to function properly one must have faith in the existence of this ability. I must again state my own firm confidence that the human organism *can* learn with very little active outside intervention, *can* evaluate itself honestly, and can accept and use non-coercive external *feedback.* The issue becomes once again, "To what extent do you trust people?" If one cannot accept these premises, he cannot accept the notion of real freedom within learning environments. Each facilitator or teacher must decide to what extent he can risk trusting others. The only way to test our faith and trust in human beings is to try freedom out. An honest try requires a real commitment and requires giving a really substantial degree of freedom. Students do not recognize "a little bit of trust" or a "little bit of confidence." Either you trust them and have confidence in them, or you don't.

Ability to evaluate one's self is a skill that people develop just as they develop the ability to create, talk, write, paint, put together a machine, cook, or do any other human activity. The way a learner develops this ability is by doing it. Many, perhaps all, people are not good at self-evaluation to begin with. It is easy to lie to oneself at first. Facilitators who allow learners working with them to evaluate themselves must be patient and provide opportunities to examine and discuss the self-evaluations their learners make. This is done by providing learners with ready access to external standards. Learners must be encouraged to discuss their work with several facilitators who may take different views of what constitutes excellence. The facilitator who refuses to give his opinions of the work of learners is not doing his job. Ultimately, however, he must say to the learner, "This is, of course, only my opinion, and you must ultimately decide for yourself whether or not your work satisfies you. You probably won't be able to get a job doing work of that quality, but maybe this kind of work is not what you want to do anyway." The facilitator's job is to help learners form their own standards, recognize the effects that outside standards may have on them, and help them to clarify their own goals and views of their own work.

Learners should be encouraged to save their best work in a portfolio of what they regard as their best product. If letter grades must be given, the learner himself can be allowed to assign the final grade, but the facilitator owes it to the learner to let him know whether he agrees with the self-evaluations or not.

Teachers and facilitators are commonly asked to submit letters of recommendation on learners. Any real facilitator owes it to the people working with him to show them the letter he feels he can send out. Personally, I usually go ahead and send out what I consider to be a good letter and send a copy to the learner. If the letter is either neutral or negative, I ask the learner *first* if he wants me to send the letter. If not, I tear it up. In case of a negative letter I give the learner my reasons for having a low opinion of him or of his work and let him know ways in which he can help me change my opinion if my opinion is important to him.[12]

---

[12]A book that has just appeared as this book is in production warrants the attention of readers interested in more documentation on revision of grading systems: Howard Kirschenbaum, Sidney B. Simon, and Rodney W. Napier, *Wad-ja-get?* (New York: Hart Publishing Co., 1971).

ACCOUNTABILITY AND STANDARDS

The learners who work with me are accountable to themselves and not to me. As a paid facilitator I am accountable to them as well as to myself.

I will provide external standards to learners who wish to measure their performance against standards of the real world. If the learner fails to meet the standards and does not wish to work to meet them, I can help him to foresee the consequences of his refusal, but he is the one to decide in the light of his own goals whether or not he wishes to invest whatever effort is necessary to meet standards.

Those who pay for the maintenance of the learning environment have a right to see the product of learners who work in this environment with me. If they are dissatisfied with the product of these learners, I accept their right to dismiss me. I trust learners in a free environment to take responsibility without my attempting to coerce them enough to stake my job on it.

I will suggest to the learners that they keep a portfolio of things (products) that they think give evidence of their learning. I will help learners who ask me to do so to evaluate the things in their portfolios. I will also provide suggestions for possible work to learners who ask for such suggestions. The learner will decide for himself whether or not to pay heed to the comments or suggestions he has solicited from me. I will try not to be disappointed when a student does not meet *my* expectations. It will be hard, but I shall learn to accept. The only person I really have a right to have expectations for is myself. We will show these products to members of the community who ask us to show accountability. Products provide better evidence of learning than standardized test scores, grades, or other such trivial indicators. Products can be *anything* created by learners.

THREAT, RISK, AND VULNERABILITY

Students take most of the risks. Teachers have control. Teachers can always steer a discussion in a direction they feel comfortable with. When they lecture, they generally have things all laid out for them with notes to help them remember the formula they might forget or the rule they might misstate. They're the ones who grade the exams, evaluate the term papers, make the home assignments, and all the rest.

How often does a student get to evaluate a teacher? These days student groups are sending around evaluators to judge and report on the teaching of various instructors. This makes some instructors very nervous. Colleagues in a department almost never sit in on each other's classes. In the six years I taught at one university, not one of my colleagues ever sat in on one of my classes, and I never sat in on theirs either. Now I'm sorry. But it won't happen again.

Some teachers ask their students to fill out rating sheets on their courses—at the end of the semester when it won't do them any good. Not many students sign their names to these forms. They feel too threatened to let the teacher know who they are and how they feel. Yet sometimes those students write beautiful things. Here is a beautiful thing that was written by an anonymous freshman student of mine on one of my course evaluation questionnaires:

> It is somewhat tragic, I suppose, that in my freshman year I had the best teachers in the subject which interested me least. When I came to the university there was at least a small part of me which wanted to go into medicine. I became interested in it more or less spontaneously, in spite of rather than because of the fact that my father and both his parents were doctors. The math and the chemistry involved scared me away. I toned down my ambitions past the point of being a biology major to the lowest level—taking a course in it.
>
> When registration came around I discovered that I could not take biology because my social security number put me in the very last

group to register and there were no more openings by the time I arrived. So I realized I had to fulfill a requirement and got into line for physics. When my turn came, a fat German physicist started shouting at me, and I picked up my papers and left. I walked over to geology as a last resort because there weren't any people crowding around, and a lab assistant looked at me and asked if he could help me. The funny thing was that he seemed to be wanting *me* to take the course. I felt funny, almost as if I were *needed.*

At any rate, my first year has ended. I've fulfilled a lot of requirements in courses that I never wanted or needed to take. With college one fourth complete I suppose I'm technically one fourth "rounded out," but all of the courses I took were either the last thing I ever wanted or the last resort. I'm no brighter than I was in September; perhaps even less than when I began since this was like an extension of high school. It was also a very unhappy year for me personally, which wasn't helped by my general lack of confidence in the faculty. Geology was a big surprise. This course, along with religion, perhaps had more far-reaching effects on my life than any other educational experience to date. What may be somewhat confusing to the faculty of these two courses is that I got different things out of the courses than were intended. In religion, for example, instead of becoming a more aware, religious, church-going person, I rebelled against it. I saw them for what they were and not what they claimed to be. In geology, something different happened. Here I became more interested in the way the course was taught than in the rocks. I wrote down notes, not so much on the material but on the method by which things were expressed. I have no doubts that if I had had this instructor and had been in a biology course I would have gotten an A for the course.

It might be considered a waste that I let my grades fall for the sake of *learning* something, but I don't believe in grades too much. (The pass/fail system you used in your course is excellent and very flexible.) It was the only course this year in which my instructor cared whether I was doing my work instead of saying, "Well, I'm too busy; if he wants help he can come and get me." It was a pleasure going to the office even if my problems weren't related to geology—a sort of return to self-sanity, from worry to self-confidence. It was the only time that a teacher *cared,* and it is sad that this will be the exception rather than the rule in the coming years. (It's also interesting to note that the only two courses I have any confidence in at all—geology and religion— both pass out these questionnaires. The other courses are statues of powerless ex-gods on orange-crate pedestals.)[13]

---

[13]Reprinted from the *Journal of Geological Education* 18 (1970):54. Reprinted with permission.

This student, whose identity I think I know but cannot be sure of, taught me something very important in what he wrote to me. For one thing, he taught me that I want to be close enough to him so he and others like him feel that they can sign their names to anything they want to write to me.

A group of graduate students at one university recently ran what they called a "reprisal" survey. They asked the questions: Do you feel that if you do not toe the mark, some of the faculty might carry out some reprisals against you? (Eighty percent answered *yes*.) Can you identify any specific instances where you think that reprisals were actually exercised against a student? (Forty percent thought they could.) I predict that any faculty that allows itself to be evaluated in this way will receive similar results. I know those fears existed among my own fellow graduate students at that time of my life. And I know that the same fears existed among graduate students who confided in me while I was just beginning my own teaching career.

Students grow up in a school environment full of fear. If I want to be a human being interacting with human beings called students, I must take the risk of trusting them in ways that I have not trusted them before. If I know what they will do, I am not really taking a risk at all. I must somehow find ways of taking as many risks as they are taking. I must become as vulnerable as they are.

Unfortunately I can't write a formula that will suggest a way for *you* to become vulnerable, reader, for I am sure that you and I are threatened by different things. But both of us need to look for ways of rejecting the power and control images we project by virtue of the simple fact that we are called "teachers." Only when we become willing to risk as much as our students do can we work on a truly human plane with them.

NOURISHING CREATIVE ACTIVITY

A good many people suffer under what is to me the misapprehension that creativity is restricted to artists, inventors, composers, writers, and Nobel prize winners. I am convinced that each of us is creative to a greater or lesser degree, and that creativity, like any other ability, can increase with practice. Native creative ability, if such a thing really does exist, can also decrease and be stifled under adverse psychological conditions. Creativity, which I define here as *the ability to combine ideas, things, or approaches in new ways,* is perhaps a state of mind more than anything else.

To create is to take a risk. A cook who throws away the recipe book and tries drastic new things takes the risk of producing an abomination that no one will eat. The greater the departure from standard, time-proved recipes, the greater the risk and, in case of a real success, the greater the satisfaction of all concerned. When Picasso and Georges Braque began experimenting with cubism, they abandoned their relatively "safe" earlier styles. But between 1906 and 1914 they "changed the look and function of painted surfaces radically and forever."[14]

Thus, the main way of nourishing creativity and helping it to grow in young people is to allow them to play and to create as extensively as possible. In a sense, every workbook assignment or other assignment where an "acceptable" form is specified merely reduces, or in the case of very strict assignments, may remove entirely, the possibility of real creativity. This may be an overstatement in that a prescribed form need not exclude creativity: Sonnets other than the first one ever written have been highly creative. The invention of the form was one creative act, but the expression of thoughts and feelings within the framework of that form have also been acts of high creativity. Writing

---

[14] *Time,* December 14, (1970), 81.

up the results of a scientific experiment in a prescribed form need not reduce the creative insight that leads to a new conclusion or to the formulation for the first time of a fundamental law. Rediscovery is to a learner a no less creative act than the original discovery was to the world as a whole. Recognition may not be as lavish, but a real facilitator of learning will take great joy in seeing a young person discover that something is personally relevant to him. Jean Piaget has stated that a thing is learned only to the extent that it is discovered or rediscovered. If we accept his view, every act of real learning is a creative act for the learner. The learner needs to value these acts as such, and the facilitator will treasure and value the learner and his creations.

A beginning geology student of mine was once involved in studying some cliffs in the Schawangunk Mountains of eastern New York. As she mapped and examined the area, she came up with the idea that the cliffs, through erosion controlled by certain layers of rock, were retreating with time, parallel to their original position. This discovery had been made years earlier by other geologists, but her rediscovery of this relationship entirely on her own gave both of us great pleasure. This and other similar experi-

—Photo by Robert Samples. Courtesy of Environmental Studies project.

ences had a strong influence on her career plans. It is only when students have real freedom to determine their own goals and to design and carry out their own studies in an environment free from threats that they will take the risks necessary to make significant creations. Freedom to fail without penalty is essential to creative activity. It is through trial and error that important creations are discovered.

Kenneth Koch of Columbia University has been working with elementary school children on writing poetry. He ignores problems of form related to rhyme and meter and tries to get at feeling through "assignments" such as, "How about a Christmas poem today?—Like what would the ocean do if it really cared about Christmas? Or the eagles, sparrows, robins—what would they do?"[15] The creative activity of Koch's young friends—ordinary elementary school children in an ordinary New York public school—is demonstrated in a collection of their poetry, *Wishes, Lies, and Dreams.*[16]

Professor Donald Murray of the University of New Hampshire has been helping English teachers become better facilitators of writing skills by letting them write. His approach is to invite students to write every day and then to write along with his students. Individual papers are not graded, and revisions are encouraged. At the end of the term students select what they think is their own best work for evaluation.

One of my junior high school daughters had a student teacher who used a similar approach. She asked her students to write two pages a week of anything they wanted to. As for evaluation, she said that all she wanted to see was two pages covered with writing. It could be copied from a book if the child decided, although this was not encouraged. Said the teacher, "If you'd like for me to *read* what you've written and give you my comments, I'll be glad to." This approach removed the threats, and the students wrote with pleasure and in a creative way.

Paul Goodman in a discussion recently held at Michigan State University stated that when he "taught," he merely suggested to students that he would be glad to have them write with him. So he and his students would go off, write together, and discuss each other's work.

---

[15] *Ibid.,* Dec. 28, (1970), 26.
[16] Kenneth Koch, *Wishes, Lies, and Dreams* (New York: Chelsea House, 1971).

Another example of how a facilitator, also in the area of art, helped his students is given below. The description was written by Lucretia Romey:

> I was scared my first day of class, partly because I was late and partly because I felt older than the other students. Aidron asked us all to tell a bit about ourselves and why we were there. Some said because they needed sculpture as a requirement; some said they wanted help in making sculpture; and I wanted a place to work and a model occasionally. We were given an assignment to cast a piece or block of plaster and then carve into it and give it some color. I'd forgotten how to mix plaster but managed somehow and came up with a form which was pleasing to me.
>
> After this we were pretty much left alone as to what we wanted to do. Most of the time a model was there to work from, or if we wanted to carve or assemble, we could do that. Aidron took all of our efforts seriously and would discuss them with us. Even our jokes he would take seriously, or rather he would laugh but consider them from the standpoint of "art." He would help us do anything from teaching us to weld to helping some kid cast polyester resin. He helped if we asked him to. Sometimes he'd let us flounder a long time before he said anything. Sometimes he would get very excited over some of the things we were doing. I liked being listened to as if I really had something to say. I liked being treated as another human being. I liked walking around his studio seeing what he was working on and hearing him talk about his work. I liked his remark that he'd entered two things in the local show, one traditional and one far out and they were both rejected. How reassuring when my things had been rejected too.

The same kind of atmosphere can exist where young people study science, mathematics, history, social studies, and other "subjects." Creative involvement is needed in every area of learning. Some of the techniques of helping people become involved in creative activity are described in the work of Calvin Taylor[17] and W. J. J. Gordon.[18] Gordon, who is organizing "creativity groups" for industry and in other areas, describes the use of word play, metaphors, and analogies in inventing and creating. David Hawkins[19] extolls the virtues of "messing about" in creative learning situations. Avoidance of external sequencing of activities and ideas provides people with the opportunity of inventing their own sequences and thus becoming involved in far more

---

[17]Calvin Taylor and Frank Barron, eds., *Scientific Creativity* (New York: John Wiley, 1963); Calvin Taylor, ed., *Creativity: Process and Potential* (New York: McGraw-Hill, 1964).
[18]W. J. J. Gordon, *Synectics* (New York: Collier Books, 1968).
[19]David Hawkins, "Messing About in Science," *Science and Children* 2, no. 5 (February 1965).

meaningful learning experiences in association with an effective facilitator.

The problems that face our world in the next few decades require intense activity by every citizen. The more people we have involved in creative attempts to solve our problems, the greater chance we have for survival as a species.

LISTENING

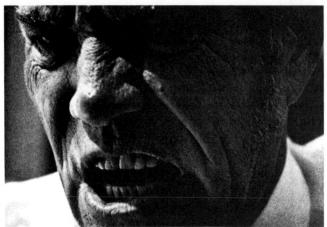

—*Courtesy of Campbell-Mithun, Inc.*

Teaching is all too often equated with talking done by the teacher. Studies by Professor Ned Flanders of the University of Michigan and his colleagues and by other educational researchers using Flanders' techniques have measured the amount of time that teachers spend talking versus the time that the students are allowed to talk. On the average, teachers spend more than seventy-five percent of their time talking, and most student talk in the classroom consists of direct student responses to teacher-asked questions.[20]

Herbert Kohl describes a teacher who wanted his students to listen and learn ". . . and yet never thought to listen, respond, or learn from the children, who remained unresponsive, even sullen."[21] Moore quotes a teacher who said to her class, "When I have everyone's attention and your hands are folded, then I will listen to what you're really trying to say."[22] My nine-year-old

---

[20]Ned Flanders, *Analyzing Teaching Behavior* (Reading, Mass.: Addison-Wesley Pub. Co., 1970).
[21]Herbert Kohl, *36 Children* (New York: New American Library, 1967).
[22]Alexander Moore, Jr., *Realities of the Urban Classroom* (Garden City, N.Y.: Doubleday Anchor Books, 1967).

son recently brought home a school paper of phrases his class had been required to copy. One of the sentences read, "A listener should easily follow the happenings of a story," and yet I know that he is seldom listened to seriously in class.

The fault of not listening is not restricted to teachers in schools. It probably is the single greatest hindrance to real communication in all human interaction. Carl Rogers, a very sensitive facilitator of learning, has become aware of the need to listen deeply through his interest in psychotherapy, where small, seemingly unimportant statements are often clues to deeper meaning. Rogers' technique of psychotherapy consists primarily of providing people who come to him with a truly sympathetic ear. Rogers identifies some of his own times of greatest personal frustration as the times when he is trying to express an important feeling and no one will really listen. Likewise, as a facilitator, he expresses great dissatisfaction with himself when he suddenly realizes that he is not really listening to a person who is trying to be heard.[23]

I recently served as a consultant, along with four colleagues, at a small college in the northern Middle West. Our task was to evaluate the curriculum and plans of one of the academic departments. We decided to ask the students who were majors in the department to join us for many of our deliberations. We presented various issues to the students and asked their opinions. The students answered frankly and made it clear that they were upset about some aspects of society and of their college experience. Three of my colleagues from the consulting group proceeded to counter the remarks of any student who made a negative statement even before the student had a chance to finish what he was saying. The tone of many responses made by panel members was centered around comments such as, "When you're a little older you'll understand what I mean," or "If you want to be successful [like we are], you'll accept your program, which has been made up for your good by people who know what is important for you." When so-called mature adults are so outragingly patronizing and refuse so obviously to listen to, to *hear,* and to sympathize with the genuine anguish of young learners who are trying desperately to find out who they are and what they want to become, is there any wonder that we live in a time of student unrest?

---

[23]Carl R. Rogers, *Freedom to Learn.*

The published text of a television interview between Vice-President Spiro Agnew and student leaders from five different college campuses provides another example of the failure of older people to listen to young learners.[24] The text of the interview sounds as if Mr. Agnew were in one room making a speech while the students were in another room talking to a loudspeaker carrying the vice-president's comments. Rarely in the ninety-minute interview did Mr. Agnew address himself directly to the real questions posed by the students.

Listening to a question or a comment and accepting it is not easy. Frequently it may be necessary for a facilitator to try to find out what the *real* question is. In a mineralogy class I recently taught for a friend, a student called me over and asked me, "What is this mineral?" I realized that his question was not really clear to me and thus asked him the following clarifying questions: "Do you really want me just to tell you the name of the mineral, or are you asking me to help you go through the routine of determining the mineral by using the equipment and determinative tables you have? Or are you just indicating to me that you want to get acquainted better?" The discussions that ensued enabled us to enter into a more fundamental kind of communication about his real needs.

One of the most devastating experiences is to be talking to a person who asks you question after question without ever really listening to your answer or allowing you to expand on your thoughts. And yet this is what classroom questioning usually involves. Questions should facilitate communication rather than be used as a device for establishing a relationship in which the questioner assumes higher status and therefore power over another person.

What about the time when a facilitator is just not in a mood to listen? After all, even a facilitator is human. In such circumstances it becomes his responsibility to seek the reasons for his own inattention and to let the person with whom he is talking know that he is simply not listening for some reason or other. "Polite" listening is soon recognized and hinders communication as much as patronizing responses or interrupting. Real listening requires effort, courtesy, acceptance of feelings and views, a willingness to wait, and, above all, real honesty.

---

[24] *"Agnew's Talk With 5 Students,"* U.S. News and World Report (Oct. 12, 1970).

COMMUNICATION

One of the most difficult problems I am encountering as I work toward helping to create more open learning environments is how to facilitate communication among members of a community. The problem arises in workshops of short duration and in long-term group situations such as courses or departmental programs. For communication to occur naturally, an attitude to want to communicate must first develop. Each group really has to invent and then keep reinventing modes of communication. Even then, knowing what other people are up to and what alternatives are being generated within the community is difficult when there are no required meetings and few formally scheduled optional events to bring people together.

We are trying informal newsletters at two colleges where I am involved this year. Bulletin-board approaches are being used also. I have begun writing lots of short letters to people whom I value but don't seem to be seeing, just to let them know I want to be in touch. I find myself using the telephone more than ever and seeking informal meetings with small faculty-student groups and with individuals.

We have to trust each other to make communication go, and everyone in a community has to work at trust. It is especially important to provide a regularly available forum where members of a learning community can get their hostilities out in the open. In that way we can identify problems among people, and once these are identified we can work with them.

I especially feel the need for highly informal contacts that may have little or nothing to do with the cognitive things we are working on. If deeply personal communication is established, communication about shallower level, intellectual matters is rarely a problem.

If communication is lost, community cannot exist.

TEACHERS AND FACILITATORS ON FIELD TRIPS

GEORGE

I recently went along on a junior high school earth science field trip which illustrates what students do when they are heavily restricted and controlled. It was a beautiful spring Rocky Mountain morning. We all met at the school—several people who had agreed to drive, the teacher, whom I shall call George, and about twenty-five students. Up the canyon we drove, to a roadcut where the sun glinted brightly from a beautiful micaceous rock surface. As I got out of the car, my first reaction was to grab my hammer and dash over to this outcrop. Left-hand Creek, full of the spring melt, was tumbling down along one side of the road, and an old mine shaft with much interesting debris at its mouth stood there beckoning. There was a movement of students and drivers toward these inviting opportunities for exploration. Then George bellowed, "All right, all of you, let's all sit down in a circle here."

Students turned away from all that beckoned to them and sat in a large circle facing inwards toward George rather than outward toward the fascinating environment around them. George said, "Get out your guide sheets now, and let's look over the questions about what I want you to learn. And don't forget that I'm going to collect those sheets and check your work when we get back." The questions had nothing concrete to do with the field trip itself, but instead concerned the definitions of such terms as sedimentary, igneous, and metamorphic rocks, weathering, erosion, and the usual abstract claptrap you find in any elementary book on rocks, be it used in first grade or in college.

During this half-hour "lecture-discussion" I alternately looked hungrily at the things nearby that attracted me so strongly, at the students, and at George. Within four or five minutes I saw that most of the students were drawing pictures in the dirt, piling up pebbles, looking at the beautiful purple sky, or were otherwise occupied except when George would single one of them out and ask a question. As often as not, the question had to be repeated before a bored answer could be obtained. The students were informed that they were to keep together during the five-mile walk down to where the trip was to end that afternoon.

George pulled the whole group down to one outcrop and allowed them to look the rock over. He resisted the temptation to turn the trip into a complete "show-and-tell" affair. When he felt that time enough had been spent at the first outcrop, he started down the road, insisting that all students should follow. The trip became a five-mile hike with strictly controlled stops.

One group of students stopped to examine feldspar and quartz fragments in the bottom of a beautiful little brook. I stayed behind with them, and we talked together about them. Before long, George stormed up to us, insisting that we must stay with the group. Because George found nothing fascinating about the material in this brook, we were not supposed to either.

Several students crossed the road to watch the overfull brook coursing along through its narrow gorge. George quickly herded them back to look at the rock he intended for them to be observing.

Within the first mile students began to straggle far behind and to ask, "How many more miles do we have to go"? In the rear ranks little of the conversation had anything to do with the trip or with anything related to earth science. Mainly, the rest of the day became a time of complaining. Students tried various subterfuges to avoid the walk. One girl pretended to have a hurt ankle when George was looking, but walked marvellously well when his back was turned. She eventually got permission to be picked up by a following car, thereby avoiding the rest of the walk.

George had a compulsion to have every student see the same things—his things. He was cordial and friendly with his students, and four or five out of the group stayed close behind him, eager to use his obvious expertise. He knew the area and he knew his geology, but he knew very little about most of his students, and he cared little for their interests.

ROGER

Roger, another teacher, took his students to this same area. He began when people left the cars by cautioning the students about snakes and spiders and then said he would be glad to talk with individual students who found things they were interested in. At the first outcrop, Roger said, "There are lots of neat things here if you want to look around." One group found some black widow spiders which they proceeded to observe; they fed one spider a grasshopper and watched her wrap it up for dinner. Others watched some geese on a nearby pond. A few settled down to examining and tasting rose hips and cactus pears. Then someone found some fossils, and the whole group was soon examining these without any direction from Roger.

The group proceeded up the hill. This trip, although in exactly the same locality as George's trip was run "backwards," with the students having to walk five miles uphill rather than downhill. As they walked along, Roger asked some questions he was interested in and also pointed out some features that he personally found to be of special interest, but the students were not held accountable for looking at any particular feature or for remembering any particular relationships. Among other things, Roger, who is much interested in conservation and environmental concerns, would stoop over every now and then to pick up an empty beer can or other bit of debris. These he placed in his pack without any flourish or comment. Soon several students in the group began picking up debris too, obviously influenced by Roger's quiet example. Some students stomped on the cans so that they stuck to their shoes and clanked along the road with their tin-can overshoes. Roger accepted various games of this type.

Occasionally students would lag behind the group, but Roger showed no real concern. He merely slowed down a bit and allowed them to explore widely and at their own rate. At lunch time in a little park some students waded in a stream and got very wet. Roger admitted that three years ago he would never have allowed this. His only rule was that students must stay within sight of him. The students respected this rule and seemed to enjoy great freedom within this minor constraint. The first complaint about tiredness wasn't heard until after lunch, and even this person later said she guessed she wasn't so terribly tired after all and would like to come back. In general there was less horse-play on this trip than on George's, and yet students seemed to be having a better time. Roger showed great enthusiasm for things he was interested in, but made no real attempts to coerce students to look at any particular things or to answer questions. Many students responded naturally to Roger's enthusiasm by sharing their own. Roger did not try to confine students' attention to rocks, but seemed himself to be deeply aware of the wholeness of the environment. Students on this trip also seemed more at ease and more open with the other adults on the trip than they had on George's trip.

At the end of the planned walk there was a forty-five minute wait for the vehicles. Roger allowed almost complete free ex-ploration during this period. He asked that students please not to go into the stream again because it might look funny if they returned to school that way, and he might get into trouble. Even though many students obviously wanted to go into the water (and could have since Roger was not trying to control them), none did. They understood that he didn't really care if they went in, but they accepted the responsibility of helping him to preserve appearances.

Much of a teacher's attitude toward field trips depends on his goals. If he is a facilitator, he subordinates any goals of his own to those of students. But if he has goals, these should be made clear. In George's situation he had specific content goals, and these were made clear to the students. But the students did not accept most of his goals, and, for them, little learning took place. Many left the trip with poor attitudes as well. Roger's goals related more to general awareness of the total environment with the hope that some students would look at things related to earth science as well. Roger's chief goal was to allow his students to explore and find questions which they were personally interested in asking. The whole atmosphere of trust, mutual respect of each other's interests, and enthusiasm indicated that his goals were met. On the basis of my own past experiences I am certain that a year after the field trip Roger's students will not only remember their trip more fondly, but they will also remember at least as many if not more specifics from the field of earth science than will George's students.

ED

Edward C. Stoever, Jr. of the University of Oklahoma describes his own conversion from the highly directive kind of field
trip role to one of facilitator. Teachers turned facilitators find
certain frustrations. With a group of earth science teachers who
were his students, Stoever had planned a long walk to see some
special features in southern Colorado, but at the same time he had
decided to let the teacher-students stop to examine any features
in which they became interested. A few yards from the cars the
teachers found a small outcrop which Stoever had never even
noticed. They spent a couple of hours examining and discussing
this one feature. By mid-afternoon the cars were still in sight, and
Stoever's special feature was far ahead. Ed finally announced that
he intended to go ahead to look at what he had come for and that
anyone interested was welcome to accompany him. A few of the
teachers went with him while others stayed behind. Upon reflec-
tion, Ed decided that the trip couldn't have gone better. The
attitude of the teachers was excellent; they had pursued observations of their own choosing, and they had learned a great deal of
geology, although not necessarily the particular geology origi-

—*Photo by John Thompson. Courtesy of Earth Science Teacher Preparation Project.*

nally intended by Stoever. The facilitator-instructor's role in such a trip is, as termed by Harold Stonehouse of Michigan State University, "sitting on a rock and waiting."

JOHN

In the past few months, I have discovered a new kind of field trip—retreats where the primary goal is interaction among people. John Carpenter of the University of South Carolina expressed the idea well when he wrote to me about a geology field trip on which "maybe they would look at some stones," but where getting to know each other was of greater importance. I have attended several such retreats recently, including one of Carpenter's, and I found that people did discover something about the natural environment around them as well as about themselves, their relationships with each other, and their relationships with their environment.

TEACHER TRAINING: LETTERS FROM MEG

Teacher training programs are notorious for not practicing what they preach. Many go so far as to preach "facilitation" and to assign books such as this one as *required* reading. I wonder how many beautiful young people who would make splendid facilitators end up doing as Meg Hayes has told me she would do in the letters reproduced below.

FIRST LETTER

. . . Although we in the geology department are fortunate to have_____ and_____on our faculty, I wish that some of our faculty in education would realize that teaching is not totally divorced from the concept of learning. (I guess this is unfair, but right now I'm kind of surly since I am in my educational psychology class and hating every moment.)

I intensely dislike the expository manner of teaching. The prof I am supposed to be listening to is a strong proponent of that school, teaches in that manner himself and has yet to understand that I will NOT be that kind of teacher. Oh well, I guess education courses have a way of being generally poor. But they should not have to be. Education, because of its role in forming the "molders of society" (that's us) should be the BEST department and have the best courses in the colleges and universities.

Because a highly structured "schedule" of learning is not desirable, it should not imply that a disciplined approach must be forfeited. Self-discipline is one of the most valuable lessons a student can learn, but I really doubt that it is something that can be taught. The role of the teacher is to facilitate the learning of such concepts. I wish I knew how to go about doing that. . . .

SECOND LETTER

Just a note to tell you that I have finally been driven out of the education program here. This doesn't mean I'm not interested in teaching earth science. Only that I'm bored out of my skull with the classes necessary to teach. Can you really be "taught to teach" anyway? I don't think so. . . .

Sincerely,
Meg

LITTLE THINGS

As I try to become a facilitator of learning and to throw off the teacher's role, I find that many little things are important in helping me feel like and perhaps become a more real person with the people who come to me wanting to learn something.

The biggest of the little things is how I treat people.

From the receiving end, Eliza Doolittle explains to Colonel Pickering that he, rather than Professor Higgins, is responsible for her real education. Higgins has taught her to speak like a lady, but that was ". . . like learning to dance in the fashionable way: there was nothing more than that in it." What made her really a lady was how Pickering treated her. "Your calling me Miss Doolittle that day when I first came to Wimpole Street. That was the beginning of self-respect for me. And there were a hundred little things you never noticed, because they came naturally to you. Things about standing up and taking off your hat and opening doors . . . things that showed you thought and felt about me as if I were something better than a scullery-maid; though of course I know you would have been just the same to a scullery-maid if she had been let into the drawing room. You never took off your boots in the dining room when I was there. . . . you see, really and truly, apart from the things anyone can pick up (the dressing and the proper way of speaking, and so on), the difference between a lady and a flower girl is not how she behaves but how she's treated. . . ."[25]

In a series of workshops for university teaching assistants, some colleagues and I recently have been helping some potential university teachers explore their perceptions of their roles. One of these teaching fellows, Kenneth Czyscinski, of the University

---

[25]Bernard Shaw, *Pygmalion,* in *Complete Plays with Prefaces,* Vol. 1 (New York: Dodd, Mead, and Co., 1963), p. 270. Reprinted with permission of The Society of Authors, on behalf of the Bernard Shaw Estate.

of South Carolina, went back to his students and made it clear to them in various ways that he trusted them and that his job was to facilitate learning rather than to be their taskmaster. His students were asked to go out and make a photographic essay of the environment near the university. Czyscinski was astonished and highly pleased by the quality of his students' performance under relaxed conditions. He wrote the following to me: "Some of the things we got were just great. Our freshmen didn't seem as dumb as I thought. Could it be that our methods of teaching made them look so stupid?"[26] Mike Hansen, a teaching assistant at the University of Illinois, described to me an open, individualized approach that, in his opinion, ". . . has already produced results far exceeding anything in my teaching experience prior to this semester and has uncovered much more depth of interest in geology and related areas than we had expected in our beginning 'idiots'. It seems we've made a serious misjudgment concerning their capabilities. Given the freedom and flexibility, many go wild over science."[27]

Involved here is the well-known "self-fulfilling prophecy," the same one alluded to by Eliza Doolittle in the passage quoted above: People will generally perform according to your expectations. If they are treated as failures or potential failures, they will fail. The converse also seems to be true: If they are treated as people of intelligence and worth, they will perform well.

Good humor and laughter seem to go along with a facilitative relationship between learners and those who help them learn. Paul Zaloom, a student who spent an exchange term at Putney School in Vermont, expressed this feeling as follows: "At Putney, there's a lot of . . . exuberance. People are really into living and life. Man, in one lousy assembly here there's more laughing than you hear in a year at . . ."[28]

During recent months I have attended several conferences of science educators in which this association of good humor and a facilitative approach has come to my attention. At each of these meetings the group has broken down into three major subgroups:

[26]Earth Science Teacher Preparation Project, *Teaching Assistant Bulletin #1*, 1970.
[27]Earth Science Teacher Preparation Project, *Teaching Assistant Bulletin #2*, 1970.
[28]Richard H. and Susan T. de Love, "John Dewey Is Alive and Well in New England," *Saturday Review* (Nov. 21, 1970):85.

(1) Some of these educators are basically authoritarians and wish mainly to impart their knowledge to their students. They are convinced that there is a single body of knowledge that all students must learn, and students must be put through this body of knowledge in a prescribed sequence. Many of these people are especially attracted by programmed instructional techniques and by behavioral objectives. For the most part they serve the interest of their disciplines first and their students second. (2) A second group includes educators who are willing to allow their students a somewhat greater degree of freedom. They limit the student mainly by limiting the environment in which he is expected to learn. For example, if they wanted him to learn certain aspects of physics or of Elizabethan drama, they would surround him with the appropriate equipment to perform certain experiments in physics or with material that relates to drama in Elizabethan England. The student might have a good deal of freedom to explore within that environment, but generally the teacher still has certain more or less definite outcomes in mind. (3) The third group includes educators truly interested in helping the learner explore ideas or skills that he himself has elected to pursue. These people feel that the student should be as free as possible to explore whatever physical and social environments surround him or whatever intellectual environments he wishes to create or invent. Such facilitators come to realize that they may not be able to help or may not wish to help a learner investigate certain ideas very effectively because their own interests may lie in different areas. No single area of knowledge is essential, in the eyes of these facilitators, unless the learner chooses to view it as important to *him.* This kind of educator is involved in learning new things along with the young people rather than teaching what he already knows.

These three groups follow interesting patterns. People in groups one and two are basically interventionists, and, to intervene or manage, they conduct long, serious discussions, quote educational theory a great deal, and make a strong distinction between their own roles and the roles of their students. The people in the third group hold highly unstructured discussions punctuated by a great deal of joking and laughter. They engage in extensive word play, think in terms of analogies and metaphors, and frequently seem to be clear off the topic assigned—until one examines what they are producing. Out of their humor and word play come warm personal relationships and in several instances I have observed that the group members invent new ideas and potentially useful new ways of approaching new problems. By dealing with each other in highly personal and human ways and with their natural good humor they seem to cut through some of the barriers which keep members of the first two groups working at a relatively superficial level. Members of the third group seem to be more comfortable with students, and before long, especially with secondary school and college students, it is not easy to determine any longer which are the "students" and which are the "educators."

There is no question in my mind that relaxed good humor is a very big "little thing" in a facilitator. Real humor enables learners and facilitators to laugh *at* each other and *with* each other without offense on either side and with the growth of warm personal feelings. Learning proceeds more rapidly under such conditions.

Dress is another factor I have recently become aware of. As a college teacher at Syracuse University, I always felt I needed to wear a coat and tie while lecturing. As soon as I was out of the lecture room, the coat would come off and the shirt sleeves would go up. In certain lab situations the tie would come off too. Being a geology teacher I scheduled a certain number of field trips, and there was a good rumpled old pair of pants and a sweater that went along with this activity. My relationship with students seemed, as I look back, to be related to dress and to situation. There was lots of joking, good humor, communication, and *lots* of learning in the informal field situations. In the more formal lecture and laboratory situations there was tenseness and, probably, less learning. What students talk about remembering was what happened in the informal field situations.

Recently I was visiting in a middle western university. I was feeling glum because of the unwillingness on the part of the faculty and administrative officers to engage in any kind of meaningful innovations. Many of them fully accepted the mindless successions of requirements and rigid schedules of dull lectures and meaningless examinations. I had also had several opportunities to chat with undergraduate students in their institution and had been much impressed by the maturity and competence of these young people and what I firmly believe to be their ability and willingness to take responsibility for their own learning without the conventional coercion.

As I walked across the campus after a particularly disappointing session with some faculty members, I greeted a number of students who smiled at me as I passed them. Suddenly I felt terribly uncomfortable. As I sought the reason for my feelings, I realized that I was identifying with the students rather than with the faculty, and yet I was wearing the faculty uniform: suit, white shirt, tie. Clothing may be a little thing, but when it helps to reinforce the distinction between one group of human beings and another, it probably makes the facilitation of learning by an older person more difficult. I rarely wear a coat and tie on a Saturday or Sunday or when I'm on holiday and am really feeling like *myself*. Therefore if I don special clothing, which is not quite comfortable anyway, when I am involved with other people in learning situations, I am playing a role rather than being myself.

First names are another little thing. I started out calling students "Mr. Jones" or "Miss Hendricks," but that didn't feel very comfortable to me. So I started to learn their first names and call them "Tom" or "Mary." When I first arrived at Syracuse University, I had a teaching assistant, Jim Street, who was just about my age and easily knew as much geology as I did. Furthermore, he had had a good deal more teaching experience than I. I asked him please to call me "Bill." Nonetheless, in front of students he called me "Dr. Romey." So I started to call him "Master Street," a title earned by virtue of his M.S. degree. Soon we were off on a real first name basis, and I, at least, felt better. In recent conversations with Jim, he tells me that he, too, felt equality between us as human beings.

For a geologist, informality is a part of life. When you're out on a field trip with younger or older people, there is something rather absurd about titles. For instance, imagine a distinguished professor slipping and falling into a stream, his students helping him out, saying, "Here, Dr. Schmaltz, let us help you out". And yet some geologists insist on their titles! They can't get out of their roles and into their real skins. It works both ways: Fear and the formality we instill in our children make it difficult for some young people to go over onto a first name basis with a teacher. I have had many graduate students who, even when asked, "Won't you call me Bill?" still can't seem to bring it off. Usually when the tone of informality is set early, a few braver students will go ahead and use the first name. Soon afterwards everyone passes over to the first name when it is clear that there are no threats or reprisals lurking in the shadows.

Ennis Geraghty, a graduate student friend of mine, describes an experience he had with Jim McLelland of Colgate University, a facilitator in the truest sense of the word. Ennis describes the facilitator-learner relationship he had with Jim as follows:

> At the first meeting we found ourselves sitting at tables arranged in a sort of semicircle, Jim sitting with us, not standing at the front of the room. He talked to us from a sitting position, carefully avoiding anything that hinted of lecturing. He was one of us, not a "little g" god lecturer, one who knows all.
>
> He suggested that we call him Jim. He preferred it to doctor or professor. Calling an instructor by his first name is not easy after four years of titles, especially when you're still calling his colleagues by their titles.
>
> By the end of the first meeting we had decided on the grading system, with everyone getting As. No tests, no papers. We completely abolished the stigma of grades hanging over our heads.
>
> The course was set up with a tentative schedule. At each session Jim would mention papers pertinent to the next class discussion, and if we'd like to read them we could. Everything was "Would you like to . . . ?" not "You have to. . . ." We would ask Jim to lecture infrequently, only to clear up a point or to get some needed background. He was present as a source of information. Every other Sunday the class met at Jim's house to discuss how the course was going, what improvements could be made, how we felt about this type of class.
>
> The class was a most rewarding but frustrating experience. Frustrating because I was taking three other courses for a grade. I was learning, developing myself educationally, in Jim McLelland's course; I was fighting for a grade in the other three. I felt at the time I hadn't done justice to Jim's course, that I wasn't ready for such a course. I see now that the course has affected me more educationally than any other course in my undergraduate or graduate years.[29]

---

[29] *Earth Science Teacher Preparation Project Newsletter #2,* Winter, 1970.

—Photo by Robert Samples. Courtesy of Environmental Studies project.

Paul Zaloom, after an exchange term at Putney School, Vermont, put his feeling about first names as follows: "Peter (Putney's director) just raps on issues—his and yours—and I can talk to Peter as Peter. First names. I know, they don't make much of a difference. But they do, do you know what I mean?"[30]

Why am I concerned about such a trivial thing as a first name? When a learner with whom I am working closely calls me "Dr.," "Professor," or even "Mr.," he labels me as if I am in some arbitrary class of people comprised of all other doctors, professors, or misters. I am *not* one of those; I am myself and want to be accepted as a person with a name, with virtues, with faults, with knowledge, with ignorance. The learners who work with me tell me they want to be received as people, but this "peopleness" must be double-edged if we are to slice through the barriers that separate one human from another.

I am commonly asked, "What if I don't want to call you Bill or am not comfortable leaving out your title?" My response to this statement is, "Address me in any way that makes you feel comfortable, but remember that you make *me* feel uncomfortable when you treat me as a distant, titled object rather than as a

---

[30]de Love, "John Dewey Is Alive," p. 85.

person. This is my hang-up, not yours, but as a result of it I intend to try in every way possible to get to know you well enough and to help you know me well enough so that you will feel comfortable in addressing me as you would a friend rather than a taskmaster or boss. In any case I will refuse to establish required tasks for you or to boss you, even if you ask me to do so."

The physical setting in which facilitators and learners interact may seem a little thing. I think of my own feelings when I am in a typical classroom with its horrible sterility as opposed to the feeling I have when I am sitting in my living room or in my messy but homey office or laboratory. A number of colleges have put in what are called "conversation pits"—carpeted areas with no chairs and only pillows to make sitting on the floor more comfortable. The dictum "less is more" espoused by a number of architects (and so well represented in Japanese homes) perhaps holds true here. Get rid of conventional classroom furniture and create a setting that demands informality. It is easier to call a teacher by his first name and to think of him as a person if you're all lying on the floor together.

In a project group I have been working with (The Earth Science Educational Program) we decided to turn a part of our conference room into a "conversation pit" or "rap pad." Since this change was made, we have had several conferences in this room, and I have been much impressed to see how much more rapidly than before workshop participants get on close personal terms with each other and with our project staff.

At the Wilson Campus School in Mankato, Minnesota, every learning area has at least one informal corner equipped with an old rug, a bunch of big floor pillows, and perhaps an old sofa or some easy chairs. Children ranging in age from five to eighteen lounge around in these areas to chat, play word, number, card, and other games, and relax when they are not involved in activities that require tables or special equipment. Adults, in the role of facilitators, join the younger people in exchanging ideas or simply in relaxing—an essential part of learning.

More and more schools are making specific plans to establish special areas for informal interaction in learning situations. The Evergreen State College in Olympia, Washington, for example, has plans for faculty "offices" that are actually learning studios to be furnished in the style of living rooms and where learners will gather, as it were in their own homes, to discuss, study, and learn. Such studios may largely replace conventional classrooms entirely in the future.

It is about time to get away from the barrenness of the conventional classroom that young people occupy from kindergarten through graduate school. I become almost ill when I walk through my children's schools—good modern ones in fine new physical plants—and see bare walls, bare floors, bare blackboards, chairs or desks lined up in rows, with the teacher's desk (a handy object for an insecure person to hide behind) confronting the class or hiding behind the desks in rows. The more universities and colleges I visit, the more I am depressed by this overwhelming barrenness. Classrooms occupied only occasionally, when a teacher is preaching, by large numbers of people sitting in rows are both wasteful of space and sterile in function. Actually it is less expensive to furnish attractive, homelike spaces than it is to buy some of the horrible office and classroom furniture we allow ourselves to live with. A further way of alleviating space problems in schools is to use the school building as a headquarters from which young people go out into the community to study, interact, and learn, rather than as a place in which they are to be confined for many years.

In my own present office I suddenly realized the other day that when people came in to see me I generally sat on one side of the desk while they sat on the other. It finally dawned on me that I could be closer to people if that barrier were removed. Now the desk is against the wall, and I, at least, feel that I can participate in a little conversational group with people who come to talk to me. Sometimes we sit on the floor, too. This informality does, I think, facilitate communication, as small a thing as it may be.

In visiting schools and colleges recently I have been impressed by the way in which faculty perpetuate their separateness from students. Not only do they dress differently, talk differently, cause students to call them by titles, and erect barriers in the very way they arrange their furniture, but they set up separate teachers' rooms, lounges, locker rooms, and eating facilities in order to avoid informal contact. Jerry Farber describes the situation eloquently: "If I take [students] into the faculty dining room, my colleagues get uncomfortable, as though there were a bad smell."[31]

Furthermore, faculty colleagues frequently do their best to discourage their associates from going into the lairs of their students. I take a risk when I approach students on their ground instead of forcing them to meet me in my territory. They may reject me, and that might hurt. In a recent visit on the campus of an eastern college I decided to take most of my meals in the student dorms. The first time I went in I wondered, just like a freshman, if I would have the courage to go up and sit down with a bunch of students. Then one of them got up and invited me to sit down with him and a group of his friends. I felt warm all over.

At the Wilson Campus School students and teachers go to eat whenever they feel like it. The same lunchroom is shared by facilitators and their young students. Staff members are generally found seated with groups of young learners. It gives you a good feeling to see a seven-year-old girl come up to a table, climb up beside the shop "teacher," tweak his moustache, and then proceed to have lunch with him while carrying on a very important conversation about her interests.

The same kind of scene occurs at the Jefferson County Open Living School. Students and teachers all bring bag lunches and small groups sit down together to eat whenever they happen to get hungry. Some of the more voracious children start lunch at 10:00 A.M., while others don't get around to eating until late. The main thing is that there are no special teachers' rooms. All spaces are for all people in the school.

I am thoroughly convinced that real facilitators of learning must come to share their homes and all of their spaces in the school with the learners who work with them, and they must visit and come to feel comfortable in the living places of these learners. They must feel comfortable eating, drinking, living, and loving in community with the young people who have come to them to learn.

Facilitation of learning, in the final analysis, is directly dependent on the accumulation of a large number of little and seemingly trivial things that are involved in human relationships and feelings.

---

[31]Jerry Farber, *The Student as Nigger* (New York: Pocket Books, 1970), p. 90.

I AM NOT AN ENCYCLOPEDIA

Last week I went to spend a day in class with William in his grade school classroom. His teacher, eager to use parents to help enrich the learning environment, asked me to talk to the class about geology. I decided that rather than presenting something through a short talk I would merely respond to the children. They began to question me. Questions were about all sorts of different things and were usually unrelated. One little fellow in the front of the room looked at me and smilingly said, "Let's see, now what will I ask you?" Most of the questions dealt with how much diamonds cost, where you get gold, and a number of other things dealing with monetary values associated with geology.

The role I had gotten myself into was that of an encyclopedia —only they didn't have to leaf through the pages. Just press the button and out comes either an answer or an "I don't know." Very little conversation took place among the children. Each question resulted in a two-party conversation between one or two children and me. I felt bad after this session in front of twenty-nine children all lined up in rows and *directed* to ask questions.

A former colleague of mine in a western university has turned his introductory geology "lecture" into similar "responding" sessions. He sits in the front of a room filled with a large number of students and only speaks when asked a question. He too has assumed the encyclopedia role. "Ask and I shall answer."

Another colleague, a renowned petrologist, tries to avoid little children who approach him, rock in hand. One of the worst experiences for a petrologist is to have a child bring him an unknown rock and ask its name. You can always fake it, but assigning a name and producing a reasonable story about a rock and its origin is commonly a complicated procedure requiring analysis and thought. My colleague doesn't like to play the role of a determinative table. I agree with him.

A story often heard concerns the young boy who approached his science teacher and asked how his little radio worked. The teacher responded, "Why don't you ask your Dad? He works for RCA." To which the boy responded, "Oh, I don't want to know *all* about it." Encyclopedias sometimes get to be heavy reading —or listening.

I once took the oral examination for the U.S. Foreign Service. I had expressed an interest in work as a cultural and scientific attaché. The exam consisted of questions such as, "Name all of the countries in the common market," and "Name all of the American authors you can think of." One examiner gave me the names of large numbers of people, mostly artists and writers, and asked who they were. Must diplomats be encyclopedias who spout off such information on command? Does it impress foreign diplomats when our own diplomats stay one-up in the game of "whose country has the most well-known authors"?

Most courses taken by people planning to teach and by those going into other professions and occupations as well stress memory of factual information. Look at school examinations. Fortunately, once a student has repeated the appropriate information on an exam, he commonly forgets it just as a magnetic tape is erased before re-use. Many students at least have sense enough not to attempt long-term memorizing of the encyclopedia.

When I give a lecture, I have to prepare for it, rememorizing much of what I will say. After all, an encyclopedia can't be caught short without the answers!

I decline the role of encyclopedia, and I think that anyone who wants to become a facilitator of learning must also do so. If I perceive myself to be a learner rather than a storehouse of information, I can work more comfortably in helping other learners find information that they and I wish to seek together.

I can no longer force them to drink up the things I know. I can no longer require them to sit at my feet and listen. I know that I will continue to talk about what interests me, but I can no longer require other learners to ask me questions that allow me to show them how smart I am. I can share what I know, but I will not be disappointed if someone else finds it less exciting than I do. I am a person, not an encyclopedia. You are a person and not a page upon which I write my information. If we both perceive each other as equal people, *then* we can learn together effectively.

FEELINGS OF SOME FACILITATORS

Several people I know have been trying to shift their roles from the managerial approaches of teaching to the responsive approaches of facilitating. Change of this type produces many different feelings of fear and frustration as well as of joy and satisfaction. When I change the way that I behave with my students, the rest of my life changes too. And I have a whole new set of things to think about in my life style and my concept of me. A person who undertakes to be a real facilitator should be forewarned about the probability of deeper personal changes within himself.

The following short essays are brief statements written by friends of mine who are in the throes of becoming real facilitators. The first four have been published in uncopyrighted newsletters of the Earth Science Educational Program, sponsored by the American Geological Institute and supported by the National Science Foundation. The fifth is from a letter I recently received which has also been published in Earth Science Teacher Preparation Project Special Paper # 2, *The Cutting Edge: How to Innovate and Survive,* 1972. They are all reprinted here with permission.

Openness scares the hell out of me—it also makes me feel good! It scares me because of:

SAFETY—A kid fell off the mountain once on a field trip, a light bulb blew up in a girl's face, hot paraffin spilled in a guy's lap.

DOUBT—Am I really on the right track?

NOISE—Constant, the sound of busy students.

LONELINESS—This occurs in a school where my openness is an island.

MESS, CONFUSION, IMPACT—Inevitable and ubiquitous, answering questions, rapping, always on call, a constant barrage of demanding, inquisitive students, broken glass, mud on the floor, spills, no time for meditation or reading, no respite from pressure. I yell a lot!

It makes me feel good because of:

DECREASED FEARS—I am less afraid of extrinsic intervention, the administration, bureaucracy, myself, the kids.

INCREASED TRUST—Much less soul-searching when I am asked for permission to do this or that; I try to consider things as legitimate as long as nobody gets hurt.

DECREASED DISCIPLINE PROBLEMS—Nuff said!

SHARED LEARNING THROUGH INQUIRY AND DISCOVERY—Excited girl peering through microscope at snow crystals: "Wow, look at this, teach!"; Boy experimenting with electro-magnetism inadvertently produces copper carbonate: "What's this weird blue stuff? Where'd it come from?"—he follows this for weeks, happy and excited; Others surprised when they put alcohol and salt in snow and frost forms on outside of container: Someone says "ice cream"—they learn much more than this, for they fool around for days; in fact they turn the whole class on to their "freezer."

Students do learn in an open environment. They learn about the excitement and importance of discovery, about their capabilities, their limits, self-discipline, and responsibility. They also learn facts. How many? Who knows? I just know that they learn some facts. They know this, too. I don't think I ever *really* knew this before, and I don't think that they did either. It makes me feel good to *really* know something and to know down deep that we are learning.

Openness promotes happiness and joy, it has good karma, it's groovy, Aquarian, cosmic. Somethin' else—it's like Zen; stop it to describe it and you've lost it. You've got to experience it, live it, do it!

One more thing. I have been frank as promised in the title. If you don't believe, then that's your problem. I have shared this with you because you're part of me and vice versa. But, you've got to learn to swim by yourself and only when you're ready. No coercion, no justification. O.K.

Roger Hudiburg

The door was open and a steady line of fourteen-year-olds trooped in and out with plastic bottles of water. The water was being dumped on a hillside near the back of the school building. Some who didn't carry water stood around and encouraged the workers. Some just talked among themselves about pep club, boy or girl friends, and what they intended to do after school. However, everyone's attention became immediately focused when a great event took place in "North Arvada Canyon." Cheers went up when a pebble that had long resisted the stream flow tumbled over and slid to the channel floor. With such heightened drama providing emotional release, the students returned to conversation. Sometimes they would pause to note how the errant bursts of water made side streams that became more and more molasses-like as they ran down the slope. Some became fascinated by the way the mud "froze" near the bottom.

Bored by the progress of the canyon a small group broke away to continue a study that they had started two days ago ... they were trying to find and prove the existence of a million of something in the environment. Just before they got out of earshot they were arguing about which solution to attempt. Grass blades and bricks were being dismissed as being "too obvious."

Inside the room a girl trying to make a wave tank in a plastic shoe box chastised two boys for offering her advice she didn't want. The teacher, Ed Maruna, came over when asked and just smiled at the boys, who stood for a moment, grinned and then walked off. I became conscious of the fact that the two boys and the girl had been arguing for a while before Ed walked over.

Somebody yelled, "Flood!" ... so I went outside again. Five plastic bottles were being emptied into the canyon at once. *It was a flood!* The delta at the bottom grew remarkably. Upstream more pebbles were exposed and bigger chunks of rock had been washed down. Ed was teasing the group in search of a million and, though I couldn't hear what they were saying, I could see them laughing with each other as he rejected the trick proof they had laid on him.

I didn't know what they would do tomorrow, nor did I care. I found that this comfortable, relaxed class had filled me with data. It had filled me with information most of which would be called forth from me in instances like now while I am writing. Someday my preconscious memories of the viscous mud may help me paint or dig into a lava flow. All of what happened to me happened to each class member and Ed. It happened. No one demanded its sterilization into words or numbers. Now I am putting it into words, yet I find the words come much more easily than if I had been required to report at the time. I have much higher recall of Ed's class than any convention talk or college lecture I was forced to listen to. Convention talks and college lectures are best when I feel a need to engage myself in them, just as writing is.

As I left there was a very pretty girl holding hands with a dark-haired boy watching the canyon form. I hadn't seen them involved in any of the activities. Back in my role as an observer I asked about it. "Oh, they aren't in this class; they just come here to hold hands where nobody will hassle them." Ed grinned at me . . . he grins a lot.

Robert Samples and Susannah Lusk

Having taught more or less "traditional" science for my first four years, and having constantly tried to make class interesting and relevant, I have moved readily into an open classroom situation. I am now teaching seventh grade life science in what I consider a comparatively free environment. My students may select any topic of study they wish to pursue, as long as they can legitimize it as being related to man or his environment. This requirement is solely to protect me and, in reality, limits the students very little. They are required to fill out project contracts, which I keep as a record of work attempted and completed, and to grade themselves, supplying written reasons for the choice of grade. Students may work anywhere on school grounds, with anyone they wish, for as long as they wish—or they may not work at all. I am available for advice, criticism, ideas, and materials, as requested. I encourage the students to be open and honest with me, and do not punish them for being so.

I believe it is fair, however, for me to express my feelings and opinions, but I try very hard not to force them on my students. The cardinal rules of the class are to be fair to others; to treat everyone as a human being; to give respect; and not to interfere with other people's work.

In this environment I am happier and feel more human; I enjoy getting to be friends with my students, rather than maintaining professional distance. I feel free to ignore small and unimportant matters of discipline and meaningless regulations, and my students appear more comfortable and open when I don't sweat the small stuff. Most of my students respond warmly and positively and seem to appreciate honesty and trust. My classes never bore me; they are always challenging.

I have had some important problems with my open approach. There has been criticism from fellow teachers, administrators, and especially parents. I have occasionally had doubts that I am fulfilling my obligations to the board of education, parents, and students because of my nonadherence to curriculum and refusal to force structured work on my students. There is some friction generated by sharing classrooms and equipment with teachers who are not sympathetic to the open situation. Above all, I have been discouraged and frustrated when students failed to respond, choosing to ignore my every effort to interest them.

Nevertheless, I feel I am accomplishing my goals: to remove punishment as a stimulus to work and to foster a spirit of inquisitiveness, candidness and pleasure in learning. I want the student to feel free to try things without fear of failure. I want to provide an atmosphere which excites students so they want to know more about themselves and their environment. These are not easily achieved goals, but the rewards are well worth the efforts.

Lawrence Crowley

Free and open learning environment means I can do whatever it is that interests me now. What do I want to learn? Wow—I don't know. I don't know what I want for me. I'm so used to your telling me what to do that when you stop, it's hard to find me. I feel empty, confused, unsure. I want you to tell me what to do, to take responsibility for me—if you do, I'll feel secure again. Sure, give me lectures and exams. I don't like them, but at least I won't have to confront not knowing me. And anyway, how can I do what I really want to? If I do, I'll hurt my parents, and my friends will look at me funny, and I'll probably screw up my future. How will I ever get a job if I don't learn all the stuff society wants me to? What does society want me to learn? Well . . . uh . . . I don't really know. I suppose all the stuff I'm required to take. No, it may not have much to do with any job I get, but . . . if there aren't any requirements, maybe I won't find something that interests me. Hell, no! How can learning be fun with all these requirements? What I really want to do is to go to Mexico—but that's not going to help me get into law school. Do I want to go to law school? Well, not really, but I might be able to do something with it afterwards. But I don't know what I want to do. . . .

Help me become AWARE of what I feel, see, hear, smell, taste, think, of what I want to do, of what I want for me, of all the alternatives I can choose among if I allow myself to be aware of them.

Let me CHOOSE. I need lots of choices, as long as I don't block my awareness of all the exciting things there are in the world to do by getting in a rut. One of the problems with moving in a rut is it gets so deep you can't see over the edge.

Let me have RESPONSIBILITY: response-ability. I must be able to respond, and to accept and work with the results of my responses. I can be responsible only for me, not for you. However, I can choose to obligate myself to respond in certain ways to you or a situation.

Jonathon Swinchatt

Still running my groups and am seriously thinking about changing my educational psychology course *from* learning theories, learning climate, growth and development of humans, etc. *to* personal growth through encounter. I emphasize this latter through the vehicle of the class, but I'm coming more and more to realize that understanding concepts, the intellectual sphere, is not the answer. First and foremost those teachers-to-be, more than ever, must be facilitating human beings and strongly aware of and in touch with themselves and their feelings. The most important part of the teaching process is the humanness of the teacher. Everything else can be written, taped, movied, or lectured, but the humanness is rare and unique. Oh, well! All I can do is *be* what I am and *be* with my students, and that's O.K.

Hugh Gunnison

PANICKY LITTLE MEN

I know a principal who is scared to death of change. I'm sure you must know one, too. Several of his teachers have decided to be facilitators. He seeks ways of undermining what they try to do.

Can you believe a principal who refuses to allow live mice in a biology room?

Can you believe a principal who tries to deny use of a court-yard to a science class because some paper blown in by the wind when the class was not even there "might offend visitors."

Can you believe a principal who tries to force his teachers into rigid lesson planning "because the rules say you have to."

I wrote to this principal asking that grades no longer be given to my children. The superintendent of schools responded by letter that every effort would be made to accommodate my desires. The principal responded that the administration required him to submit grades for all children. Hmm!

One day I visited the school to sit in on some classes. As I emerged from a classroom where I had gone to talk to a teacher friend, I saw the principal tongue-lashing two girls.

"Do you know what they just did?" he shouted to me. "They kicked the locker door!"

One of the girls said, "But that's the only way we can get any of these lockers open."

Sure enough, every locker in the row had a dent in it, and the lower part was covered with dirty scuff marks indicating a long history of being kicked.

"You go see the janitor or the assistant principal for help when that happens," roared the principal.

One of the girls said, "Well, we'll just do without our books today, then." And the two started to walk away.

Less sure of himself, the principal called them back and offered to help them open the locker. He pulled a master key from his pocket, and, after considerable effort, was able to pry the door open without a kick. (His possession of a master key indicates again his lack of trust of the students, and the fact that he periodically searched student lockers was confirmed by the girls later. This raises an interesting legal question about illegal searches!)

After the girls had gotten their books, he again cautioned them to go get the janitor or assistant principal the next time rather than kicking the door.

When he had left, one of the girls turned to me and said, "Have you ever tried to go get the janitor or assistant principal to open a locker for you when you only have four minutes between classes and when you know that the teacher in the next class is going to shout at you for being late and then send you right back to the assistant principal's office to get chewed out some more?"

The school administration, rather than working to correct the basic cause of locker kicking—namely the lock-step system of regimented formal schedules—remained satisfied to stick to their rule book and to browbeat the students. Panicky little men preserve the institution or the system at the price of the people.

I once knew a university department chairman who wouldn't "allow" his faculty members to drink with their students. "There are the officers and the enlisted men, you know, and you are the officers." I knew another who wouldn't allow students to call any faculty member by his first name, even when the faculty member desired it. I know several principals who go into a purple funk when teachers ask to be called by their first names. Panicky little men standing on their status because they have nothing else to stand on!

A young professor in a midwestern university recently decided to allow his students to choose their own topics for study. He gave no tests, allowed his students a large measure of freedom, allowed the students to grade themselves, and served as an effective resource person and facilitator. At the end of the term, he got a note from the dean of the college informing him that the academic policy committee had reviewed his performance and that he would be expected in the future to teach "in the traditional way, with normal required lectures and examinations." Renewal of his contract was made contingent upon his agreement to do so.

The young professor insisted on a student survey of all of the members of his own department, including his chairman who had initiated the policy committee action. In the survey, the young man came out with very high ratings from the students. His students considered him to be an effective and easily approachable facilitator. (The department chairman resigned his chairmanship after the survey—on which he got a relatively low rating.) The young professor is still trying to establish closer relationships with his students, but he has had to become much more cautious.

A mother recently phoned me and told about her ninth grade son. His IQ, she told me, was in the genius range, but the rigid curriculum he was in was causing severe emotional problems. He couldn't stick it out when his classes involved so much repetitive and boring work. Her son had missed more than fifty percent of the school days last year because of emotionally induced migraines, and yet he had still received a passing average. The school district administrator in charge of special education suggested that the boy be assigned to a vocational-technical center for three hours each day this year. The boy is especially excited by electronics. The principal of the boy's school, however, is trying to deny the boy permission to have this opportunity. "It will confuse his schedule" is the excuse. The principal will agree only if the boy has a medical certificate with a doctor's recommendation. The boy's application has already been accepted by the vocational-technical center in spite of the fact that students must normally be in the tenth grade to be admitted for work there. The mother is hesitating to send her boy, though, for fear that the principal of his regular school will make life unbearable for her son during the three hours each day when he would be in his regular school building.

At Colorado State University, a young history professor was recently fired because, according to newspaper accounts, his dean felt that among other things he allowed his students to evaluate their own work and he allowed too many As and gave too few Fs!

Panicky little men who live by the rule book will continue to plague those of us who want to facilitate. I will do all I can to expose and root out such little men. I will close my classroom door and do as my students and I please. I will enter the arena of political activity to facilitate learning for learners who choose to work with me. Young people are too important to me for me to bow to panicky little men who fear tomorrow.

"BUT YOU HAVE TO START THAT
IN GRADE SCHOOL"

When I propose freedom, democracy, and full rights for secondary school and college students, I receive from someone in virtually every group the response, "But you have to start that in grade school. By the time they're beyond elementary school it's too late."

I am unwilling to admit that everyone who is over twelve and who has never experienced a free learning environment can never learn to be free. I am struck time and again by how mature most young people are and how willing they are to learn to be free when they are recognized as human beings of great intrinsic value.

Age or position of people who come to learn in my company is not a factor I will take as an excuse for using power that the system may make available to me.

Some older students who have had bad experiences in learning or who have accepted the idea of being dependent may require longer than others to learn how to be free. I accept this as a human problem and will deal with our human relationship in helping each learner become more independent.

WHAT IF?

What if some students cheat when you let them grade themselves?

What if the students make noise and disturb the other classes?

What if parents don't like what you're doing?

What if the students don't do anything when you give them freedom?

What if someone gets hurt on the field trip?

What if people think I'm an idiot?

What if I fail?

What if the sky falls in?

One of the easiest ways for me to avoid trying new things is to play *What if?* I like to be ready for contingencies so that I will have confidence in my ability to cope with situations.

But the easiest way for me to change is to trust my intuition when I want to do something. I feel less and less need to ask permission. I want to *do.* Sometimes I *will* fail. But I'll probably learn from that failure, and, if I don't take myself too seriously, life will probably go on. I will respond to situations that arise as a consequence of the things I do. I take responsibility for my actions. But my life is too short to waste precious time and energy playing *WHAT IF?*

"THEY WON'T LET ME"

Lots of people I meet say they are dissatisfied with the way they are teaching and claim that they want to change. They profess a desire to give their students greater freedom in the classroom. But to each possibility for change suggested to them, their response is "I can't do that. *They* won't let me."

When I ask who "they" are, these teachers name their principal. Principals blame the superintendent for preventing them from doing what they say they would like to try. Superintendents blame their boards; college professors blame their department chairman; department chairmen blame their deans—none of them will take responsibility for their own decisions and actions.

If I mean it when I say that change is necessary, I accept responsibility to act. If I fail to act, then I do not really want to change. I take a risk when I act to change the way I do things. If I really want to change, I will. Most of the really important changes don't require permission. Often it is better not even to bother asking. I will not blame higher-ups for my own unwillingness to act. I accept responsibility for what I am and for what I choose to do or not to do.

PRISONER OF MYSELF

I can do what I want to do. I can be what I want to be. Any time I blame my problems on the outside world I had better look inside myself.

If I feel that I am a prisoner, I know I am not a prisoner of someone else. I am a prisoner of the constraints I build within myself.

AWARENESS

The more I get involved in problems of humanistic education, the more I find my awareness of my own hang-ups increasing. I am getting to be more aware of times when I am not listening to other people, of times when I am failing to communicate, of the sources of a whole host of both discomforts and joys. More and more, when I feel there is a problem, I am inclined to try looking inside myself. When I am uptight, I can more and more frequently find the source of the discomfort within myself. This makes it easier for me to deal with the outside world.

I want my awareness to keep increasing. For this I depend partially upon an open, facilitative relationship with people I come in contact with and partially upon introspection. Honesty on the part of other people helps increase my awareness and permits me to work on my own problems as a person and as a learner. Honesty on my part lets me help others in the same way. If there is trust between us, we know that we won't hurt each other too badly and that we will grow by helping each other to become more aware.

JOY

Two colleagues who have reservations about "open" class-rooms recently reported on an informal classroom in which they observed "dull, cheerless faces of students aimlessly, rather than purposefully," doing various activities.

Not long ago I visited a college in which a highly touted facilitative program has been introduced. I detected a slowness and lack of enthusiasm in some of the students and faculty there, too.

I have been in some encounter groups this year where things got "heavy" and where some people left with bad feelings and with a sense of lack of support.

Joy and enthusiasm are essential components of a facilitative environment for learning. Of course, when people experience real joy, they also become capable of experiencing real sadness and sorrow at other times. The least interesting existence from my point of view is to be a neutral person who can experience neither joy nor sadness fully.

Joy is possible for me when I do not take myself too seriously. I depend on the group I am in to get feedback on when I begin to take myself too seriously. Gradually I develop greater aware-ness of myself and my moods, and I can analyze my feelings and then do something to change them if I don't like them.

Enthusiasm comes to me when I get deeply involved in some-thing and enjoy doing it. If I am to be a good facilitator of learning, I want to pursue my own interests actively and openly as well as responding to the interests of students who are learning with me. If I have my own enthusiasms and if I share them regularly with those around me, I think I can help to generate a "WOW!" environment of electric enthusiasm within the whole group in which I am working. Joy comes to me through this kind of electrified atmosphere.

Several members of the geology department at Boston University recently formed a "Committee on Enthusiasm." I feel that clearer identification of the need for joy everywhere will facilitate learning and make learners feel and learn better.

OPTIMISM

A facilitator of learning is basically an optimist.

I have confidence in the innate ability of humans of all ages: in their ability to determine what is relevant, in their desire to learn things that are important to them when they have access to learning facilities they desire, and in their ability to make decisions about their own lives.

The degree to which adults and young people become involved in non-credit night school and extracurricular activities makes me confident that my optimism is justified. As I watch my own children, their friends, my friends' children, and college students play, I perceive that much of their play is learning. It has been pointed out by numerous educators that play is the work of the child. I know that people like to play. Play usually is a learning experience to a greater or lesser degree. Therefore, I am confident that they will learn on their own if I will keep out of their way when they do not want or need me.

I was recently discussing ideas on curriculum with a staff member of a national curriculum project who works in a slightly different area than the project I am associated with. He defended the need for requirements and his project's structure. I suddenly realized the difference between us. He is basically a pessimist and does not really trust young people to learn on their own. I am an inveterate optimist. I will trust the people who elect to come learn with me.

If you cannot share my optimism, then that is your problem. The quality of interaction with learners in the learning situation will differ greatly depending on whether you are an optimist or a pessimist. Pessimists may make fine managers or "teachers," but they will not be likely to operate efficiently as facilitators of learning.

4

Some Problems of Schools, Society, and Implementation of Change in Education

ALTERNATIVES

In the 1800's kids could learn more inside school than outside; in today's world, with all of the richness provided by technology and the media, they can learn more outside than in: school actually interrupts learning.

Paraphrase from Marshall McLuhan,
The Medium Is the Message

It's an odd thing that in as big a country as ours we limit ourselves to a single kind of school system. Because the schools are locally controlled, you might expect to find different kinds of schools in different kinds of communities. But that's not the way it works. You can go into a school in New York, Indiana, Pennsylvania, Colorado, California, North Dakota, or anywhere else, and it's the same school. Students sitting in rows in front of a teacher who spends most of his time talking. How we can generate such uniform mediocrity without having a fully centralized mediocrity control bureau is beyond me.

Ask a school administrator what kinds of alternatives his own system offers for students, and you will hear about college prep tracks, vocational tracks, business tracks, elective courses, and so forth. Some systems have been forced to adopt small alternative programs for highly alienated student dropouts and slow learners. But almost all students are expected to learn in the same *way*. Little effort is made to create alternative learning environments for young people with different learning styles.

Many private alternative schools have been founded recently, but the average life of these is on the order of eighteen months. A movement is in progress to create a voucher system in public education whereby parents could send their children to approved private schools and receive their own tax dollars back to help pay the tuition in these schools. The voucher system has many public school administrators worried.

In recent extended discussions with a group of school district officials, several colleagues and I have been trying to get a local school district to sponsor within the system an open-curriculum school of the type described in chapter two (The Wilson Campus School) and in chapter five (Fantasy). The officials admit that our ideas are good ones, and our volunteer student population of over 300 students indicates a need for an open-curriculum school. We hold to our premise that we want an alternative school, using the normal per-pupil expenditure for students in the district, and with a student body consisting entirely of students who have signed up specially for the open school program with full permission from their parents. The parents have even volunteered for extensive participation in school programs and a large university nearby has offered extensive volunteer support and assistance in instruction, curriculum development, and program evaluation.

Yet the school district administrators keep asking us to compromise. They want to "split the difference." Their goal is to make their schools slightly more student-centered and open and our proposed school much less so. They want to move the whole system and to keep a concept of The School. Equal opportunity, they sometimes call it. Equal deprivation, I call it. Young people learn differently, and schools should thus be widely different rather than striving to be all the same.

Dwight Allen,[1] dean of the University of Massachusetts School of Education, has recently suggested that every school district should allot ten to fifteen percent of its total budget for alternative schools which are freed from *all* of the conventional rules of the system. It is through examination and observation of real alternatives that the educational system as a whole advances.

A group of citizens in Jefferson County, Colorado, persuaded their school board and administration to create an open-curriculum, student-centered elementary school which opened in Fall, 1970. (See chapter two for a brief description of the school.) Some of the conservatives in the district have complained bitterly about the school district's allowing such freedom in a school, even though their own children are completely untouched by this

---

[1]Dwight Allen, "Seven Deadly Myths of Education and How they Mangle our Children," *Psychology Today* (March 1971):71-72, 106.

freedom and remain in conventional schools. In the spring of 1971 the same committee that managed to get the open-curriculum school into operation has requested that another alternative school be started: one for the conservatives who desire a highly regimented environment and a return to McGuffey's Reader. The open-school group believes that any alternative is acceptable in the system as long as a sufficient number of students and parents can be found to make it economically feasible to set up the alternative program.

A country like ours is rich enough and big enough to support alternatives. In alternatives lies the potential for growth and for evolution. Without alternatives within the system, the system is doomed to more disruption and ultimately perhaps to destruction.

THE UTILITY OF LEARNING IN GROUPS

The young have been trained and educated in groups for thousands of years. In primitive societies training was intended to develop courage and skills rather than knowledge and intellect. Vigorous group training for maturity and the tasks assigned to adults can still be observed in primitive and aboriginal societies that exist today. In some primitive societies candidates for admission to official adulthood were given arduous duties during the daytime and then prevented from sleeping at night. Whipping and torture of young people in some primitive societies are common during their training.[2]

In more complex societies, such as the one that existed in ancient Sumeria over 3000 years ago, schools existed in the temples. Ancient school tablets recovered from the temples indicate that groups of children studied writing, arithmetic, and something akin to social studies.[3] Thus, the grouping of young people for the purpose of transmitting to them the accumulated knowledge of a civilization is as old a procedure as civilization itself.

Some of the most fundamental skills needed for survival in many societies, however, have been transmitted in a very informal fashion. The curiosity of children and their desire and ability to imitate lead them to learn complicated tasks efficiently and quickly. One need not go back to ancient civilizations to see informal education occurring.

I observed some good examples of informal education occurring during two summers I spent doing geological field work on a small island called Flagstadöy in the Lofoten Islands of Arctic Norway. My family and I had settled into a small fisherman's cottage located in a small village enclave consisting of about six

---

[2]Will Durant, *The Story of Civilization Part 1, Our Oriental Heritage* (New York: Simon and Schuster, 1954), p. 75.

[3]*Ibid.,* p. 129.

houses plus numerous out-buildings. About two dozen Norwegian children ranging in age from two to twelve lived in the village of Nesland. We were struck by the way the children followed adults around and performed the same kinds of tasks they saw their elders performing. Children accompanied the adults out to set the salmon nets and to recover salmon that had been caught in the nets. When haying time came, the children imitated and helped the adults. Because of the damp conditions, it was necessary to erect hay fences upon which the new-mown hay could be dried. We noticed groups of children putting up their own hay fences and having considerable difficulty getting them braced so they could stand alone. Occasionally an adult passing by would help them with some aspect of the construction they were engaged in. Before long the children had learned, without any formal instruction, to erect a sturdy fence. Important concepts of practical geometry were learned in this way. The children had extensive knowledge of the habits of the salmon and the ways in which nets could be constructed to catch these fish. Their knowledge was acquired strictly by observing and playing the games that adults play.

My wife spent much of her free time sketching. Commonly she would go out onto the stone pier in front of our little house and spend hours sitting there drawing. Small groups of children would come out and watch her. One day she took with her extra pads of paper and extra crayons and pencils. So the children then asked if they might not sketch too. One evening when I came in from a field trip, I found her sitting on the end of the pier surrounded by a dozen small children, all of whom were sketching. The children and she got together and decided that they would set up an art exhibit showing their sketches to their parents and friends. In this situation, the experience the children were having with art was entirely an informal one with the children grouping themselves around an adult who was doing something they wished to imitate. The drawings done by the children demonstrated their intimate knowledge of construction of salmon nets, of the things their parents did for a living, of the mountains around them, and of the animals that lived there.

The natural tendency that people have to watch and observe can be seen at any construction site where people proverbially gather around the fence to watch the construction machinery in action. The way people watch railroad trains and the way they gather at airports are other examples of the watching tendencies we have. There is a natural tendency for people to gather and observe someone who is busily engaged in some task or other. This kind of observation leads to participatory involvement where the watchers begin to play with a kind of activity they have been observing. Those who find the play sufficiently interesting become involved in a more disciplined, yet still informal, effort to do the things they have observed being done. The craftsman, whatever crafts he is involved in, is often called upon to give advice and to evaluate. Natural groupings seem to form a fundamental part of the fabric of learning during human growth. Schools at all levels have, consciously or unconsciously, attempted to exploit this grouping phenomenon. But schools usually establish rigid, scheduled, mandatory groupings rather than allowing the growth of informal groups that are transitory in duration and membership.

Up until about one hundred years ago the young were expected to learn primarily through apprenticeships, grouping themselves with adults and observing and imitating. Of course, there were provisions for entry into scholarly life, and young people who followed this route were commonly involved in class-like groupings. With the Industrial Revolution, however, came exploitation of children. The old apprenticeships were replaced by having children work long hours in factories. Society finally reacted strenuously against this inhumane treatment of children by passing child labor laws. In addition, however, compulsory schooling laws were also passed. Children were, thus, excluded from the working force and were, instead, required to participate in enforced schooling groups. Basically, children were not trusted to attend to their own learning. Schools and teachers, perhaps interested as much in their own survival as in the education of children, caused children to be confined to rigid classroom schedules. Tacitly, teachers and schools were trying to build a case for their own indispensability.

In the early one-room schools that characterized many rural communities informal groupings continued to exist and, in some rural districts, still exist. Teachers, faced with the problem of helping educate children of a wide range of ages, simply could not enforce rigid adherence to schedules. Students cooperated with each other and much of what they learned was from their fellow students rather than from the person identified as "teacher." The informal groupings characteristic of one-room schoolhouses have nearly disappeared, however, with the prevalence, even in rural areas, of large consolidated schools replacing the smaller one-room schoolhouses.

In the cities and other populous areas, schools that differentiated students by age and, thus, placed them into patterns unlike those that exist in real life rapidly developed. The number of students per teacher grew larger and larger. There were two real alternatives available to teachers: One of these was to allow the students to group themselves informally and to allow them to pursue their education without a great deal of interference. The other alternative was to force a rigid grouping of the students and to require all students to proceed in their studies in more or less lock-step fashion. It is the latter course that was followed in most schools. This course of action, forcing students to march along through their education lock-step, testified to a great lack of trust on the part of the schools and teachers in their students. The patronizing attitude adopted in the school system was that students were not able to group themselves intelligently or to learn individually. Thus, in the view of the school system, learning became tied to the teaching acts performed by the teacher. It was assumed that students would learn what the teacher taught. The whole concept of school became centered around the idea of forced groupings of students performing tasks assigned to them by teachers.

The net result of this development was that the school took on a coercive character, not unlike the coercive character of the system under which children were forced to work in factories for many hours each day. When they were forced to work in factories, children lived in a physical environment that led to ill health and high mortality among the very young. In today's schools children are generally in reasonably good physical health. However, many are forced into situations that cause psychological strain. The coercive nature of today's schools may be causing psychological damage that is equally as bad for children as the physical damage they were subjected to during the early days of the Industrial Revolution. Children are regimented and forced into highly competitive situations rather than becoming independent, eager to learn, and willing to cooperate with their fellow men in an increasingly complex society that demands creative activity, independent thinking, and yet highly cooperative behavior.

Many educators have become increasingly concerned about the barrenness of the schools. One of the chief villains they have identified is the lock-step system of teaching that exists in most of the schools. One of the popular solutions that has been adopted by many educators is a movement toward the individualization of learning. Programmed instruction, computer assisted instruction, and other such techniques are being widely tested as ways of removing children from the rigid, forced groupings that exist in conventional classrooms. With the introduction of these kinds of individualized instruction many educators are beginning to speak of inhumaneness and depersonalization. The machine is identified as another possible villain. Of course, some of the people who cry the most loudly against the use of these techniques are the very teachers and systems who are most inhumane in their treatment of children in forced groupings.

Going to a scheme of individualized instruction is over-compensating for the evils of forced groupings. Forced individualization is merely the opposite extreme of a continuum ranging from individualized instruction to large group instruction.

A way out of this dilemma is to stop focusing on the act of instruction or the act of teaching and to re-orient our thinking toward the process of learning. A great many studies have been performed on how the learning process occurs. It is clear that people learn best when they work in an environment of great trust where they can build real self-esteem. One has only to look at how very small children learn to walk, talk, manipulate objects, and so forth, to observe situations in which children learn complex tasks economically and efficiently. One also observes that, when left to themselves, small children regularly form small informal groups. When children and young people are allowed to form their own groupings informally and are allowed to enter and to leave groups whenever they wish, the chances of having significant learning occur are probably greatest.

I have recently observed patterns of informal grouping in a number of places and am quite convinced that a focus on learning rather than on instruction is necessary. Permission should be granted for children to work individually, to form groups, and to change groups whenever they wish to do so. In the Wilson Campus School at Mankato, Minnesota, students ranging in age from three to nineteen are permitted to wander through the school, to work independently when they wish to do so. Some formal groupings are also scheduled, but no student is compelled to attend any such formal group. In the informal groupings, one finds six-year-olds grouping with twelve-year-olds for certain kinds of activities. In other activities groups of seventeen- and eighteen-year-olds may group together with faculty members for informal seminars on various topics. Those who participate in these seminars have frequently spent a great deal of time preparing in advance by mutual agreement to discuss a topic the informal group has chosen. The composition of such a group, however, may change from seminar period to seminar period.

A characteristic of informal groupings is a phenomenon I shall call *migrating leadership.*

I recently observed an informal group in which migrating leadership was occurring during a summer workshop for environmental studies teachers. Four of us were officially the staff of this teacher training institute in which there were about thirty participants. We had announced to the participants at the very beginning of the conference that we would not impose any groupings upon them and that each participant was free to pursue whatever interests he wished to in the area surrounding a Y.M.C.A. camp at Tabernash, Colorado, in the Rocky Mountains where the group was staying. We made it clear that there were to be no competitive pressures imposed by us as a staff by announcing that each participant would assign his own grade (for graduate credit) at the end of the session.

One day during the workshop, a number of participants decided to go to Toby Lake, a few miles from the main camp, to study the lake and the surrounding countryside. In searching for the lake we took a wrong road and came to an impasse where it was necessary for the several vehicles to turn around and seek another route. As we stood about deciding where we should go, I realized that we were quite high on a mountainside near some spectacular white cliffs I had hoped to visit at some time or the other. I, therefore, decided that I would like to walk over to the white cliffs and from there try to find my way down to Toby Lake. When I announced my plan, four others (Bill, Don, Jack, and Bob) announced that they would accompany me. Bill acquired a topographic map from one of the participants who decided to remain with the informal group that would seek to reach Toby Lake by another road.

The five of us began to walk along the ridge line. From time to time one or another of the members of the group would stop to look at some plants or to study a soil profile or examine the nature of a burned-over or logged area. Had I been alone, with my own geological proclivities, I would have passed these features by without a second glance. Bill picked up the leadership at these times. He, too, was one of the staff members of the workshop, and he quickly placed the rest of us in the position of students. He tried to use guided inquiry techniques of leading us to guess the answers to questions that he posed. The group seemed willing to play his game.

—Photo by Robert Samples. Courtesy of Environmental Studies project.

Several times, being unsure of our location, we had to look at the maps and discuss our location. None of us was certain exactly where he was, and no one in the group assumed a real position of leadership. Bob suggested routes back to Toby Lake several times, and we generally followed his lead.

At one point we were about to walk by several rock outcroppings. Bill picked up the leadership in a very directive way. When we arrived at the white cliffs, each individual found several things of special interest to him. Rather open, leaderless discussion ensued, although I was picked out as the prime resource person to come to for problems of rock identification. Bill, also a geologist, was used by the group in a similar manner. Bill continued to use guided inquiry techniques, whereas I generally discussed openly without asking the other members of the group to guess what was in my mind.

Once we reached the top of the white cliffs we were able to see Toby Lake. The group decided to go straight downhill, and since we had no compass, the idea arose that we might navigate in the heavy woods by observing the position of our shadows. Bill assumed the leadership role in the group, and we all arrived directly at the lake.

Once we arrived there Bill decided that we should go one direction around the lake. The other four of us decided to go the other way. When we reached the far side of the lake, it was clear that the other, larger group that had hoped to reach Toby Lake by road had not been there. It became apparent that we had a long way to walk back to our camp. A group decision was made that we would cut across country in order to find the shortest route back to camp. As we navigated across country, leadership switched back and forth many times. In one case, we came to a road not shown on the map, and I led three of the group along this road until we realized that it had circled back in the wrong direction. The three of us had to backtrack to find the other two. Later we came to another road, and I immediately started out again on this one as if it were the correct one. The rest of the group questioned whether or not to follow me since I had made a questionable navigational move on the road we had previously encountered. Nevertheless, all finally followed me, and we did come out in the right place.

The group operated primarily in a democratic fashion, and individuals within the group took over leadership roles whenever the rest of the group perceived that they would be led to interesting features or to the right road home.

On another day I went to the main meeting room of the group to see if anyone had posted a notice that he was going to do something interesting. None of the participants had volunteered to lead any groups. A few people were looking at films or books that were available. I walked back outside with no particular goal in mind. Upstairs I found Don. He had on field clothes, and I asked him where he was going. He said that he and several others were on their way to visit some geologic features about twenty miles from the main camp. I wondered aloud if I might not join their group and was invited to do so. Lloyd and Bob A., two participants who had not been along with us on the previous day's trip to Toby Lake, had already been to visit the Willow Creek dikes, the goal of our expedition, the day before. They had found these features so interesting that they wished to go back and take some other people. A total of eight of us gathered as an informal group with the Willow Creek dikes as our destination. Lloyd and Bob A. clearly took the initial leadership role, having identified the features and brought the group together.

As we drove to the Willow Creek area, Lloyd and Bob A. described the various things along the road as we traveled. Jeanne, Lloyd, and Fred called upon me as a resource person to answer questions about the nature of the topography. We discussed these questions at some length, but I made it clear that I could not really answer their questions in any authoritative way. As we approached our destination, a question arose as to whether or not we had already passed the dikes we had intended to visit. The leadership role was nearly relinquished by Lloyd and Bob A. as we were on the verge of taking over the trip until they convinced us that we were on the right track. When we finally arrived at the first of the Willow Creek dikes, Lloyd and Bob A. still held the primary leadership role. The group fanned out, and people started to look at things in a general sort of way. Lloyd then led me off on a small trail, telling me that he wanted to talk over some features that he had observed the day before. Three or four members of the group immediately teamed up with us in a small subgroup. Lloyd then showed me several volcanic features which I became very excited about. However, I was not able to provide any pat answers to Lloyd's questions because the configuration we were examining was a very complex one. We began a period of hypothesis making and started to throw ideas back and forth. The other members of the group, hearing our loud discussion, joined us. I walked away from the group shortly afterward and started to look at other things that attracted my attention. The group as a whole moved down to a small shack at the bottom of the hill where another subgroup was examining entirely different features. Leadership during the discussion passed back and forth among members of the group as they started showing things they had observed to the group as a whole. When I returned to the group my opinion was asked about several features. My role in the group was strictly that of a resource person rather than a leader, however.

Some of the members started back to the car. Meanwhile, I walked over to an outcrop that had attracted my attention and found a very interesting feature that led me to exclaim, "Wow!" in a very loud voice. Don came running over, and several other members of the group converged on us when they saw that we were having a very animated and excited discussion. As I proceeded to give my own ideas, some of the members agreed while others disagreed. A few of the members of the group proceeded to look for other evidence relating to the discussion we were having.

Fred later took the leadership role and started a discussion about crack patterns in some of the rocks. My first feeling was to move on and pay no attention to his discussion, but I was gradually drawn back into the discussion and a number of us became involved.

On another morning several members of the group decided to study a small pond near the camp. Upon reaching the pond many of the members stood around expecting one of the staff members to make suggestions and to pick up the leadership role. When the staff members did not pick up this role, several members of the group began pursuing various kinds of activities, and several small groups, each with a project of some kind going on, formed spontaneously. In each of these groups only one or two people were really doing much, and the others were mainly observing. One group went off to examine plants. In a second group attempts were made to core the bottom of the pond. Although one member of the group was the focal person, other members in the group were giving him instructions as to where to core and soon began to do a great deal of work in cutting cores in half and trying to interpret them. Another group became interested in the chemical qualities of the water.

A visitor who was present at our institute mentioned his distress at the seeming disorganization and migration of participants from group to group. He felt that the groups should have been called together regularly so that they could share their data and review their work for each other. I pointed out to him my feeling that the desire to share had to come from the group, rather than being imposed by the staff. Imposing a sharing from without would have led to the same kind of staff and teacher domination which ultimately leads to rigidity and lock-step activity. If we as staff members had issued extensive procedural instructions in the early stages of these investigations, we would have established a dependency of the group members on us. This would have set the pattern rather than letting patterns come from the group as the need for them arose. In our position as staff members who had decided to be facilitators of learning rather than "teachers," it was apparent that we had to learn to play a waiting game. As should be clear from the examples above, however, our own natural enthusiasm for certain features we observed and our acceptance and valuing of the enthusiasm shown by the participants for other things that they had found frequently thrust us into an informal leadership role. We considered it extremely important, however, to allow the leadership to migrate away from us in such a fashion that the independent creative activity of the participants was not inhibited. By not imposing leadership from the outside we hoped that the learning situation would be more like real life. In practice, as the institute continued, it was our opinion that the participants did begin to function more independently and more creatively. Furthermore, a number of the participants began to operate in a more facilitator-like role in their own classrooms.

—*Photo by Robert Samples. Courtesy of Environmental Studies Project.*

I feel strongly that the concept of instructional groups, in which the teacher is identified as a strong leader who imposes activities upon his students, must be replaced by informal learning groups characterized by democratic procedures and migrating leadership. Students must feel free within the group and must feel free to enter or leave the group when they wish to do so. Many such informal groups are highly transitory and may last for only a few minutes, as when a shout of excitement from one student causes others to gather around him and find out the reasons for this display of enthusiasm. Other informal groups may become highly task-oriented and may persist for long periods of time. As a case in point, small research teams of scientists or humanists who decide to collaborate on a study would be an extreme example of a persistent learning group. In learning situations in the schools, however, it should be noted that the more persistent the group is, perhaps the more likely a definite leadership pattern is to emerge and the more likely the group is to become formalized.

Learning is primarily an individual enterprise, but the formation of informal groups can facilitate learning in each of the individuals who join them.

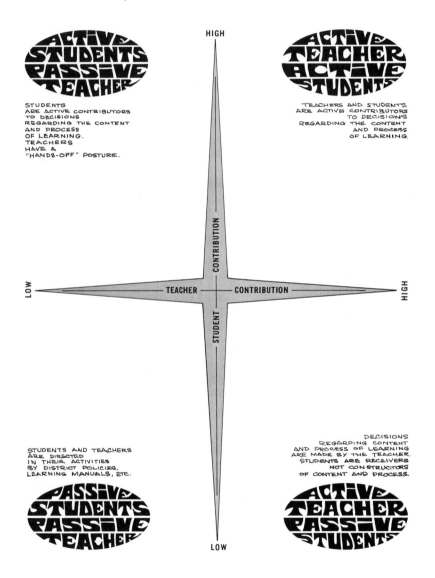

HIGH

ACTIVE STUDENTS PASSIVE TEACHER

STUDENTS
ARE ACTIVE CONTRIBUTORS
TO DECISIONS
REGARDING THE CONTENT
AND PROCESS
OF LEARNING.
TEACHERS
HAVE A
"HANDS-OFF" POSTURE.

ACTIVE TEACHER ACTIVE STUDENTS

TEACHERS AND STUDENTS
ARE ACTIVE CONTRIBUTORS
TO DECISIONS
REGARDING THE CONTENT
AND PROCESS
OF LEARNING.

CONTRIBUTION

LOW — TEACHER —|— CONTRIBUTION — HIGH

STUDENT

STUDENTS AND TEACHERS
ARE DIRECTED
IN THEIR ACTIVITIES
BY DISTRICT POLICIES,
LEARNING MANUALS, ETC.

PASSIVE STUDENTS PASSIVE TEACHER

DECISIONS
REGARDING CONTENT
AND PROCESS OF LEARNING
ARE MADE BY THE TEACHER.
STUDENTS ARE RECEIVERS
NOT CONSTRUCTORS
OF CONTENT AND PROCESS.

ACTIVE TEACHER PASSIVE STUDENTS

LOW

—*Modified from "Analysis of an Approach to Open Education," an interim report by Anne M. Bussis and Edward A. Chittenden, published under a USOE grant to the Educational Testing Service, Princeton, N. J., August, 1970.*

COMMITMENT

Over the past several weeks I have been involved with a seminar composed primarily of graduate teaching fellows and faculty members. The seminar is a required part of a program in which all of us are working. We have been assigned to subgroups based primarily on our disciplines. Most of the people in my subgroup are science-oriented, even though the announced purpose of the overall seminar was to work toward interdisciplinarity.

At our first planning meetings the question arose as to what we should do in this required seminar. When many different ideas were proposed, one of the faculty members forcefully suggested that we all read a classical paper on physics (vintage 1850) and spend the next seminar period discussing it. The group accepted the suggestion because they were unwilling to endure the uncertainty of no agenda for the following week.

At the discussion section one of the faculty members took over the seminar and began quizzing people about the paper we had been asked to read. There was very little reaction from a large number of participants. Few members of the group had committed themselves in any real way to the assignment.

For several weeks now the group has floundered. One group wants to read papers and discuss them, but there is little agreement on what papers to read. A second group wants to meet without agenda and work with whatever ideas are generated at the meeting. Other groups have other wishes, and one person has dropped out completely to work on a special problem in lieu of attending the seminar. The group is actively questioning why it is required to exist, what its goals should be, and whether or not the members really want to commit themselves to preparation leading to any more meaningful sharing of ideas.

Some of the faculty participants want to impose rules and requirements that will force involvement. Such forced involvement would be superficial at best.

I am willing to commit myself to the activities of a group only under certain circumstances. One reason for committing myself is that I find a topic intellectually or emotionally stimulating enough to me personally that I am willing to set aside time to prepare myself either through reading, thought, or discussion with others for an intense group interaction session. A second reason is that I may value the people in the group enough to agree to devote some of my time to a favorite topic of theirs in order to help them explore in the same way they have helped me explore areas that have special relevance to me. I never derive my commitment from another person's feeling that I ought to commit myself to his topic because it will, in his opinion, be good for me. Commitment is intrinsic, and I am the only one who can commit myself. For a commitment to be meaningful, I must make it willingly and without outside coercion.

Thus, I refuse to commit myself to a group until I have a positive feeling about that group of people. For me, the way to begin a seminar experience is not to be assigned to a group. First I need to explore with a group of people, in an open way, what our individual feelings and perceptions are like. This may be done in an encounter-group setting or in some other way. From my point of view, the group needs to generate many alternative topics, directions, and means of interacting. I like to work with groups that are generating alternatives because I always learn a lot about the ideas and feelings of people in the group. Just as important, a large group generates many more alternatives than I could ever generate by myself. The more different kinds of people present in the group, the greater the number of alternatives possible.

What I have suggested implies that the members of a group, coming together for the first time, are willing at least to commit themselves to the process of generating and exploring alternatives. This commitment requires no special advance preparation. Advance preparation for the generation of alternatives consists of each group member's total previous experience.

Once alternatives are generated, several things may happen. First, the group may be composed of people like-minded enough that they decide to continue meeting as a group of the whole, and each member may agree to commit himself to pursuing a given topic or schedule of topics. Second, and more likely, several smaller, like-minded groups may assemble. These smaller groups may then meet separately, with each member of each group voluntarily committing himself for any particular advance preparation. Third, there may be so many alternatives that few or none of the members are willing to make any commitments to each other. In this instance, the group has no basis for further existence.

I am most comfortable in a situation in which alternatives are regularly generated by groups and subgroups and in which channels of communication are established that allow me and others to know of alternatives generated by other people to whom I have not yet been willing to commit myself. I also want them to know about alternatives I have generated. If we agree to make this commitment to communication of alternatives, there is a possibility of my finding ever greater numbers of people to whom I want to commit myself. And more people may be willing to try a session with me.

I do not like groups with rigid, closed membership. I want to seek out new people who can help me grow both intellectually and emotionally. I want to join any group on a voluntary basis, and I want others to join me only because they choose freely to do so.

There will be many different kinds of subgroupings of people in groups I will choose to enter. Some will be narrowly based groups comprising mainly specialists in my own special areas of interest. Others will include specialists from many different areas of interest. Yet others will have specialists and non-specialists sharing what they have in common. And in others, all of us may be non-specialists sharing our feelings.

Commitment cannot be imposed. I want to help provide learning environments in which enough alternatives are generated so that members of the learning community can find other people with whom they want to share and to whom they are willing to commit themselves for longer or shorter encounters related to all varieties of intellectual, aesthetic, and emotional happenings.

TERRITORY

I have heard many teachers invite students to come to them with problems. Using the phrase "My door is always open" gives many people a feeling of having done their duty.

It is very easy for me to receive someone else on my own territory, be it physical, intellectual, or emotional territory. When someone visits me in my office, lab, camp, or home, I am the master. My visitor watches me to see what is the proper way to behave—especially if I am a teacher and he is a student or if he perceives that in some other way I could have power over him.

I feel discomfort myself when I go onto foreign territory until someone goes out of his way to help me feel comfortable. The only way I can be aware of how someone else might feel on my territory is to risk going onto his. If I am a facilitator, I want to risk seeking out people who are working with me as learners in just the same way that they are asked to seek out teachers who say, "My door is always open."

Being aware of territorial risks helps me deal with other people as I try to help them feel comfortable in learning with me.

At a recent workshop in which the participants were considering ways of implementing humane learning environments, we became aware that everyone was locking his door, guarding his territory. After we all became aware of what we were doing—not trusting each other—a few people took the risk of leaving their doors unlocked, then just ajar. Before long, all of the doors ranged from unlocked to wide open. Nothing disappeared.

In a college department where students were invited to move into the department physically and to set up and maintain their own working spaces, the first thing that happened was that all of the students wanted keys to lock up their territories. Gradually locks became less important as people came to trust each other.

A young man from the University of Texas recently sent me a hastily scrawled note. He had found himself about to write his name—his territorial mark—on a set of materials our project had produced urging students and teachers to trust each other. His note said, "Suddenly, I realized how ludicrous it seemed to write my name on the packet."

Intellectual territorialism is one of the real problems of research and teaching institutions. The teacher who says, "You can't possibly do that until you've had my course," is guilty of intellectual territorialism. A geologist friend of mine once wrote to a well-known volcanologist and expressed his interest in working on volcanic rocks in Oregon. He received a reply that said, "Go right ahead, as long as you keep east of the 120th meridian."

Desire to have my ideas recognized is a very human characteristic. My product is part of the portrait of myself that I build up and that each person builds of himself. Being aware of my own intellectual, emotional, and physical territorialism helps me to work better with others.

Territorialism is part of our basic biological heritage, if we are to believe Robert Ardrey,[4] Desmond Morris,[5] and others. Yet awareness of the problem can lead to cultural evolution in a direction of greater cooperativeness and trust and can diminish the animal territorialism practiced by man. Our territorial instincts must evolve if problems of nationalism, overpopulation, private property, and war are ever to be reduced. Marx felt that the only solution was violent revolution. I prefer to adopt the optimistic outlook of Charles Reich.[6]

---

[4]Robert Ardrey, *The Territorial Imperative* (New York: Dell Publishing Co., 1966).
[5]Desmond Morris, *The Naked Ape* (New York: Dell Publishing Co., 1967).
[6]Charles A. Reich, *The Greening of America* (New York: Random House, 1970).

HOW WOULD YOU LIKE TO BE OPERATED ON BY A SURGEON EDUCATED IN ONE OF THOSE "PERMISSIVE" SCHOOLS?

I think that in almost every discussion I can recall on freedom in education, strong decision-making powers in the hands of students, and a facilitator role for educators, someone has brought up the hackneyed question, "How would you like to have one of those free students operate on you?" In the first place, when I examine my own basis for choosing a physician, dentist, plumber, auto mechanic, or any other professional, the last thing I would ever think of looking at is his academic credentials. Where he was trained is of little importance to me. His reputation in the community and especially with my friends is what leads me to him.

As a matter of fact, however, if I were to look at credentials, I would be highly impressed to find out that a surgeon had gone through an "open" educational system. The reason for this is that I have a deep trust in how responsibly people behave when given real freedom and when allowed to study independently in the company of effective facilitators. If a surgeon had developed the sense of responsibility that is one of the foremost goals of open systems, he wouldn't even consider trying to remove an appendix until he knew he could do a competent job.

In a free environment learners have a chance to identify their own personal goals early, without all of the trivial and generally useless "distribution" and "general education" requirements. This is not to say that I disapprove of "liberal education." On the contrary, I merely feel that forcing "liberal education" on anyone is more likely to make him hostile to any intellectual activity than it is to "give him a liberal education." A true liberal education is more likely to result when a student is allowed to pursue his own interests without being confined to artificial subdivisions and courses that have little to do with real knowledge and real cultural value systems. Once personal goals are set, learners generally are the first to recognize what things are important to learn. For our prospective young surgeon, he would be likely to search out facilitators who could help him learn about appendixes, lungs, hearts, or bones. He would be likely to become an apprentice to a competent surgeon, and the competent surgeon would very likely insist that the young man learn appropriate amounts of anatomy and other things that are important in performing operations.

For one thing, the young prospective surgeon in a free learning environment would probably jump directly into a *clinical* apprenticeship rather than into a series of pre-sequenced "courses" in elementary biology, invertebrate zoology, vertebrate zoology, general chemistry, embryology, and all of the conventional (and commonly useless) premedical courses. In the process of working as a clinical apprentice he would soon find the need for learning various *useful* aspects of biology, chemistry, mathematics, anatomy, histology, and other important subjects *in the context of his goal for the future: to be a surgeon.* Learning in his own sequence and in the context of the needs he perceives from the very important viewpoint of a clinical apprentice allows the young man to learn more efficiently, to make mistakes that harm no one, to relearn what is really appropriate to remember, and, most of all, to prepare effectively for the day when he becomes a full-fledged surgeon. All of this means that "open" medical schools would have to reorganize drastically the learning environments they provide and to humanize the relationships between faculty and the "clinical apprentices" (formerly called medical students).

People who express fears that a poorly prepared, dangerous surgeon would result from an open learning situation have little understanding of what an open learning situation involves and implies. One of the key things they refuse to hear us say is that the learner is working with a group of skilled facilitators of learning whose function it is to help the learner or trainee (a word that I dislike) find the resources he needs to meet his personally set goals. Facilitation is not equivalent to "permissiveness." Permissiveness would imply lack of human concern for both the prospective surgeon and his prospective patients. Facilitation involves the deepest possible personal and human concern for our young prospective surgeon both as a person and as a surgeon. If a learner tells me he wants to be a surgeon I will go out with him to find what a surgeon *really* needs to know. I will not, however, prescribe for him a set of course titles which generally have little to do with a surgeon's needs. Ask any surgeon how much of his premedical or even first- or second-year medical-school training was of use to him in learning the art of the surgeon.

You may now fault me for presuming to say, as a geologist and science educator, how I would help a learner work toward becoming a competent surgeon. One of the most important things I would personally have to do if a learner asked me to help him work toward this goal would be to scurry around and help him find other facilitators more qualified than I to help him use his freedom to learn effectively and efficiently. I would owe it to a learner working with me to disqualify myself as a person competent to offer any real technical assistance in the process of his becoming a surgeon. Encouragement I could continue to offer.

A special brand of honesty can be developed between a real facilitator and a learner working with him. In the case of the prospective surgeon, a facilitator who feels that the candidate does not have the psychological characteristics and physical skills necessary to become a competent surgeon would make this clear as early as possible and would then help the learner identify other goals. He would also let the learner know his reasons for feeling as he does. If an honest personal relationship between the facilitator and the learner has been established at the outset, and if the learner is involved very early in experiences based on a clinical apprenticeship, most young people genuinely not suited to become surgeons will be honest enough and will have an opportunity to *select themselves out.* If their relationships with their facilitators are those of whole people working together in clinical situations, there will be an opportunity for early and continuing re-evaluation of goals. A learner can thus change his goals and emphasis early, when many options remain open and when relatively little time has been invested.

For the fearful who still want to ask the question, "But what about the ones who might slip through?" I must add that schools are not the ones who finally "certify" surgeons anyway. Furthermore, there are plenty of very poor surgeons who have gotten through the existing system anyway. No system will guarantee that all of its products are equally competent. Given the watchfulness of medical societies and the rigor attached to surgical internships and residencies, the notion is absurd that medical school or premedical course work has very much to do with who is allowed finally to operate on people!

What I suspect is that if more surgeons had their premedical and medical education available to them in free learning environments (involving a clinical element that starts as soon as the goal of being a surgeon is identified by a young person), we would find qualified surgeons being certified in many fewer than the total of over ten years presently required. One need only think of how competent some surgical and maternity nurses come to be without much of the technical training a surgeon has. An even more dramatic testimony to the effectiveness of the apprenticeship route is found in the competence of many medical corpsmen in the military services. Many of these corpsmen have been forced to perform complicated emergency battlefield surgery and have, with virtually no "formal" education or training, shown a high degree of competence. What is sad is that, in order to become "real" surgeons, such highly motivated and competent medical aides would usually be required to go back through a sterile and dull premedical and medical school training "course" rather than being allowed to proceed directly into a full-fleged internship or residency. The waste, redundancy, and dullness of present professional requirements in most areas—law, medicine, science, mathematics, humanities, business, etc.—causes minds and faculties to become dulled rather than sharpened as they should be. When I go to a surgeon, I want him to be quick of mind and reflex in a way that only a creative, inventive free learner can be. I want to feel that he will be able to cope with the unforeseen and not just be able to duplicate a "standard" procedure that someone showed him how to do.

A typical example of the kind of irrelevant argument used by people who ask the, "How would you like to be operated on . . ." question is found in the statement printed below:

Anti-Intellectual Nonsense

In these days of substituting "pass-fail" for grading, "open enroll-ment" for admissions standards, and "relevant activism" for scholar-ship, it should be no surprise that anti-intellectualism would hit Phi Beta Kappa.

At a recent New York meeting of the society founded on scholastic excellence, some members supported the notion that the organization should be open to every one who possesses "a love of learning."

It is doubtful that the proposal will get far, but it is significant that even in that elite group some who have qualified for membership by their scholastic achievement have somehow managed to become "edu-cated" without a sense of values and scholastic standards.

Carried further, their attitude would condone the conferring of an engi-neering degree on any youngster who possesses "a love of Erector sets," a scientific degree on any one who has "a love of science-fiction movies," an architectural degree on the "lover of building blocks," and so on ad infinitum. [Italics mine.]

Fundamental in the structure of civilized life is measurement. Without standards there is chaos. One of the proper jobs of education is to teach students what the standards are or ought to be. Unfortu-nately some educators are leading the anti-intellectual about-face to-ward mediocrity.[7]

I must reject totally the implication that certification stan-dards, "intellectualism," and real scholarship for engineers, scien-tists, and architects are incompatible with free learning models, pass-fail grading systems, and "relevant activism." One need only sit down with some of the finest engineers, scientists, and architects and analyze with them the relevance of the lock-step systems they came through and the system of extrinsic rewards to get a sense of how these factors actually impede creative ac-tivity and the acquisition of skills in a *personally* relevant order. More and more "teachers" are coming to realize that lock-step systems of "preparing" professionals are wasteful of time, en-ergy, and emotion for the simple reason that no one has yet been able to write a single formula for producing a competent, *creative* professional surgeon, engineer, scientist, or architect. It is through practice and intense, personally directed involvement in profes-sional work that real competence and creative abilities are fos-tered. Education of professionals needs to be done in a real-life

[7]James D. Corriell, "Anti-Intellectual Nonsense," *Boulder Daily Camera* (Colo.), 27 December 1970. Reprinted with permission.

setting rather than in the sterile environment of lock-step, largely irrelevant "schools." Open environments for self-directed learning can certainly do no worse or less economical job than present professional training schemes. Indications from many competent educators indicate confidence that openness in the system will improve competence and creative ability.

RESEARCH VERSUS TEACHING — A PHONY ISSUE

For years students have argued that professors should do more teaching. For years professors have tried to organize their schedules so they can teach less and do more research. People get promoted on the basis of scholarly productivity. Many say that only a special person can be good at both research and teaching.

The dichotomy between research and teaching depends on what you mean by teaching. If teaching is laying on last year's lecture notes, or making up a new lecture on an obscure issue (or even on an important one!), or making up, giving, and grading another exam, or tearing a bunch of student term papers to shreds, then I agree that teaching hinders research. But that kind of teaching hinders learning, too, and that kind of teaching needs to become extinct.

What happens when good research is done? In this day of complicated problems, team approaches to problems are producing some of the most promising results. Research is being done more and more by "learning teams." Research at its best *is learning*.

If in the educational system we all stopped worrying about teaching people things and concentrated more on having everyone work together to learn things, education would consist of having both the beginner and the experienced person totally involved in learning things.

The trouble with most teachers is that they have really stopped learning. If they concerned themselves more with learning—and learning in the company of their students at that—they would be doing *research*. With lots of research associates. The people they used to call "students."

If I have fifty to seventy-five students ranging from beginners through graduate students working with me during a given period of time, I have fifty to seventy-five research associates. If each of us is searching (rather than re-searching) and if each of us perceives himself as a learner, the dichotomy between teaching and learning disappears. All of us are involved in the vital kind of learning that counts. And we can treat each other as human beings of equal value while we learn.

TWO CULTURES?

C. P. Snow has discussed the fragmentation of western society and has deplored the way that men educated for different disciplines fail to communicate. In *The Two Cultures*[8] he points up the increasing separation between scientific and literary people. Most of what is happening in our schools is designed to maintain and accentuate the idea that there is a science way of life as opposed to other ways of life. Writers such as Theodore Roszak now say that many young people belong to a "counterculture." As long as teachers impose knowledge that they and the textbook writers have fragmented artificially, the maintenance of separate cultures and the lack of communication will continue. And young people will resist and turn to countercultures.

On the other hand, when young people are allowed to integrate knowledge in their own ways in free, humanistic social and learning environments, the two cultures and the counterculture may merge so that intellectual activity can involve the whole person with all of his feelings, interests, and joys. When people use labels such as "scientist," "literary man," or "hippie," they tend to become what their labels say they are. I have difficulty in attaching a label to myself even when I fill out my income tax return these days. If I say I am a teacher, I imply that I am different from students. If I say I am a scientist, I imply that I am that more than I am a musician, athlete, actor, outdoorsman, linguist, or PERSON. I am I, and I contain many interests, skills, talents, faults, and pleasures. I do not fit into anyone else's system of fragmented cultures or countercultures.

---

[8]C. P. Snow, *The Two Cultures: And a Second Look* (New York: Mentor Books, 1963).

THE SCHOOL AS A SCREEN

Headline in a newspaper advertisement for a college of business in a large eastern city:

YOU'RE NOBODY TILL SOMEBODY HIRES YOU!

Schools in the United States have begun to perceive their role as that of a screen. From grade school on, parents bug their children about making grades to get into college. Once in college, students are bugged about getting properly "certified" for jobs with industry or business or for getting into graduate school. The student leaving graduate school has to be "certified" for his job a little later.

The worst part is that the schools have mainly accepted this role of screening students for schools higher up the chain and for jobs. One of the first cop-outs I always hear from educators—from first grade teachers all the way through graduate school professors—when we talk together about the need for dramatic change and humanization in the educational system is "But how will my students get jobs or into Harvard [Yale, Berkeley, or you name it]?"

If we accept the idea that the function of the schools is to separate sheep from goats, officers from enlisted men, and Yalees from students at West Overshoe Junior College, our system is really sick. Schools should be there to educate people rather than to certify them. John Leonard[9] defines education as change. If a person has not in some way been changed by a learning experience, he has not been educated. "Certification" for the next level invites people to devise strategies for beating the game, while education involves deeper change in personality, ideas, and behavior.

---

[9] J. Leonard, *Education and Ecstasy* (New York: Dell Publishing Co., 1968).

There is an easy way out of the role of screening people: Individual teachers need only refuse to evaluate their students comparatively. To protest that "we have to give grades because the school requires it" is another cop-out. If the system requires grades, we need only give all students As or let them grade themselves in order to subvert the system effectively. If groups of teachers—even small groups—band together in this effort, the system can be destroyed.

"Irresponsible!" shout the screeners and, unfortunately, some of the parents and students who have been so brainwashed that they fail to see what the system has done to them. Does subverting the system in this way give us a license to spoil the chances of our own students? It certainly does not if we accept the responsibility of helping our students in other, more humane ways than giving them transcripts and secret letters of reference.

Take letters of reference as an example. Writing them has always made me dreadfully uncomfortable. And I know that many of my colleagues share my hatred of this secret evaluation system. Then Jack Carter of Colorado College suggested to me one day that I ought always to show each letter of reference to the person who requested it and to allow *him* to decide whether or not he wants me to send it in. I feel much better about letters of recommendation now that I, too, have put this scheme into operation.

The lack of standard kinds of grades and comparative evaluation need not hurt a student either. As I have stated elsewhere in this book, I strongly favor having each student, from kindergarten through graduate school, keep a personal portfolio of what he considers to be his own best *product.* No one knows better than a student himself what he is truly capable of doing. It is my job to provide him with access to external standards, but he is the one to decide what work best represents his capabilities and interests. I refuse to take responsibility for rating his capabilities. He must take responsibility himself both for his own learning and for choosing the product he wants to stand as evidence of his capabilities.

I accept another responsibility, too, if I give up the role of screen-holder. I will help to educate graduate school admission committees and outside employers about how they can have a basis for comparing my students with students from the screeners. I will help my students make personal contacts with people who hire and with people who admit to higher school levels. Someone has to persuade the employers and graduate school people to take an honest look at my students' portfolios and to conduct in-depth interviews with them.

I also must let my students know in advance that my refusal to act as a screen may deny them entrance to certain companies and to certain graduate schools that are too rigid to humanize their own admission procedures enough to look at special credentials in a special way. If one of my students *really* wants to work for Company X, which does not accept my refusal to act as a screen for them, I will have to suggest that he seek another teacher or school in which to get himself "screened."

Fortunately, most of the first-rate companies and schools that have real confidence in their own product are not threatened by the kind of scheme I favor. Only the second- and third-rate outfits exhibit such rigidity that they refuse to consider different kinds of performance records. Enough colleges and high schools have now begun experimenting with mildly to radically different reporting and recording schemes that I have no fear about the potential my own students will have for being admitted to the schools and jobs they wish.

As more of us reject the role of screener and encourage our students to take more personal responsibility for developing a product they can demonstrate, the "consumers" of our students will themselves humanize their own staff and student selection procedures.

COMPETITION

I'll bet that using non-coercive, open learning schemes I can turn out better prepared, more creative, more productive, happier graduates than you can in your conventional classrooms!

That statement shows how hard it is for me to throw off the competitive spirit that has been educated into me. A couple of my colleagues who are interested in free learning environments for students and in greater internal freedom for all human beings participated in a meeting we conducted recently. They spent several weeks competing to see who was freer!

I was taking my daily swim last week when I sensed that the man in the next lane was pulling ahead of me. I poured on the steam to get back ahead of him.

On a recent ship voyage I watched a group of fifty- and sixty-year-olds participating in a shuffleboard tournament. The non-players were betting on the outcome of the games. Soon they were arguing over rules for the bets and who was ahead of whom.

It seems sordid. But that's the way we are brought up through the schools. Fred Hechinger[10] points out that most parents do not believe that their children can be educated for life in a competitive world without going through a competitive school. If that's what they believe—and I accept that they probably do believe it —I don't agree with them.

The great American competition is one of the things that pleases me least in our society. It exists in just as vicious form in the Soviet Union and in Western Europe too. Changing our attitudes in the schools is one of the only ways I know of to combat the sordid side of our competitiveness. Will children educated in a non-competitive society survive in a competitive society? I have faith not only that will they survive, but that they will begin to

---

[10]Fred M. Hechinger, untitled essay in *Summerhill: For and Against,* ed. Harold Hart (New York: Hart Publishing Co., 1970), pp. 35-46.

cause society itself to change. If it doesn't change, we'll soon blow ourselves clear off this planet.

Maybe we in the schools had better begin listening to what many young people in the counterculture are saying about the ills and waste of human and natural resources caused largely by our madness to get ahead of the next fellow.

Animals are fiercely competitive. Man is an animal. Therefore man must compete, according to some people. But there is a difference. Man got where he is through a complex evolution that gave him capabilities possessed by no other animal. Man's evolution from lower life forms was through biological evolution. But man's development as a species is now controlled more by cultural factors. Man is the first animal with the capability of shaping the environment to fit him rather than adapting or dying. There is no reason to assume that just because man is highly competitive today he needs to remain that way in order to survive. A highly cooperative environment for learning may just have within it the seeds of the highly cooperative society I think we must develop if we want to survive. Out of the diversity that naturally arises in people who learn in free learning environments may come the creative talents to allow our cultural evolution to overcome the environmental, political, and social problems that threaten us.

Don't get me wrong, by the way. I like games and I think most people do. But do games need to have stakes? Being in them for the sake of playing is where I want to be. I like the kind of competition where I *choose* to compete according to standards I think are important. I reject the kind of competition in which someone tries to force me to compete according to an external set of standards about which I have nothing to say. This latter type is the kind that prevails in most educational institutions today.

COURSISM — ONE OF THE GREATEST ILLS OF AMERICAN EDUCATION

Most of the things I have been reading about deal with changes in courses. A recent study of elementary and secondary schools by the National Education Association indicates that most of the major curriculum changes reported in kindergarten through twelfth grade involved changes in courses.[11] In this book I have referred in some places to things I have done, do, and will do in courses. But in the long run the whole idea of courses is abhorrent to me. Most people come out of an educational system with the incredible notion that you have to have a group of people sit down in front of a person called a teacher for some fixed period of time—six, ten, fifteen, thirty weeks—with a fixed, externally imposed schedule, in order to learn anything.[12]

I remember a doctoral student who came up to me in a super-market parking lot several years ago while he was in the throes of his dissertation work. We talked about his progress. He said to me, "You know, what I need right now is a really good course in stratigraphy." His comment fell on me like a lead weight. Unfortunately, I have discovered since that encounter that a large percentage of students—and, worse, an even larger number of faculty members—share the view that studies must largely be directed from outside *even for themselves.* Anyone who has fre-quented college or high school faculty meetings or who has sat on a curriculum committee knows how tied we are to the ideas of courses, courses per semester, students per course, course grades, and all the rest. College teachers receive "credit" not for the number of human beings they help in the learning process but rather for the number of courses they teach.

---

[11]"Curriculum Change Is Taking Place," *N.E.A. Research Bulletin* 48 (1970), pp. 103-105.

[12]See, for example, the essay by Max Rafferty in *Summerhill: For and Against,* ed. Harold Hart (New York: Hart Publishing Co., 1970), pp. 11-25.

Courses mean people laying their knowledge on other people and holding these people accountable for what was laid on. Courses mean fragmenting knowledge and skills into packages that generally come to be used over and over again regardless of how irrelevant they may be to the learner. Courses lead to rigidity of mind and spirit.

Any innovation in education that does not directly challenge the assumption that learning occurs in courses is unlikely to bring much improvement. I can personally and unaided by others subvert the system by teaching "non-courses." Regardless of titles in the course catalog I can have each of my students determine the course of his own learning and evaluate his progress toward his own goals. I shall create an informal, self-directed learning environment regardless of course titles, credits, and other such trivia.

Because I disagree with the system, I also accept responsibility for trying to change it in a direction away from a highly specified course orientation. I shall take aim first at my immediate colleagues, then at my department, then at my college, then at my university as a whole, at other universities, at the public school system, and at the whole educational establishment.

IN A TIME OF DISSATISFACTION

An essay I wrote for the professional journal *Geotimes* in March, 1971, led to the exchange reproduced here.

THE ESSAY:

During the last twenty years there has been a remarkable growth of Earth science in the secondary schools. The 1970 U.S. Registry of Junior & Senior High School Science & Mathematics Teaching Personnel lists 15,524 Earth-science teachers. A recent survey of enrollments in Earth-science classes, made by the Earth Science Curriculum Project, indicates that more than 1,300,000 students were enrolled in Earth science this year.

This is a time of disruption in schools at all levels and of widespread dissatisfaction in the educational system. Charles Silberman (in *Crisis in the Classroom*) and others have painted a bleak picture of education in 1970. What is the position of Earth science at a time like this? Having just emerged from a period of several years of curriculum reform that led up to the ESCP program, can we be satisfied with Earth-science education?

Some Earth scientists are asking, "What's wrong with the old ways? Why change them? We succeeded under them." One of the things wrong with the old ways is that they are alienating our youth from science. Teaching more Earth science or more physics, biology, or chemistry in the secondary schools will be of little use if it continues to make people afraid of science rather than making them comfortable with it.

Why does Earth science seem so dull and humdrum to many students although it seems so vital and exciting to us? Could it be because we are involved with Earth science on a creative level while we regiment our students and deny them the very creative involvement we find exciting?

Perhaps it would be better if we did away altogether with "courses" called Earth science, biology, physics, and chemistry. Why, in 1970, should any student at any level be forced to study something called 'Earth science' every day of the week at some set time? Perhaps he doesn't want to study about it at all for several weeks and then might like to study nothing but Earth science for several days.

The trouble with the old ways is that they treat all students as if they were alike. If we care about learners, and if we care about education in the Earth sciences, it behooves us to seek ways of providing students with large numbers of alternatives, including alternatives the students themselves have chosen. It behooves us to release students from our power—the power of the grade, the threat of physical punishment, the threat of being humiliated in front of other people. It behooves us to demonstrate to students by our actions that we trust them and that they can trust us.

This is a time when we need creative people who can deal with new problems. If we are content to teach students how to solve yesterday's problems, where does that leave us?

I recently received a letter from an acquaintance who expressed fear that the present environmental-education craze might displace Earth science and Earth-science teachers from their hard-won place in the junior high school. It seems to me regrettable that students should study Earth science in the eighth grade or in the ninth grade and never think of it again. Our mania for specialization in the long run makes young people fear science. I look forward to the time when a great deal of Earth-science equipment and many Earth-science resources will be available to every student between the ages of one and eighty-five. Schools need to develop along "open curriculum" lines where the student elects what he will study on any given day and at any given time rather than having the teacher make this decision for him. When we get away from arbitrary subdivisions in science we will have a better chance for people to develop sympathetic attitudes toward scientists as people and toward science as an area of human activity. I am eager to see Earth science (and physics, biology, chemistry, environmental education, English, French, social studies, music, art and all the rest) disappear as discrete fragmented subjects that children are forced to study. I am convinced that, given freedom to select for themselves hour by hour what they will do, large numbers of students will pursue subjects in the area we call "Earth science." It remains critical for us to produce teachers who are highly competent in the area of the Earth sciences but who have enough sense about people not to try to force them to learn things these people may perceive to be of little value.[13]

A REACTION FROM PAUL

Please note the date of this letter—April 2, 1976. It is just five years since I read Bill Romey's editorial in *Geotimes,* March 1971, entitled "In a Time of Dissatisfaction." I was impressed by the admonition that

---

[13]William D. Romey, "In a Time of Dissatisfaction," in *Geotimes* 16 (1971):9. Reprinted with permission.

students be given ". . . freedom to select for themselves hour by hour what they will do. . . ." While Romey's editorial specifically referred to junior high school and to ". . . subjects that children are forced to study," I thought the ideas ought to be equally applicable to students at the college level, where I happened to be teaching. I thought, too, that responsibility toward others was a mutual affair.

So, try to appreciate the dismay I felt yesterday when the decision was made that despite my tenured status I would be fired. Even more, try to appreciate the dismay I feel that this action is completely supported by the students.

You see, I began conducting "open" classes. I didn't insist that students come to lecture (I *never* have in over fifteen years!). As I *always* have, I expected that students that were really interested in the kind of geology I talk about would do work at times of their own choosing. As always, I had laboratories open as long as possible—i.e., as long as we could be sure that someone would be nearby to respond to any emergency that might develop.

The changes after I read Romey's editorial were that I insisted that neither students *nor* I be restricted to studying at a given time of a given day. I began giving lectures when I felt I would give them best. Gradually I saw that I should not hamstring myself by adhering to a pre-determined set sequence of topics. The result was that my lectures also became freed from constraints on content. I found them getting better and better. I was particularly impressed by the one I gave on the end of Deadman Point looking into Dark Canyon. (It concerned the textural effects in the series of paintings I was doing using shales and siltstones in linseed oil.) It's a shame none of my students found me to hear that one; more exciting and relevant (to my interests at the time) Earth Science you've never heard! And the laboratory exercise I demonstrated when I got to the junction of Dark Canyon and Woodenshoe Canyon. It was tremendous!

I have talked with my lawyer and he tells me a grievance procedure will fail; the local AAUP Chapter says they won't support me in a complaint; a colleague told me he doesn't think anyone else will hire me in spite of the fact that I think I can justly claim to be as liberated from the old ways of failure as anyone.[14]

MY RESPONSE

The basic difference from my point of view that would be present in a person who would write the April 2, 1976, letter is

---

[14]Thanks to Paul Reitan for sending me this response and for giving me permission to print both it and the further notes that follow my response to his letter.

the self-centeredness of the instructor and his failure to respond to the needs his students identify. A truly free learning environment of the type I'm interested in can only exist if I care enough for students who are working with me to know in great detail what each of them is interested in and how I can best support his interests. Sometimes I can best support these interests by giving a lecture, at other times by organizing a laboratory session of some particular type, at others by keeping entirely out of the way. The one thing that I personally decline to do in the future is to use my professorial power to require students to do the things I prescribe. My role becomes that of helping a student clarify the consequences of his own actions. The responsibility for what he elects to do remains on his own shoulders. As an example, if a student asks me what skills he will need to pass the U.S.G.S.[15] Exam, I accept the responsibility for providing him with the yardsticks against which he will be measured and to give him all the information I can obtain about how to succeed in this examination. The responsibility to learn the things necessary to pass the U.S.G.S. Examination belongs to the student, and I shall not bug him about reaching his own goals. At regular intervals I will talk with him about what he is doing and give him my opinions about whether or not he can expect to succeed. If he refuses to take responsibility for meeting these goals that he has set for himself, I accept responsibility to talk to him about these goals. Perhaps he really doesn't want to work for the U.S.G.S. Perhaps he doesn't really even want to be in college. The decision is always his, and I will not lay my ratings on top of him. I will provide them for his information.

Your letter gives an example of lectures that an instructor gives but which are attended by no students. Here we come to the responsiveness of the individual teacher. I happen to like to lecture and will continue to give lectures about things that interest me. As I see the attendance at my optional lectures decreasing, however, I shall seek the reasons for this decrease by talking to my students and trying to find out whether or not lectures on other topics may be more suitable for them. If they simply do not like to have any lectures because I don't communicate well with

---

[15]U.S.G.S.—U.S. Geological Survey.

them in that way, I will seek some other means of communicating with them.

Your letter implies a lack of trust, loving, care, and responsiveness on the part of the instructor. If I show a lack of these qualities in a free learning environment, then I shall be prepared to lose my position as a faculty member because if I am not willing to accept this set of responsibilities to other human beings, I am sure that I would probably be far happier in some situation other than a university teaching position as I conceive it.

I emphasize that my response here is strictly a first person response. I don't care to impose my system of values on my colleagues or my students. I recognize that the particular framework I favor for myself and my students may not be suitable for other teachers and other students. In a sense I wish to see a set of alternatives, one of them with a very wide degree of freedom, which are not presently available on the American educational scene in any substantial degree.

Incidentally, the models I speak about are not experimental ways of dealing with students. There are a number of faculty members and a number of students operating in very free educational frameworks in public schools and colleges in various parts of the United States. I personally have no fear about being in the position your 1976 letter puts your hypothetical teacher in. If he finds himself in this position, it becomes his problem for not being responsive to the situation in which he operates.

A NOTE BACK FROM PAUL

You note the self-centeredness of the writer of the "1976 letter" and his lack of trust, love, care, and responsiveness. Exactly right. That is the major satirical ingredient of the letter. Your approach demands self-sacrifice, trust, responsiveness, love, and consideration on the part of the teacher but does not seem to require anything more than self-interest on the part of the student. If I object it is not because too much is demanded of me, but because success in improving the educational process must depend on mutuality of trust, responsiveness, respect, and effort.

We agree that one approach, framework, or style may not be best suited to everyone, either teachers or students. I am convinced that much of our activity in traditional forms aimed at education in schools at all levels is not helpful to some proportion of our students. In consequence we agree on the need for alternatives to the present dominant style or scheme of education. I think I may have understood your *Geotimes* editorial as championing a different method rather than appealing for alternatives.

POLARIZATION AND POLITICIZATION

Two junior high school teachers I know are in the process of becoming facilitators of learning. Both are in a single school building. Their openness is well received by their students; these students want openness in more of their classes. Discussion among students makes other students wish for the same openness in their classes. Non-responsive teachers and facilitative teachers find themselves polarized. Both sides begin political activity, the first to defend the status quo and to try to force it on all other teachers and on all students, the second to be allowed to continue their own facilitative efforts but not to force other teachers into a facilitative model and not to force young people into an open framework unless they desire it.

One of Cricket's teachers attracted her into a discussion of open curriculum schools. Several other young people participated. The next day Cricket was called to the principal's office and asked to explain why she was trying to "influence" the other children in favor of an open curriculum. Cricket was apolitical. But if you treat her like a radical, she can become one.

How many of our radical young people have been politicized by the schools in this way? It's a self-fulfilling prophecy: Those whom we treat as radicals will probably become radical.

"WE CAN'T DO THAT WITHOUT MORE MONEY AND MORE PEOPLE"

—*Photo by Robert Samples. Courtesy of Environmental Studies project.*

Some people suggest that it costs more money and takes more people to create a free and humane environment for learning. I have seen enough teachers simply change the way that they do things to know that this is just another "cop-out." The statement shows unwillingness to take responsibility and indicates that the person who makes it is not really interested in change or, more likely, that he fears it.

The most important changes cost little money but much commitment. I can no longer use this statement as an excuse for my own inaction. Reallocation of efforts and financial resources threatens the status quo of the system. It does not require more money or more people.

5

Fantasy

INTRODUCTION

In the preceding chapters I have written about myself, about the role of facilitators of learning as I see it, and about problems that seem to help prevent change. Thinking about these things causes me to fantasize about what I would do myself in various school situations. The next few sections contain the results of some of my fantasy. One danger of putting such fantasy down on paper is that the models proposed may be taken as blueprints to be followed in their details by others. My undulating fantasy causes my own models to change continually as I am stimulated by things I see, read about, and feel and even more so as I come into contact with people whose fantasy seems more beautiful than mine. The models that will be described here represent a record of where my fantasy stood at the moment of this writing, and, because I live in a world of change, you may find me in a different place the next time we meet.

I have not written down the results of my fantasizing about how I would behave as a teacher in a self-contained elementary school classroom. Many other people like Sylvia Ashton-Warner,[1] John Holt,[2] Francis Hawkins,[3] and Joseph Featherstone[4] have described what I consider to be different and exciting models. I have never spent much time with young children in school situations, and so I leave the writing down of ideals in that area for others to do—at least for now.

The greatest fantasy I could engage in would be to describe my ideal system for society with special attention to education

---

[1]Sylvia Ashton-Warner, *Teacher* (Baltimore: Penguin Books, 1966).
[2]John Holt, numerous books including *Why Children Fail* (New York: Pitman Publishing Co., 1964).
[3]Francis Hawkins, *The Logic of Action* (Boulder, Colorado: Elementary Science Advisory Center, University of Colorado, 1969).
[4]Joseph Featherstone, "The British Infant Schools," *The New Republic* (Aug. 19, Sept. 2, Sept. 9, 1967).

within it. I could, like Paul Goodman, advocate the end of compulsory education and urge great changes in the overall position of schools and universities in society. But I haven't yet gotten to the point where I want to put that particular fantasy down on paper. That fantasy might require the complete overthrow of existing systems, and this kind of overthrow smacks of open rebellion and violence. There is already enough of that around. I am still a man of the system. I still believe that evolutionary change within the system is possible. Thus I want to talk about me and what concrete things I know I could do if I were . . .

IF I WERE A JUNIOR OR SENIOR
HIGH SCHOOL TEACHER

—Photo by Robert Samples. Courtesy of Environmental Studies project.

If I were a junior or senior high school teacher alone in my own classroom, and the school as a whole were the usual rigid, conventional, sit-in-straight-rows and go-to-the-same-room-at-the-same-time-every-day kind of place, I would make a pact with the kids. I would say, "Look, you people, we're all locked up in this box together for one hour every day and we're supposed to be studying _____ (fill in the blank). There are lots of things in _____ that I know a lot about and I'll be glad to talk to you about them. There are lots of things in the world and even in _____ that I don't know much about. But if you get excited about them, I may, too. Then I'll be glad to go help find out about them. So come and talk to me when you want to about things that grab you.

"I'd feel more comfortable if you'd call me by my first name, which is Bill. If that makes you uncomfortable, call me whatever you like." That invitation may lead to all sorts of things!

"You'll be responsible for what you learn in here, and I'm not going to lay assignments on you. Since this is supposed to be a course' in _____, you probably ought to do some _____ or else transfer to some other class. But I'm not going to be bothered if I see you doing other things. If you prefer to think of this as a general purpose alternative learning environment, instead of a class in _____, perhaps we can work something out along those lines. I care very much about you as people, and I also care about your education, so help me to help you and we can have a beautiful time together.

"You people arrange the furniture any way you want when you come in.

"Each of you gets a permanent hall pass, library pass, and bathroom pass which I will not take away from you regardless of what you do. If someone else takes it away from you, that's tough luck. Then you're stuck in here. If you want to take some field trips, we'll work together to set them up. We may need help from your parents if you want to go very far.

"I want you to have the best possible chance to learn what you want to learn in _____. In exchange for the freedom you get, please don't get me into more trouble than I can talk my way out of. There are other people in classrooms around us, and your freedom (and mine, too) stops where their freedom begins. I get mad when I see people interfering with other people's freedom. You have a right to get mad at me just as much as I have a right to get mad at you.

"I'll try to provide as much stuff for studying _____ as I can. I'll also try to suggest things to do if you want suggestions. Help me to find out what you're interested in, and I'll try to help you find stuff to satisfy your interests.

"Sometimes you'll want to work alone. Sometimes you'll want to work with me. Sometimes, you'll want to work with a group of other people. That's your choice to make—not mine.

"When there are problems or troubles, I'll call a class meeting, and we'll see what you want to do about the problem. We'll vote on what to do, and I'll have one vote just as each of you will have one vote.

"Incidentally, I'm not going to grade you, but the school requires a grade. So you'll have to grade yourselves. I'll want to talk to each of you about your work several times a grading period. If you want some outside standards to measure yourself against, I've got lots of standard tests and old tests I used to give, and you can test yourselves if you think that gives you a better feeling of having learned something.

"I'd suggest that each of you keep a folder in this file drawer up here. You can put any of your own work in that folder as a sort of permanent file to show what you've done in the area of _____. _____ is just about as broad as you want to make it, too. You can write papers, poems, use drawings, put in results of what you did on self-tests, or just keep a diary of what you did. Or you can put nothing in the file folder.

"Why keep a folder? When your parents want to see what you've done, you can show them. Or next year when some other teacher says, 'Oh, you were in that stupid classroom where you didn't really do anything or learn anything,' you can lead that teacher in here and show him your folder and say, 'That's what I did, buster.' Only maybe he wouldn't like it if you called him 'buster'!

"You're the only one who can add or subtract anything from that folder. That folder should contain stuff to show your idea of your own best work, and you're the only one who can be responsible for how good or bad it is. If you want me to write a letter for the file telling what I think of your work, I'll be glad to write one, but you must decide, once you've seen the letter, whether or not you want to put it in. If I write down that I think your work is terrible, you may want to do some better work and ask me to write another letter later. Or you may not care *what* I think of your work. That's fine, too.

"If you write something that you'd like me to read, I'll be glad to read it. I may even ask to read something you've written, but you have the right to say no any time you want.

"Now, let's talk over the whole business for a while to see what suggestions, questions, and ideas you have about the hour we'll spend together every day."

From that point on, what happens in the classroom depends on the people in the room, and I'm sure that every classroom will be different. The next day the students are free to do what they wish to do, and my job becomes that of responding to them.

Sound like something you want to do, but you just don't think it's possible? Well, it is! I've visited a whole group of science teachers this past year in very "straight" schools, and some version of this model is in action. Some of the other teachers in the buildings seem terribly threatened by it, but it's working and the kids are learning and feeling good about learning—at least for that one period a day.

IF I WERE A PRINCIPAL

If I were a principal, I would get all of the teachers together and tell them the schedule was done for. I would tell them—and the students, too—that each student would decide for himself, every minute of the day, where he would be, whom he would talk to, what he would study, whom he would work with, *if* he would study, and for how long.

I would invite the teachers to suggest activities, seminars, demonstrations, films, plays, concerts, sporting events, classes, and other things that they thought students might like to do and to request space and time for individual activities on a day-by-day basis. I would invite students to do the same thing. Then we would prepare a big, daily master schedule to hang in the hall so everyone would know what would be going on where and at what hour.

I would deny teachers the right to impose work on any student and deny them the right to impose grades. I would urge them to let students know what they thought of their work, and I would urge students to tell the teachers directly what they thought of their teachers' attempts to facilitate learning. In this way teachers and students could grow together. I would urge teachers to make external standards routinely available to their students, but I would deny them the right to force any student to use these standards.

I would offer any teacher a chance to transfer to another school, and I would offer the same option to any students who would be unhappy in the environment we would provide.

I would schedule voluntary encounter groups for teachers, students, and parents so that all could come to know each other as human beings and to recognize and work with problems that would occur in the learning community.

I would have each student select a teacher or an administrator to be his "personal advisor" to help him with his learning and to help him learn to cope with his learning problems and personal problems. The student could change advisors whenever he wished to do so.

We would set up a master file of portfolios for individual students, and each student would assemble his own "stuff" to show others his best product or whatever product he wants to represent him. Only the student would be able to add items to this portfolio-record or to remove items.

If I were a principal, I would be a teacher, too. I could not accept the role of "administrator" because I think everyone in education should work directly at helping other people learn. I would expect to be regularly engaged in learning myself. I distrust high-salaried, full-time administrators. Most of them can be removed with no detrimental effects to learning by the students.

I would provide every opportunity for every teacher to become comfortable with the role of facilitator and counselor rather than "teacher."

I would jealously guard the rights of students, for my focus is on the students and their problems. I would have compassion for the feelings and problems of the teacher, but in most disputes I would probably take the side of the student. I recognize that teachers are humans, too, and I would guard them against threats from both outside and inside the school.

If I really had my way, I would start from the beginning and select teachers in the first place who agreed with my goal to provide a free learning environment full of caring people. Then we could establish a horizontal structure in the school rather than the kind of vertical hierarchy that now exists everywhere.

It's been done much this way, incidentally.[5] It works best when the teachers volunteer for the program. But in some schools where this kind of system has been imposed on the teachers, they now say that they wouldn't go back to the old system for anything.

---

[5]See D. Glines, *Creating Humane Schools* (Mankato, Minn.: Campus Publishers, 1971).

IF I WERE TEACHING A REQUIRED
INTRODUCTORY COLLEGE CLASS

Almost all introductory college courses I know of are either teacher-centered or curriculum-centered. Students enter a teacher-centered course on a prescribed date, and the teacher informs them of *his* goals. The students meet with instructors at prescribed times and are periodically asked to demonstrate in some way the extent to which they have met the teacher's goals. The teacher's goals are commonly related to the structure of a discipline as the teacher perceives it, to the skills of the discipline as the teacher perceives them, to information selected by the teacher, or to a combination of these. The student's job is to meet the teacher's goals.

In a curriculum-centered course the teacher imposes an externally prepared curriculum on his students. He sets the cadence and calls the dance, but the song has been composed elsewhere. Many high school science teachers "follow" a curriculum, and a surprising number of college teachers "follow" a textbook and a laboratory manual. Most college teachers use a combination between teacher-centered and curriculum-centered models. In all of these courses, after exposure to the given program, the student is supposed to have "had" the course and therefore not to "need" any more for a "liberal" education.

Student-centered introductory courses are rare. In the completely student-centered course I would offer, each individual student would determine the curriculum for himself, and my functions would be to respond to needs identified by my students. Ideally no grades at all would be involved, and the student would decide for himself how long he wished to be involved in my "course." Practically, if a "credit" system existed, the student would be able to designate how much credit he should receive for his work. If a grade system existed, I would ask the student to evaluate himself. I would provide external standards to help students determine credit and grade, and I would discuss each student's work with him periodically, but final decisions on these matters would always be made by the student. In short, such a student-centered introductory "course" would look like an independent study, tutorial experience in which I respond rather than present and in which I accept and clarify rather than judge. A good description of a student-centered upper level "course" in psychology is given by Samuel Tenenbaum.[6]

When I give this definition of a student-centered course, many instructors whom I talk to in both large and small colleges throw up their hands and say, "It can't be done here." The excuses are many, but the principal ones are that numbers are too great and that "the administration won't let me." These excuses are not valid in most places. The real reason why teachers hold onto teacher-centered and curriculum-centered models of instruction is that they are afraid to trust their students, to trust themselves, as people, to work with students on the highly personal basis required in student-centered models, and to give up the power they have over students. Honest steps toward the introduction of student-centered learning environments are being successfully attempted by a number of colleges associated with the Earth Science Teacher Preparation Project. More details on the operation of student-centered introductory courses are included in the following section.

---

[6]Samuel Tenenbaum, *"Carl R. Rogers and Non-Directive Teaching"* and *"A Personal Teaching Experience,"* in Carl R. Rogers, *On Becoming a Person* (Boston: Houghton Mifflin Co., Sentry Editions, 1961) pp. 299-310 and 310-313 respectively.

IF I WERE DEPARTMENT CHAIRMAN IN COLLEGE

In my own ideal college department, education would proceed in a highly informal manner. There would be no courses, no requirements, no credits, no grades assigned by faculty members, no required examinations. In their place a close personal relationship would exist between faculty members (who will commonly be referred to below as "senior learners") and students (who will commonly be referred to in the following paragraphs as "junior learners"). Senior and junior learners will be involved in learning together about the discipline or area of interest which the department has facilities for exploring. "Teaching" in the sense of having faculty present information and train students in skills will not be a frequent activity. The more experienced will help the less experienced to pursue their own investigations. This program is based on the idea of *operational humanism* in which faculty members relinquish much of their control and evaluative function and assume roles as co-learners and advisors to their students. It attempts to create a collegial atmosphere of mutual trust and cooperation between and among older and younger members of the department. The department is governed by a committee of the whole, including all majors, graduate students, and faculty.

ENTRY INTO PROGRAMS OF THE DEPARTMENT

FIRST EXPERIENCE

This department would ideally exist in a college or university with no distribution requirements that would force students to study in the area concerned. Comments will be made at the end of this section about colleges with distribution requirements.

People wishing to pursue beginning, non-professional studies in the department would have available to them a wide variety of optional stimulatory activities which would help them plan individual and group studies aimed at helping them to explore the area of departmental responsibility to whatever depth they desire.

The members of the faculty as a group would schedule a minimum of one major public departmental lecture each week—to be held in a large auditorium and to be open to all who are interested. A minimum of two or three small group discussions or as many as necessary to accommodate the number of interested students in groups of about fifteen would also be scheduled each week for those who wished to attend.

A laboratory for people wishing to carry out further activities related to lecture and discussion group activities would be kept open a sufficient number of hours so that those interested could work with the paraphernalia related to the "topic of the week." Faculty members could also schedule optional field activities.

All of the above activities would be entirely optional, and any given faculty member would only occasionally commit himself to be in charge of a week's activity of the type described. In smaller departments (three-four man), individual faculty members would be responsible for three to four weeks' worth of these activities per semester. In larger departments they might be called upon only once per semester or per year. The function of these activities would be to provide opportunity for interested students, other faculty members, and people from the community (if space permits) to be introduced to current topics before committing themselves to further study. All would be free auditors in these events, for which no "credit" would be assigned.

Learners wishing to have their involvement recorded on their records would choose a faculty member with whom they wished to work and would approach the faculty member and discuss with him a study they wished to perform (or they might solicit his advice about a study they wish to perform). If credit of any kind were desired by the learner, the amount of the credit could be determined *at the conclusion of the study.* It would be expected that the learner and his facilitator would be in contact several times during the course of the study. In addition, facilitators would be likely to schedule occasional seminars to which several advisors with related or unrelated studies might be invited. Students would be able to change advisors whenever they or their advisors believed such a change desirable. Upper division learners would also serve as advisors if they wished to do so. Facilitators would help provide resources in the form of bibliographies, access to facilities, assistance in the field, and access to human resources (other faculty members, upper level learners competent in certain fields, etc.).

A facilitator would not deal with more than about thirty to forty learners in this context during a given term. The number he would accept would depend on the wishes of the facilitator, in coordination with the departmental administration. Some facilitators would probably be able to serve more students effectively, others fewer. No one would be expected to spend more than about half of his time facilitating (including work with more advanced learners, as will be described below). The number that a faculty member would consult with would be subject to the condition that some of his time be free for his own scholarly endeavors and administrative or service activity. (The faculty member's own scholarly activity would very likely involve upper division students as collaborators and assistants, so that even his research activities would be closely correlated with his activities with learners.)

*   *   *   *   *

In universities and colleges requiring students to have a course in the department, the same general scheme would be applied except that students wishing to "examine out" of the requirement rather than being involved in individual studies would be allowed to do so by taking an examination on the materials covered in the lectures, in a textbook or books, in a reading list, or in some other way. Students would grade themselves on their performance (unless they wished to be examined and graded by the instructors in charge). In all cases, any student could ask to switch at any time to the individual or group studies scheme described above. Special other ways of satisfying the requirement through doing supervised readings would also be permitted. In no case should the number of students who work with a single instructor exceed the number whom the instructor could come to know personally during the semester—this may range from 50 to about 100 per instructor. Each student should have a chance to consult personally and individually with the instructor at least several times each term in addition to any optional group meetings. Only students who desired examinations would be given examinations, and all students would be offered the options of grading themselves and justifying this grade if grades were required.

The department would actively seek abolition of all science requirements and abolition of all grades with the possible exception of a credit, no-credit system if some accounting were to be done. "No-credit" would not appear on the student's transcript in any way other than by the lack of the name of a given course on the transcript.

* * * * *

Learners who wished to continue work in the department on a non-professional basis or as part of their work in another department would be encouraged to set up an individual program of readings, laboratory work, field work, or any other work suiting their purpose with a faculty member or members as facilitators.

ADVANCED STUDIES

Students wishing to pursue advanced studies leading to a major in the department or to a program involving extensive studies in the area of concern would be expected to apply for admission to the department. It would be expected that each prospective "major" (if such terminology were retained) would pursue, in advance of his entry into an advanced program, independent studies under the beginning programs described above and would thus become personally acquainted with one or several members of the faculty. The applicant would submit to the department a statement of his goals and a portfolio showing examples of his own work that he considered to be representative of his abilities. His portfolio would be examined by several faculty members (senior learners) and upper level students (junior learners), both graduate (if available) and undergraduate. The applicant would also be interviewed about his portfolio and plans.

The applicant, if accepted, would then begin a term as an apprentice in the department. (If not accepted, he would be informed of the reasons for his rejection and would receive suggestions about ways of becoming an acceptable candidate if he still wished to join the department.) At the end of the apprentice semester his portfolio—with work from the apprentice semester included—would be re-examined by a group of senior and junior learners. If the quality of his work were judged acceptable, he could be either fully admitted as a junior learner or continued for an additional term as an apprentice if the committee wished to see further work. Special interdisciplinary committees would be formed to accommodate junior learners with interests that required support from other academic areas.

During his advanced program, the junior learner would have no formal course work, but would instead work individually, with small groups, and with senior learners on projects he had conceived or on projects already designed by other learners in which he wished to participate. He would continue to add to his

—Photo by Robert Samples. Courtesy of Environmental Studies project.

portfolio reports of his work, discussion papers on his readings, data he had gathered, and other items that he wished to have represent his activities. He could add to or subtract from his portfolio at any time he wished to do so.

Junior learners would normally participate as advisors to apprentices and to beginning students in the pre-professional programs described earlier. They would also be likely to schedule seminars and presentations in which they review their own work so that their junior and senior colleagues and advisors could learn more about them and their work.

Each junior learner, as soon as he were accepted into the "major" program, would be assigned laboratory and office space within the department and would be considered a professional colleague in every respect.

All students and faculty would be engaged in helping others learn as well as in learning themselves.

GRADUATION FROM THE UNDERGRADUATE PROGRAM

A committee of senior learners and recent graduates or junior level graduate students would periodically review the portfolio of each junior learner and would certify that a given student had completed work of sufficient quantity and quality for a major program. It would be desirable each year to bring in outside consultants from nearby universities with graduate programs to consult with learners about their portfolios. The consultants would come in midyear so that a learner whose work was weak would still have time to add more and better work to his portfolio. Junior learners at earlier stages of preparation would also be encouraged to consult with the consultants. The senior learners would act as advocates for the junior learners. Outside consultants chosen from many different universities, industries, and companies would also have an opportunity to come to know the product of the department. This would facilitate the placement of departmental majors with graduate schools and into jobs. No set number of years or semesters would be set for graduation. Some students might produce sufficient work in a year; others might require two- or three-year programs.

Students hoping to go on to graduate school would be advised to keep in their portfolios lists of books and articles read, problems dealt with, etc. Senior learners would certify that this work had been done and would write reports discussing the details of each junior learner's work and perhaps try to translate the program into terms of more conventional course-work in order to facilitate entry into graduate school. It would be incumbent upon the department as a whole to publicize and make known as widely as possible the model of undergraduate education being used. Graduates of this program would have had up to two or more years of involvement in creative, problem-oriented, individual research and study of a type similar to that which graduate students pursue. In the course of these studies and before being certified as graduates, the junior learners would have acquired all of the basic skills they would have gained in a more conventionally oriented undergraduate program. It is likely, as shown by experimental programs of the type described, that many junior learners would produce research results equivalent in quality to much published research. Junior learners would be encouraged to submit their results for publication when the quality of their work was judged by themselves, their peers, senior colleagues, and outside consultants to be sufficiently high.

HOW THE PROGRAM COULD MESH
WITH PROGRAMS OF OTHER DEPARTMENTS

It would be hoped that other departments would establish similar systems for their major and non-major students. But the proposed program could operate also in a conventional system. A single department operating in this way within a normally operating academic community would schedule its offering as Geology (or Psychology, English, or whatever the name of the department happened to be) 1,2,3,4,5,6, etc. Geology (or whatever) 1 would merely consist of whatever the student happened to be interested in studying during his first term of geology. Thus Geology 1 might be mainly stratigraphy for one student, climatology for a second, environmental studies for a third, petrology for a fourth, and some kind of wild combination for a fifth. The number of credit hours attached to each course number (Geology 1,2,3,4,5, etc.), if course credits were to be granted, would be equivalent to any other normal university course. Thus a student who, in a conventional system, would have taken two or three geology courses in a given semester would enroll for Geology 3 and 4, 3,4,5, or some other set of numbers depending on how many previous "units" he had "credit" for. Obviously, this use of "units" would be merely a device to fit conventional university and college course and credit frameworks. As greater segments of the college adopted this system, it should be able to abolish such useless accounting systems. The student's portfolio, in an ideal system, and his close working relationship with his colleagues (both junior and senior learners) should make it possible to certify him without meaningless mechanical accumulations of "credits."

Optionally a block credit grant equal to the normal number of credit hours attached to a major (perhaps forty) would be made to the junior learner upon completion of a satisfactory portfolio. If the college insisted upon a semester-by-semester accumulation of credits, it would be desirable to allow the credits to be assigned *at the end of the term* rather than at the beginning, for in an atmosphere of independent inquiry, one cannot accurately predict either the quality or quantity of the work until the work has been completed. If grades were required (and it is planned that they would *not* be), each junior learner would be asked to assign his own grades and then to discuss these grades with his advisors (and peers if he desires). In each case, the grade he assigned himself would be awarded, and the purpose of the consultation would be to help the student become aware of external standards, to be a competent self-evaluator, and to come to grips with the problems of honest self-appraisal.

I would hope that supporting "courses" taken by the student in other departments could be jointly evaluated by the departmental faculty and the responsible faculty member in the supporting department. A more desirable alternative would be to have departmental majors involved in supporting courses as free auditors, with "credit" toward the major to be determined by the faculty of the learner's parent department or even to be included in a block credit grant entitled "studies in support of the major program." The student would include within his portfolio evidence of his supporting studies in peripheral areas. It could be expected that under these conditions, major students would audit only pertinent sections of supporting courses rather than sitting through lectures and exercises that would probably be useless and uninteresting to them. The most desirable relationship would be for students who enter the major program as juniors (third-year students) to be granted a sixty-hour block credit grant to be certified by the major department at the rate of fifteen credits per term (if credits must be accumulated term by term). All work in outside departments would thus be on a free-audit basis and would be *described* by the student in his portfolio but not evaluated by the outside departments.

A student's portfolio might contain not only his best product in the area of his major, but also concrete evidence of his work in peripheral science and humanities areas. As an example, he might include poetry he had written, programs of dramatic or musical events he had participated in, etc., as well as essays, reports, and data from his work in the major. Many graduate departments and employers highly value evidence of widely diverse interests and of participation in extracurricular and extra-professional activities. Portfolios could also contain the learner's statement about sessions he has led and the extent of the "teaching" he has done, in that all learners would also function as "teachers."

GRADUATE PROGRAMS

Graduate programs would follow the same model as the upper level undergraduate programs. There would be no formal course activities, only an intense personal involvement by each learner in creative scholarly activity. Each graduate would also keep a portfolio and would assist both undergraduate learners and faculty members just as both of them would assist him in the common pursuit of knowledge, skills, and professional and personal associations.

Normally, undergraduates receiving their degrees under this program would be encouraged to go elsewhere for their graduate training. The reason for this is my assumption that experiences in many different places and with many different groups lead to a richer overall learning experience. Such learners would be called back periodically to help evaluate the portfolios of those behind them and to provide suggestions that would help these younger learners prepare for graduate study.

SUMMARY OF SOME KINDS OF ACTIVITIES WITHIN THE DEPARTMENT

1. Large-group public lectures—a minimum of one per week—given by faculty, graduate students, upper-level majors, visitors. These would have a recruiting function and, in schools where there was a required course in the department, would help students see alternatives for independent studies. (entirely optional for all students)
2. Film series—weekly films (optional and free)
3. Small-group seminars and discussion for beginning learners. Discussion leaders would be faculty, graduate students, undergraduate majors. These could be related to the weekly public lecture or to other topics. (optional)
4. Field trips conducted by faculty, graduate students, and undergraduate majors. These would be aimed mainly at beginning students and would either be related to the weekly public lecture or be presented as different topics. (optional)
5. Special laboratory sessions (several per week) aimed at allowing beginning students to explore various topics or to work on individual projects for credit or for inclusion in a portfolio-application to become a major. (optional)
6. Special tutorial sessions, both individual and small group, for beginning students and for undergraduate or graduate majors. These would be conducted by any competent faculty members or graduate or undergraduate majors. *All* members of the department would both "teach" and learn.
7. Extensive independent and small group research and study activities involving students and faculty.
8. Numerous small discussion groups primarily for majors and graduate students and involving students interested in a scheduled topic. Such discussions would be scheduled by majors (junior learners), faculty (senior learners), or both. Attendance would be entirely optional at these sessions, most of which would probably be highly informal in character.

9. Many other kinds of activities would likely arise. If other institutions with departments in the same subject area were nearby, the senior learners would make every attempt to foster joint programs of research, joint seminars, joint field trips, etc., in order to share facilities and make more options and resources available to junior learners (and to themselves).

10. Encounter groups: Depending on the wishes of the learning community as a whole it might be decided to introduce encounter group activities of the type suggested by Rogers[7] or "classroom meetings" described by Glasser.[8] Rogers and Glasser would both require attendance at such meetings. I would be inclined to leave the decision about attendance to the learning community as a whole and to have my vote count on an equal basis with that of any other individual in the community. I believe that through my own efforts and those of the upper division "assistants" to seek out non-participating students and to let them know how much we *care* about their involvement most students would become involved deeply. If a student-centered model of learning is to succeed, problems such as individual involvement and group involvement must be approached as human problems, and the community as a whole must agree to recognize and deal with these problems in an open, humane fashion. A spirit of "operational" humanism must permeate the group. Recipes for "handling" situations cannot be written, but the cooperative spirit of the group will ultimately lead to the seeking of ways of supporting individuals within the group.

FACILITIES OF THE DEPARTMENT

1. Each faculty member would need a studio-office for informal sessions with other faculty and with graduate and undergraduate students. The studio would invite informality and "rap" sessions and would probably be furnished in the style of a living room or study rather than as an office. Certainly it would *not* be like a conventional classroom in any way. The room should accommodate about fifteen people comfortably. One or two extra seminar studios should be available for use by learners when a faculty member is not involved in the discussion.

2. In a science department one or two major laboratory rooms would

---

[7]Carl R. Rogers, *Freedom to Learn* (Columbus, Ohio: Charles E. Merrill Publishing Co., 1969).
[8]William Glasser, *Schools without Failure.* (New York: Harper and Row, 1969).

be used as open laboratories for beginning students who wish to explore what possibilities the science offers before applying to major. If there were a required first-year science course, these spaces would be available to students in this course. Conversation and reading rooms would be available in non-science departments.

3. Several laboratory or studio rooms would be available that could be used as offices, labs, or studios for major students. Each student would have definite assigned space and keys to facilities he might need or desire to use. Probably several learners would share a large space, with each having his own desk and bench space.

4. There would be access to a *large* lecture room, which would be needed only one or two hours a week.

5. Special laboratories and facilities: Special rooms containing expensive equipment, collections, materials, and books for general use would be available for use by all majors. First-year students would be able to use such facilities under the guidance of either competent junior or senior learners. Both junior and senior learners would be expected to be "checked out" in the use of major instruments before being permitted to use them. This caution would be necessary to preserve fine equipment and help keep it in satisfactory operating condition for the benefit of all.

6. Vehicles: Several departmental field vehicles always on call should be available for a department with need for transportation.

7. It is anticipated that there would be no need for conventional types of "classrooms," since there would be no formal "classes" in the program. Any such space would be converted into open offices for junior learners to "live" in.

8. A departmental library and reading room, comfortably furnished, would be desirable. It would be hoped that both senior and junior learners might contribute to an audio-tutorial "bank." This would consist of a tape and slide library aimed at helping interested people in the department learn certain skills when they wish to do so. Certain skills might be more easily learned if a large bank of programmed instructional materials were on hand for *optional* use by students. All departmental lectures, given by senior and junior learners or by visitors, would be taped and kept in the tape library for reference as long as needed. Building new resources for such a programmed instruction and reading center would be an on-going task for all members of the department. (Language labs would be included under the category of facility.)

9. Access to computer facilities: Among other uses, the computer could be used to store data for a data bank. All original data from

independent investigations within the department could be stored for easy computerized retrieval in support of further studies.

10. Other facilities would also doubtlessly be needed to support the wide range of independent investigations that junior and senior learners might wish to undertake, and the department would need to be flexible enough to find ways of providing resources as the need for them arises.

NOTE: We are currently implementing a model similar to the one described in this chapter in the Department of Geology and Geography at Saint Lawrence University.

IF I WERE DEAN

As I examine undergraduate programs in most colleges in the United States, I find certain common elements present in all but a small number of institutions. From these common elements it should be possible to work backward to determine what must be the basic assumptions underlying these programs. The following are some of the assumptions that I am convinced must underlie much of higher education in the United States. Many of these assumptions can be recognized as pervading graduate as well as undergraduate education.

1. Students should all study the same things at the same times in a given course. This assumption is especially true in lower level courses, but I have also observed it in a large number of upper division and graduate courses as well.

2. There is a definite track that all students should follow through a major program. This track should normally be selected by a faculty member. In some modern programs the student may be consulted about certain details of his program. Some departments introduce several different tracks, but most of these are relatively inflexible.

3. People learn mainly by taking courses. Since virtually all undergraduate and graduate programs in the higher education system of the United States are based on courses, this assumption must be present in the existing system. I cannot think of any major institutions in the United States that do not have programs based to a large extent on formal coursework.

4. The role of professors is to teach. Teaching for the most part consists of having professors talk or give relatively rigid laboratory or other assignments to their students. Studies done by many educators indicate that professors talk for well over seventy-five percent of the time that they are in a position of interacting with their students. A corollary to this assumption is that the role of students is to learn, where learning is defined as listening intently.

5. Professors have the primary task of evaluating and grading. The role of students is to be evaluated and to be graded. Students

should not evaluate either themselves or the faculty members that deal with them.

6. Courses must consist of an arrangement in which one hour of credit is given for each hour per week the student spends in lecture. In laboratory or practical work courses, two hours of laboratory work per week are granted one credit. Implicit in this assumption is the notion that learning can be measured in credits and that granting of degrees is based upon an accumulation of these credits rather than on learning per se. Implicit in the course system is the assumption that a college undergraduate experience must be divided into fifteen-week semesters. Normally eight of these fifteen-week semesters automatically qualify one to be called either a bachelor of arts or a bachelor of science. One "progressive" innovation organizes the year into ten-week quarters rather than fifteen-week semesters. Big advantage!

7. Undergraduate colleges have a duty to train undergraduates for graduate school or industry. Colleges have a duty to screen students for graduate school and industry.

8. Undergraduates, and especially lower level undergraduates, are not capable of very original or creative activity in most areas of science and the humanities. Exceptions to this rule are occasionally recognized in some departments of art, music, or creative writing, although even in these courses a heavy, teacher-dictated structure may be imposed upon the student.

9. Emotions have little place in the learning of science and the humanities. Rationalism is all-important in college programs.

10. The role of intuition in undergraduate science and humanities courses is negligible. Students learn best through following an externally imposed structure rather than being allowed to flounder and to make intuitive decisions.

11. Professors should mainly teach their specialties. Thus, students who have interests which do not coincide with the specialties of their professors should wait to follow these interests until they can find a suitable faculty member from whom to learn.

12. Professors and students should not get too close to each other because close personal relationships may cause students to lose respect for faculty members.

13. Undergraduate students should learn mainly to answer questions rather than to ask them. Examinations in most courses stress answering rather than asking.

14. Programs in both science and the humanities should begin with surveys of the field and work gradually toward greater specialization and narrowness.

15. Disciplines are learned most efficiently if fragmented into courses. Learning of a given subject is considered to be more or less complete after one has completed all of the courses available on a given subject.
16. Students will not learn without an external pressure and reward system. Examinations are the best way to uphold standards and to insure that graduates of programs in individual disciplines will know many of the same things that their professors know.

* * * * *

From the way in which I have stated the above assumptions and from the earlier chapters in this book, the reader knows that I reject them completely. Many of my colleagues in higher education and most learners I know would also reject them, and yet here we sit in the year 1972, surrounded by lock-step systems composed of restrictive majors, fragmented courses, course credits, accumulation of credits for degrees, grades which protect yesterday's standards, and coercive environments that inhibit creative activity on the part of both professors and their students. Incredible!

If I reject many assumptions that underlie the present system, however, I should propose a new series of assumptions that can replace the old ones. The reader should understand that I do not pretend to have identified all of the assumptions underlying the present educational system among the sixteen assumptions listed above. I am sure that the reader can add additional assumptions which are equally untenable. The new assumptions I propose below should also not be considered as a complete list. These are presented as a basis for a new model for higher education that I shall propose later in this chapter and that I would work toward establishing on an institution-wide basis if I were dean. The new assumptions I have in mind are the following:

1. Every student is capable of making significant decisions about what to study, how long to study it, in what order to study it, and in what depth to study it.
2. Learning involves the whole person and does not proceed from the neck up only. Emotion and intuition are essential in the process of learning.
3. Learning is most efficiently done in a non-coercive environment. Thus, examinations used for comparative evaluation, programs

based on credit systems, required course programs, required attendance, and many other paraphernalia of the present system are untenable.

4. Learning requires a tremendously diverse environment, equipped with as much paraphernalia related to the various disciplines represented as possible. Lectures, richly equipped laboratories, well-filled libraries, art and music studios and programs, galleries, etc., are essential.

5. Learners, given free choice, will rarely elect to jump into the conventional boxes represented by pre-packaged courses. No course can be constructed which even approximately meets the needs of all students in the course.

6. Freshman students, upper division students, and graduate students are all capable of original creative activity. All they need is to be given the chance to engage in such activity.

7. The role of professors is to facilitate learning along directions chosen by students and to provide the students with access to suitable physical and human resources so that they may pursue these directions as far as their curiosity makes them wish to go.

8. The professor should think of himself as a learner in his dealings with the students rather than as one who dispenses knowledge. Learning should consist of exploration performed by professors and students working jointly on new problems.

9. The closer the personal relationship between teachers and their students, the better.

10. Undergraduate and graduate students are capable of evaluating themselves, although they may wish to have help from their teachers in developing their own personal evaluation scales.

11. Learning is most efficient when each student designs his own program. Faculty members should be available to consult with students, but final decisions should always be in the hands of individual students.

12. The learner is entirely responsible for his own learning.

*   *   *   *   *

The main difference between the old assumptions and the new ones just stated is the following: The new assumptions presume that the faculty member has deep trust in his students and has complete confidence in their ability to learn by themselves if they are provided with an adequate environment.

*   *   *   *   *

It should be possible to outline a complete undergraduate experience that would meet most of these new assumptions. In the following section I propose to sketch out the program for a community of scholars of the type which I believe could help meet these assumptions. Many other models would undoubtedly do the job equally well, and my own utopian scheme is presented in the hope of stimulating others to work on similar kinds of models which focus on the *possible* rather than on the *practicable.* Members of the academic community have too long dwelled upon the restrictions of what they consider to be the practicable and have consequently overlooked what they are actually capable of accomplishing.

Events of the last several years in higher education indicate clearly that timid solutions and minor rearrangements of programs will do little to bring about the major improvement in higher education we now require. Drastic reorganizations are required if real progress is to be made. These drastic changes can be tried in experimental colleges existing within the framework of our larger institutions. Evolution is possible only if sufficient diversity is present within the system. Cultural evolution cannot occur in a peaceful way unless the system contains a large number of alternative directions within it.

In the proposed undergraduate college, students would enter, find out who they are and where they want to go. A year, two years, or more of free exploration with no evaluation, no courses, no grades and no credits attached! The student would elect a counselor or perhaps a counseling committee with whom he would agree to meet regularly to discuss himself and his growth. His counselors would help him to find and follow his interests. Each counselor's responsibility would be that of facilitating the student's exploration and coming to know the student *as a person.*

The college would provide a wide range of stimulatory experiences designed specially to attract these free floaters. There might, for example, be regular schedules of introductory lectures of various kinds. Any faculty members, upper division students, or outsiders wishing to lecture could schedule meetings. However, there would be no required attendance and no examinations attached to these lectures. The student would operate as a free auditor. Faculty members might schedule discussion groups around various topics. Discussion groups and series of lectures might extend over periods of several days or weeks depending upon the wishes of individual faculty members and on whether or not any students are showing up for the meetings. Presumably, as soon as a faculty member found that no one was coming to his proposed stimulatory lectures, he would soon look for some new topic or stop giving lectures. There would be a regular schedule of cultural events including concerts, plays, athletic events, etc. Students would be strongly encouraged to participate in musical, dramatic, and athletic groups.

Each student would be encouraged to develop a portfolio of his products. Within this portfolio he would include items which he considered to show him at his best. He might include poems he had written, music he had written, programs of performances in which he had participated, testimonials he had solicited to certify his skills, scientific essays he had written, short stories he might have written, accounts of experiments he had performed, photographs of works of art he had created, discussions of his reactions to things he had read and to concerts and performances he had attended. In short, he would include anything he considered to be representative of himself. A student would be free to add new material to his portfolio at any time and to remove items which he no longer considered worthy of inclusion.

As the student developed specialized interests, he would likely begin to gravitate toward certain special intellectual areas. As soon as his counselors discovered this, they would help the student find new counselors closer to his immediate interests. The student would be free to change counselors at any time and as frequently as he wished to do so.

Finally, as the student's interests developed further, he would submit his portfolio to a group of junior and senior learners whom he found attractive as potential colleagues and engage them in detailed discussion and interviews about his interest. Once a group of ad hoc advisors had agreed that a given student had become sufficiently mature and goal-oriented, they would agree to have him work with them for an apprentice period. If the student felt that he was mature enough but the advisors did not, a procedure would be worked out to give the student a chance to submit additional work and to get to know the advisors better.

Alternatively, the student could select other advisors and work with them. Such disagreements would be handled as human problems and dealt with in an honest, humane fashion. After a period of a few months, the student's performance would be evaluated, and if the student wished to continue to work with this group and if the committee considered on a subjective basis that his work deserved their support, he would be admitted as a full member of the learning community.

Further work would consist of no formal courses, credits, or grades, but would rather encompass independent and small group experiences of various kinds to be determined by the learner and his colleagues (junior and senior learners). The student would continue during this time to build a portfolio in close coordination with a committee which would meet with him regularly to discuss his program. The role of the committee of peers and faculty members would be to provide the student with the human and physical resources he might need to pursue his learning. Individual faculty members and upper level students would undoubtedly give talks and set up laboratory and discussion experiences of various kinds, but junior learners would not be required to attend or be accountable for the subject matter discussed. Students would be encouraged to go off campus when they wished to do so and pursue investigations related to their major studies. The only requirement would be that they remain in contact with their faculty counselors and possibly with fellow students who might also be on their counseling committees. At the same time, it must also be recognized that some learners might need to be alone for long periods of time, and their right to do so must be respected. Some learners might spend long periods of time learning about themselves rather than about subject matter, and their colleagues in the humanistic community would make known their willingness to listen and respond when asked to, but would not intrude if asked to go away.

As the student developed his portfolio containing what he considered to be his best work, he would continue discussions with his committee. Eventually the student, together with fellow students and his faculty committee, would decide that he had completed sufficient work to obtain a bachelor's degree. A student could also elect to have his work evaluated by someone outside of his own university. In some cases the faculty and peer group might decide that a student should receive a degree with distinction. There would be no set time required for completion of work. The opinion of the student's committee that his work was complete would be accepted by the university as the basis for graduation. All programs would have students involved in research, original investigation, or original creative activity from the very beginning.

The possibility of wildly interdisciplinary programs is implicit in the scheme set forth here.

*   *   *   *   *

Such a scheme as the one proposed may sound quite impossible. However, a number of people working in various efforts have already, within existing institutions, implemented pieces of this scheme. The main basis for such a scheme includes the following elements:

1. There is a wide range of real alternatives for students to choose among.
2. Faculty power as a weapon to be used against students disappears.
3. A very close personal faculty-student relationship comes to exist. The line between faculty members and students becomes blurred. Faculty members perceive themselves as older, more experienced learners, and students perceive themselves as younger, less experienced learners. But all are pursuers of knowledge together.

Among some of the programs that have attempted to introduce elements of the program described above are the following: The Unified Science Study Project at MIT; the experimental program of the University of South Carolina; certain aspects of the Experimental College at the University of Vermont; certain aspects of the Sewall Hall Project at the University of Colorado; an experimental program at Ohio University; a few biology courses taught at Colorado State College by Professor J. Carter; aspects of elementary science courses taught by Professor Stanley Harris at Southern Illinois University; paleontology and elementary geology programs taught by Professor F. D. Holland at the

University of North Dakota; the earth science program at the California State College at Fullerton; the geology and geography program at St. Lawrence University; and a number of other individual programs that could be named. Several new colleges propose to introduce elements of the utopian scheme described above, but whether or not these colleges will be successful remains to be seen. Among the colleges concerned are Hampshire College (Massachusetts), The University Without Walls (coordinated through Antioch College in Ohio), the Evergreen State College (Washington), Kresge College at the University of California at Santa Cruz, and Governors State University (Illinois).

Any institution can begin work on the *possible* through colleges within their colleges. For any appreciable amount of success to be expected, however, conventional rule books must be thrown completely away, and full cooperation for an experimental period of five or more years is required in order that a valid test can be assured. Registrars, faculty councils, and other administrative groups as well as the faculty at large at major institutions must agree to accept on a non-judgmental basis (at first) large-scale innovative programs of this type if viable alternatives to the present educational system in higher education are to be found.

Epilogue

WHERE DO I GO FROM HERE?

Don't push the river—it flows by itself
—Barry Stevens[9]

If you have read my earlier book, *Inquiry Techniques for Teaching Science*,[10] you will recognize that my own views about teaching, my relationships with learners, and my picture of myself have changed drastically. It is hard to say how I will change and where I will go in the future. I have spelled out some current fantasies in the section of this book entitled "Fantasy." The main place I expect to go from here is toward a closer, more responsive, more caring, and more honest relationship to people I live and work with. If I do this, people who come to learn with me will learn more and feel better about themselves and what they learn. And so will I.

---

[9]Barry Stevens, *Don't Push the River-It Flows by Itself* (Lafayette, Calif.: Real People Press, 1970).

[10]William D. Romey, *Inquiry Techniques for Teaching Science* (Englewood-Cliffs, N.J.: Prentice-Hall, 1968).

WHERE DO YOU GO FROM HERE?

—Photo by Robert Samples. Courtesy of Environmental Studies project.

A Warning

If You Change Your Perception of Your
Role as a Teacher, You May Find
The Rest of Your Life Changing Too!

Working at Becoming a Whole Human Being and Sharing
Your Perceptions, Fears, Joys, and Loves
Openly Is Risky Business,

But the Process Makes Me Feel Good
Much of the Time.